Culturally and Linguistically Diverse Classrooms

PEFC
PEFC/16-33-111
CATG-PEFC-052
www.pefc.org

NEW PERSPECTIVES ON LANGUAGE AND EDUCATION

Series Editor: Professor Viv Edwards, *University of Reading, Reading, Great Britain*
Series Advisor: Professor Allan Luke, *Queensland University of Technology, Brisbane, Australia*

Two decades of research and development in language and literacy education have yielded a broad, multidisciplinary focus. Yet education systems face constant economic and technological change, with attendant issues of identity and power, community and culture. This series will feature critical and interpretive, disciplinary and multidisciplinary perspectives on teaching and learning, language and literacy in new times.

Full details of all the books in this series and of all our other publications can be found on http://www.multilingual-matters.com, or by writing to Multilingual Matters, St Nicholas House, 31-34 High Street, Bristol BS1 2AW, UK.

NEW PERSPECTIVES ON LANGUAGE AND EDUCATION
Series Editor: Professor Viv Edwards, *University of Reading, Reading*

Culturally and Linguistically Diverse Classrooms
New Dilemmas for Teachers

Edited by
Jennifer Miller, Alex Kostogriz and Margaret Gearon

MULTILINGUAL MATTERS
Bristol • Buffalo • Toronto

Library of Congress Cataloging in Publication Data
A catalog record for this book is available from the Library of Congress.
Miller, Jennifer
Culturally and Linguistically Diverse Classrooms: New Dilemmas for Teachers/Edited
by Jennifer Miller, Alex Kostogriz and Margaret Gearon.
New Perspectives on Language and Education
Includes bibliographical references.
1. English language–Study and teaching (Secondary)–Foreign speakers.
2. English language–Study and teaching (Secondary)–United States.
3. Language arts (Secondary)–Social aspects. 4. Literacy–Social aspects
I. Miller, Jennifer. II. Kostogriz, Alexander. III. Gearon, Margaret. IV. Title.
PE1128.A2M5534 2009
418.0071–dc22 2009026154

British Library Cataloguing in Publication Data
A catalogue entry for this book is available from the British Library.

ISBN-13: 978-1-84769-217-7 (hbk)
ISBN-13: 978-1-84769-216-0 (pbk)

Multilingual Matters
UK: St Nicholas House, 31-34 High Street, Bristol BS1 2AW, UK.
USA: UTP, 2250 Military Road, Tonawanda, NY 14150, USA.
Canada: UTP, 5201 Dufferin Street, North York, Ontario M3H 5T8, Canada.

The policy of Multilingual Matters/Channel View Publications is to use papers that
are natural, renewable and recyclable products, made from wood grown in sustainable
forests. In the manufacturing process of our books, and to further support our policy,
preference is given to printers that have FSC and PEFC Chain of Custody certification.
The FSC and/or PEFC logos will appear on those books where full certification has been
granted to the printer concerned.

Typeset by Datapage International Ltd.
Printed and bound in Great Britain by the MPG Books Group.

Contents

Acknowledgements

We wish to acknowledge the international scholars in this book, their knowledge of the field and their responsiveness to deadlines, revisions and countless emails. We are particularly grateful to series editor Viv Edwards, who saw the value in the topic and the book as an area worthy of serious attention. Her encouragement to develop the themes and our initial proposal has strengthened the book and its contribution to the field. The Faculty of Education at Monash University provided funding towards the final editing of the chapters and we thank our colleague Nike Prince for her meticulous, efficient and supportive role as copy editor. It is thanks to Nike that the manuscript came together in a timely fashion. Thanks also to Prue Madden who helped us navigate through the contractual agreements. We also wish to thank the publishers and all those who worked on the production side so efficiently. It is with much sadness that we acknowledge the sudden passing of Professor Peter Martin in April 2009. Our condolences go to his family, colleagues and friends, including co-authors Angela Creese and Arvind Bhatt.

Contributors

Arvind Bhatt has worked in the field of community languages and complementary schooling for over 20 years as well as in mainstream teaching. He has argued the case for complementary schools and bilingualism, both locally and nationally, and has been involved in major research projects with universities of Lancaster, Leicester and East London where he was a Research Fellow. He is currently teaching advanced level Gujarati at the Jalaram Bal Vikas complementary school in Leicester.

Tracey Costley is a PhD candidate at the Department of Education and Professional Studies at King's College London, where she also works as an English for Academic Purposes Lecturer at the English Language Centre. Her current research interests include exploring the interface between education policy and curriculum practice in relation to ethnolinguistic minority students in mainstream schooling contexts, as well as academic genres and student identity in writing at university. She has been actively involved in a number of curriculum development projects for ethnolinguistic minority pupils, focussing on language and literacy development for 14–19 year olds.

Do Coyle is Professor in Learning Innovation at the University of Aberdeen, formally Director of the Visual Learning Lab at the University of Nottingham developing technology-enhanced learning spaces. Much of her research is in the field of pedagogies for content and language integrated learning (CLIL) and bilingual settings for Modern Foreign Languages (MFL). She has developed the 4Cs conceptual framework for CLIL and is an international expert, working closely with a range of agencies for promoting CLIL. She was awarded Chevalier dans l'Ordre des Palmes Academiques for her services to French. She believes that all young people should have an entitlement to positive language learning, which demands a radical rethink of current practice.

Angela Creese has worked in linguistically and culturally diverse schools as a researcher, a teacher trainer and as a consultant. Her work is on educational inclusion, multilingualism and community schooling. She has experience working in multilingual research teams and conducting collaborative research. She is a founding member of the United Kingdom Linguistic Ethnography Forum. She is Professor of Educational Linguistics at the School of Education, University of Birmingham.

Diane Dagenais is Professor and Associate Dean, Academic, at the Faculty of Education at Simon Fraser University. She is co-editor of the Canadian Modern Language Review, a member of the British Columbia Centre of Excellence for Research on Immigration and Diversity and the European Centre for Modern Languages. Her research is supported from several sources and she publishes on issues of diversity and language learning as they relate to immigration, multilingualism, multilingual literacies, second language and bilingual education.

Karen Dooley lectures in literacy at Queensland University of Technology, and has a particular interest in second language education. She has worked in mainstream English as a Second Language (ESL) settings in Queensland primary schools and as an English as a Foreign Language (EFL) teacher in a Shanghai secondary school. Karen is particularly interested in pedagogy for English language learners in mainstream classrooms, and is currently completing a study of provision for middle school students who have arrived in Australia as refugees from Africa.

Hannele Dufva is Professor of Language Education at the Department of Languages, University of Jyväskylä. She has authored a number of articles on dialogical philosophy of language and its potential contribution to contemporary applied linguistics. She has edited and co-authored several books and teaching materials. She is currently responsible for the research project The Dialogues of Appropriation, funded by the Academy of Finland.

Margaret Gearon is a Senior Lecturer at the Faculty of Education at Monash University. She specialises in languages teacher education at both preservice and inservice levels, curriculum and assessment in foreign and community (heritage) languages, and bilingual education. Her research interests are in immersion education, codeswitching in the foreign language classroom and how the knowledge and beliefs of preservice languages teachers are manifested in their classroom practices. She is currently project director for the design of a teacher-training course for community languages teachers in Australia.

Jennifer Hammond is an Associate Professor at the Faculty of Arts and Social Sciences (Education), University of Technology, Sydney. She teaches in the fields of language and literacy education, English as a Second Language (ESL) education and research design. Her research interests are in literacy development, classroom interaction, and the implications of sociocultural and systemic theories of language and learning in ESL education. She has published widely in these areas.

Alex Kostogriz is Associate Professor in TESOL at the School of Education, Deakin University. He has published widely on issues of professional practice and ethics of English language educators, teacher professional identity and learning, transcultural literacy and a pedagogy of Thirdspace. He has co-edited *Dimensions of Professional Learning* (2007), special issues of *Mind, Culture, and Activity* and *English Teaching: Practice and Critique* on learning in multicultural conditions.

David Lasagabaster is Associate Professor of English Studies at the University of the Basque Country, Spain. He has been involved in language teaching and teacher education in Spain for many years. He has published on second/third-language acquisition, foreign language teaching methodology, language learning among immigrant students, language attitudes, and multilingualism. His work has appeared in books, edited books and several international journals.

Constant Leung is Professor of Educational Linguistics at King's College London. He is Deputy Head of Department and Director of the MA English Language Teaching and Applied Linguistics and MA Assessment in Education programmes at the Department of Education and Professional Studies. Before taking up teaching positions in higher education, he taught in schools and worked as advisory teacher and manager in local government. His research interests include education in ethnically and linguistically diverse societies, second/additional language curriculum development, language assessment, language policy and teacher professional development. He has written and published widely on issues related to ethnic minority education, additional/second language curriculum, and language assessment nationally and internationally.

Joseph Lo Bianco is Professor of Language and Literacy Education at the University of Melbourne. He is best known as the author of the 1987 Australian National Policy on Languages, adopted as a bipartisan national plan for English, Indigenous languages, Asian and European languages, and Interpreting and Translating services, and now used worldwide as a model of language planning. He has more than 100 scholarly refereed articles and has written or edited 32 books and reports.

Peter Martin worked in primary and secondary classrooms, and in higher education, in several linguistically and culturally diverse contexts. His interests included bilingual interaction, multilingualism, widening participation in education, and community schooling. He was involved in research into classroom interaction, community education and Austronesian linguistics. He was Professor of Education and Linguistics in the Cass School of Education at the University of East London. Sadly, Peter died following a stroke on 24 April 2009.

Jennifer Miller is a Senior Lecturer at the Faculty of Education at Monash University where she teaches postgraduate Teaching English to Speakers of Other Languages (TESOL) courses. Her research and publications are in the areas of language acquisition and identity, the sociocultural framing of language pedagogy, and teacher's work. Her book, *Audible Difference: ESL and Social Identity in Schools* (Multilingual Matters, 2003) explores the politics of speaking and identity for immigrant students in Australian high schools. Her current research concerns low literacy refugee students in the high school mainstream, and preservice teachers from non-English-speaking backgrounds.

Danièle Moore is Professor at the Faculty of Education at Simon Fraser University in Canada, and Research Director at Paris 3 – Sorbonne Nouvelle in France. Her research focuses on the sociolinguistic and educational aspects of bilingualism and multilingualism in minority situations. Her recent publications include *Plurilinguismes et école* (2007, Collection LAL, Didier, Paris); *La compétence plurilingue. Regards franco-phones* (2008, with Véronique Castellotti); *Plurilinguismes et enseignement. Identités en construction* (2008, with Pierre Martinez and Valérie Spaëth); and *Perspectives pour une didactique des langues contextualisée* (2008, with Philippe Blanchet and Safia Assalah-Rahal).

Cécile Sabatier is an Assistant Professor at the Faculty of Education at Simon Fraser University. Her scholarly work is situated in language education and educational sociolinguistics, with a focus on linguistic and cultural diversity, multilingual competencies and language acquisition in minority contexts. Her work documents attitudes to multilingualism in families, schools and communities, as well as addressing issues of teacher education in a rapidly expanding world. As an author or co-author, she has published several articles in journals and books.

Olli-Pekka Salo is currently working as a Lecturer in Language Pedagogy at the Department of Teacher Education, University of Jyväskylä, Finland. His research interests cover a wide range of topics including, for instance, philosophy of language education, pedagogical grammar, teacher and learner beliefs and curriculum studies. He has written a number of articles dealing with many different aspects of language education in Finland. He is also participating in a project called The Dialogues of Appropriation, funded by the Academy of Finland.

Suzanne Smythe is Postdoctoral Fellow in Education at the University of Western Ontario. Her research interests include school-community relations, gender and education and critical literacies in community settings. Recent publications include 'The good mother: Exploring mothering discourses in family literacy texts' (*Australian Journal of Literacy and Numeracy Studies*, 2004, with J. Isserlis), and the edited volume, *Portraits of Literacy across Families, Communities and Schools* (Erlbaum, 2005, with J. Anderson, M. Kendrick and T. Rogers). Her current research explores the gendered work of kindergarten transitions.

Kelleen Toohey is Professor at the Faculty of Education at Simon Fraser University. Her research addresses English language learning by immigrant children and critical literacy. Recent publications include *Learning English at School: Identity, Social Relations and Classroom Practice* (Multilingual Matters, 2000); *Critical Pedagogies and Language Learning* (Cambridge University Press, 2004, with B. Norton); and the recent *Collaborative Research in Multilingual Classrooms* (Multilingual Matters, 2009, with C. Denos, K. Neilson and B. Waterstone). Her current research is with teachers and multilingual children.

Joel Windle is a lecturer at the Faculty of Education at Monash University and has previously taught in French and Australian schools. His research is in the field of comparative sociology of education, and focuses on the intersections of gender, ethnicity and class under contrasting institutional and political conditions, as well as under the changing conditions of globalisation. He has previously published on the experiences of migrant-background students in working-class secondary schools; and on the perceptions and representation of minority youth.

Part 1

Pedagogy in Diverse Classrooms

Chapter 1

The Challenges of Diversity in Language Education

MARGARET GEARON, JENNIFER MILLER and ALEX KOSTOGRIZ

A successful multilingualism policy can strengthen life chances of citizens: it may increase their employability, facilitate access to services and rights and contribute to solidarity through enhanced intercultural dialogue and social cohesion. Approached in this spirit, linguistic diversity can become a precious asset, increasingly so in today's globalised world. (European Commission, 2008: 3)

One of the most critical realities of contemporary education in a globalised world is the growing cultural, racial and linguistic diversity in schools and the problems involved in educating large numbers of students who do not speak the dominant language as their home or heritage language. The impact of this diversity is felt in many education-related fields, including policy, curriculum, pedagogy, teacher education, teachers' work and language education research. The range of diversity poses an extraordinary challenge for language teachers in countries such as Australia, Canada, the UK and many European Union countries, where students from diverse linguistic and cultural backgrounds must engage with mainstream curriculum in a new language, frequently the dominant language. Programmes to support such students to cope with the demands of the set curriculum in the mainstream are limited and varied, and provide the focus of some chapters of this book. In addition, teachers of compulsory foreign language courses must also cater for the same heterogeneous student population, as well as adapting to the emergence of content-based language teaching.

In these complex cultural-linguistic circumstances, there is a need to re-evaluate language teaching practices and curriculum in a way that is more responsive to difference. Kramsch, for instance, points out that language education, if it is to be effective and democratic, requires a shift in what and how students in multicultural countries are taught. She states:

> We are still teaching standard national languages according to a 19th century modern view of language as a structural system with rules of grammatical and lexical usage and rules of pragmatics reified to fit the image of a stereotyped Other. The 21st century is all about meaning, relations, creativity, subjectivity, historicity and the inter- as in interdisciplinary and intercultural... We should conceive of what we do in ways that are more appropriate to the demands of a global, decentered, multilingual and multicultural world, more suited to our uncertain and unpredictable times. (Kramsch, 2008: 405)

Pedagogically, this highlights a tension around the role of language education in servicing the global economy and, more importantly, in mediating the everyday life of young people in multicultural conditions. This mixture of the global, the national and the local presents an increasing need to take into account multiple languages and hybrid literacies that young people use and develop for effective functioning within and across social and cultural borders (Kostogriz, 2005).

In language education research, bilingualism, multilingualism and plurilingualism are core concerns and often contested as educational values and goals. Clearly, students need to be competent in their first language use, and also in the dominant language of their country or region, which allows access to academic success, social power, further education and work. Many require proficiency in additional languages for school curricula and in day-to-day communication in their personal or later work-related lives. While this range of language competences may be recognised and even valued in some parts of the world, this is frequently not the case in predominantly English-speaking countries such as Australia, the UK, the USA and Canada. The European Community, by contrast, is highly conscious of the need for citizens to develop multilingual competence and has developed a language policy that recognises the value of multilingualism. The European Commission's (2008) statement declares, 'Multilingual citizens are better equipped to take advantage of the educational opportunities created by an integrated Europe', while its 'Action plan on language learning and linguistic diversity' specifies the scope of strategies to build multilingual competence.

Researchers have long demonstrated the additional political, economic, social, intellectual and communicative advantages of multilingualism, yet even in European Union policy statements there is little recognition of just how challenging diverse classrooms can be, not to mention the multiple contextual caveats that need to be attached to language planning, language learning and teaching objectives. In the USA, Commins and Miramontes (2005) problematise and deconstruct some of the myths and key arguments in the ongoing debate about linguistic diversity and teaching, and, in particular, issues around language policy, bilingualism, English literacy, equity and pragmatism.

It is not surprising that the issue of a socially just and democratic language education, one that is responsive to cultural and linguistic diversity in our classrooms, has been gradually disappearing from the discourses of educational policy making (Kostogriz, 2007). The neo-liberalisation of education in some countries, with its emphasis on the self-regulation of educational markets through privatisation, competition and 'customer' choice and the de-professionalisation of teachers through accountability and performativity mechanisms, has led to a convenient oversimplification of the cultural-linguistic complexity of schooling. Educators' confusion about how to teach students who often do not share their cultural values and linguistic backgrounds is just one consequence of this simplification.

Perhaps the one certainty in contemporary languages education is that mass movements of peoples due to global economies, conflict and sociopolitical instability, and the resulting impact of large numbers of immigrants, refugees and children of guest workers' in schools have changed the face of language teaching and, by implication, language teacher education around the world. Kramsch (2008) draws attention to the urgent need to shift how we think about and do language teaching, and the kinds of courses we offer to future language teachers. This also requires research into and reflection about how best to address languages education, whether first, second and foreign languages, in order to meet the needs and interests of these students, their families and their school context/s.

Our thinking about this book began three years ago with the project of exploring how language teacher educators might engage with the changes in classrooms such as those outlined above. At that time, we asked ourselves the question of how to address the needs of pre- and in-service teachers who must face the reality of multiple languages, voices and cultures in their classrooms. We noted Kramsch's statement that:

Linguistic and cultural pluralism is more than the mere coexistence of various languages. It is primarily about the transcultural circula-tion of values across borders, the negotiation of identities, the inversions, even inventions of meaning, often concealed by a common illusion of effective communication.... The teacher trainers of tomorrow will need to be increasingly plurilingual and pluricultural. (Kramsch, 2008: 390)

The context of linguistic and cultural diversity is, therefore, a given that underlies the research presented in this book, which has several aims. These include:

- to continue the debate on the roles of language and power in rapidly changing multilingual and multicultural communities within various nations;
- to address ways in which this debate can inform policy, curriculum and language teacher education courses;
- to contribute to understandings of the tensions between home language/s and the dominant language of schooling, and to propose some ways these are being addressed;
- to present teacher and learner perspectives on mainstream participation for students who are still acquiring the dominant language of schooling;
- to problematise language pedagogy using a range of sociocultural theoretical perspectives that pay due attention to social, institutional and political contexts.

As we engaged with scholars and their work in several countries with highly diverse populations, including Canada, the UK, Australia, Spain and Finland, the book evolved beyond the scope of teacher education to incorporate policy and language planning, language curricula and innovative pedagogies, language and multimodal literacies, teachers' work, changing theoretical conceptions of language learning and use in transcultural contexts, and indeed the types of research best suited to explore these complexities. All the chapters address one or more of these areas, and the ensemble opens up to the reader a number of dilemmas and problematic issues surrounding language teaching and learning in highly diverse contemporary contexts.

Challenges in Globalised Language Education

This book focuses strongly on research oriented to language teaching and learning in multilingual and multicultural classrooms and societies. The first challenge we wish to raise regards the equity of educational provision for extremely diverse groups of students. It is uncontroversial to say that many of the culturally and linguistically diverse students that are the focus of the research in this book are also socially, economically and politically marginalised. Costley and Leung (this volume) draw attention to the entrenched disadvantage of many immigrant and refugee students, as well as to the hiatus between policy rhetoric and educational practice. When students arrive with limited or interrupted schooling, settlement, integration and academic success become even greater challenges (Brown *et al.*, 2006). In the UK, and Australia for example, the gap between state claims and aims for multicultural education and the actual conditions in state-funded schools is vast and ever increasing. In Australia, this is accentuated by the severe underfunding of government schools, which are overwhelmingly attended by the students referred to above. The dramatic increase in numbers of these students is also a factor. Lasagabaster (this volume) highlights the tenfold increase in such students in the past decade in Spain, while Hammond (this volume) provides the important insight that in some inner city schools in Australia, ethnically and linguistically diverse students form 90% of the student body. It is a useful reminder that groups often labelled as 'minority' are, in fact, the overwhelming majority in some schools – a heterogeneous majority, but a critical one.

There are three related issues in highly diverse schools. These are complex integrated issues, but are primarily social, ideological and linguistic in focus, respectively. First, successful social integration, inclusion and cohesion depend largely on academic success. Rutter (2006) argues in the UK context that a primary indicator of successful integration is successful academic outcomes, and that unsuccessful groups remain as labour in society's worst and most low paid jobs. But, as second language researchers, we must also ask, what is the role and the importance of proficiency in the dominant language in these outcomes? One problem is that there is relatively little detailed empirical research that examines the efficacy of practices in relation to students' language proficiency, school participation or transitions through school (Anderson *et al.*, 2004; Rutter, 2006; McBrien, 2005). Likewise, there is little detailed research that examines the conditions that enable schools to develop these practices in holistic ways. The need for hard-edged research that both measures and responds to the literacy needs of diverse students remains as urgent as ever. As Labov argued in his keynote address at the AAAL Conference in 2007, the failure of schools to teach disadvantaged children to read was the most serious social problem of the USA. The majority of these disadvantaged students, both in the USA and elsewhere, are from culturally and linguistically diverse backgrounds.

A second challenge is basically ideological, and concerns the neglect of difference and diversity as consequential, while attention is increasingly galvanised on national curricula and national standards (see Kostogriz, this volume). Kostogriz points out that as teacher performance and accountability pressures increasingly dominate policy and media campaigns, diversity and contextual complexity remain in the background. In addition, the scale of diversity and its educational ramifications are silenced in public discourse. In Australia, this is partly out of fear of alienating the population even further from government schools, and partly because thinking through the needs of highly diverse school populations and coming up with viable responses requires too much work and money. This serves to reify disadvantage for already marginalised groups. A point that should be made here is that there is always a danger of homogenising ethnically, racially, linguistically, culturally, socially and educationally diverse groups. The categories within diversity are invariably heterogeneous, with a full range of talents, competencies and difficulties. This should, however, not distract from the primary problem that a large body of evidence identifies highly diverse student groups as overrepresented in educational underachievement. It is also worth recalling Cummins' (1997) argument that ignoring the intersections between power and pedagogy serves to reinforce coercive and exploitative structures in education.

The third challenge we wish to raise is more specifically linguistic and academic in nature. Students who speak a range of languages other than the dominant language or language of instruction must compete with native speakers of the dominant language, who are constantly improving their language proficiency, in mainstream classrooms, often with minimal or no intensive language support. Further, there is a significant difference, often poorly understood by policy makers and many teachers, between social language and the highly specific academic language required in schools. In a body of research spanning over 15 years, Collier and Thomas have addressed the problem of how long it takes language minority students in the USA to acquire the social and academic language for successful integration into the mainstream. They stress the need to look beyond the notion of 'learning English' to the processes involved in acquiring a second language for success at school. The language needed for academic success at school requires the use of specialised forms, genres and vocabulary, which are specific to subject areas such as maths, social science, science and so on. Collier's model (1995), which illustrates the complexity of acquiring any additional language in school, outlines the interdependence of academic development, language development, cognitive development and sociocultural processes.

How is this to be achieved? There is considerable research evidence that first language competence and literacy play a vital role in the acquisition of an additional language, particularly for academic purposes (Cummins, 1991; Thomas & Collier, 1997). Bilingual research provides a strong argument for first language support wherever possible. However, in highly diverse Australian classrooms, where up to ten language groups may be in one class, this becomes impossible. This is often the case in many North American and European classrooms too. Both Lasagabaster and Dooley (this volume) highlight the language demands of the mainstream, while Hammond reminds us that 'second language' is now a mainstream issue. In this book, research related to bilingualism is presented by Windle, and by Dagenais, Moore and Sabatier.

Specific bilingual support may prove impractical in some contexts, but this should not undermine the importance of what Cummins (2003) proposes so convincingly in his paper 'Challenging the construction of difference as deficit: Where are identity, intellect, imagination, and power in the new regime of truth?' For learning a new language for success at school and in society, Cummins (2000) emphasises the 'centrality of identity negotiation' (p. 154) and 'identity affirmation' (p. 268) in effective practice, while claiming these have been consistently ignored in mainstream educational research. For minority students in particular, he argues that practice must be grounded in the lives of the students. Research projects on innovative approaches to language education that reflect a strong focus on student identity are presented in this volume by Smythe and Toohey, and by Dagenais, Moore and Sabatier. The cross-over between home and school literacies, the complex clashes between dominant language and culture with heritage language and culture, youth culture and technoliteracies, illustrated by Smythe and Toohey, highlight the challenges for teachers, students and schools as something beyond learning and teaching English. They reveal a range of tensions between institutional constraints and objectives, and the multilingual, multimodal and multicultural resources that minority students bring to school. In the context of foreign language teaching, Coyle lays out the re-conceptualisation needed to integrate traditional languages studied in mainstream schools and heritage languages or community languages taught in after hours schools.

The chapters in this book offer new insights into language learning and teaching in times of unprecedented diversity in schools. We know that the dilemmas implicated in this diversity are many and troubling for schools, teachers, students and governments. We hope that the research presented here offers many ways to re-think language teacher education. Nieto (2000, 2006) argues that diversity, coupled with the emerging sociopolitical contexts of schools, means that effective teachers now need more than strong pedagogical skills. She illustrates that teachers who are successful in working with these students also display a sense of mission, empathy for their students, the capacity to critically challenge conventional approaches, flexibility and a passion for social justice.

This book, therefore, addresses a number of issues that are encountered by language educators and researchers in their respective local contexts. The significance of the book lies partly in representing how language educators respond to the consequences of globalisation. It also provides ways to think about language education in the context of nationally and regionally embedded globalisation. In other words, insights from teaching and research in local contexts have implications for understanding the impact of the great transcultural flows and linguistic pluralism of our times. We hope that the book will help readers to think about cultural and linguistic diversity in language education, and their effects on teachers and learners.

The book is organised into three parts, namely Pedagogy in Diverse Classrooms, Language Policy and Curriculum, and Language Research in Diverse Contexts. We recognise that in most chapters there is substantial overlap across these three areas, but the parts provide readers with some indication of the primary focus of each chapter. We would like to acknowledge the valuable contributions by the international scholars in this volume, who collectively provide such a rich and insightful picture of the dilemmas for language educators in linguistically and culturally diverse times. In what follows, we provide a brief outline of the individual chapters in the three sections of the book.

Part 1: Pedagogy in Diverse Classrooms

In highly diverse school populations, Miller reminds us that both students and teachers come from an extraordinary array of cultural and language backgrounds. Although a body of literature has attended to 'difference' in student groups, less has been written about teachers. Miller's chapter presents a group of graduating Australian teachers for whom English is not the first language, and who, in some cases, were still grappling with issues of identity, their accents and the way they were heard, as well as their own perceived cultural gaps and strengths. They found that their lecturers and local peers were sometimes insensitive to the linguistic and cultural challenges they faced, yet felt they had valuable knowledge and experience that remained untapped in their pre-service course. The problematic assumptions made by teacher educators in regard to international students are raised, along with broader implications for pre-service teacher education.

Lasagabaster analyses the linguistically complex situation regarding immigrant students and the challenges it creates in the Basque Autonomous Community. He examines how both teachers and students perceive multilingualism in a context where the presence of several languages in schools is the norm. The three compulsory languages of the curriculum (Basque, Spanish and English) co-exist with the languages spoken by an ever-increasing number of immigrant students. His results show that, in spite of the fact that the social value of multilingualism was perceived as high, the participants did not really attach an important personal value to it. He argues that the European Union's concept of a personal adoptive language would be a feasible way to bridge the gap between local and immigrant languages and to counter the hegemony of English.

In her chapter on an intensive English transition programme for English as an Additional Language/English as a Second Language (EAL/ESL) learners in Sydney, Hammond argues that given the widespread diversity in many urban classrooms, 'ESL is now a mainstream issue'. She draws on her own work with Pauline Gibbons on 'scaffolding', as well as on a recent body of work that stresses quality teaching and high intellectual challenge for language learners. Hammond's project with teachers used a high challenge-high support framework in which multilingual and multimodal support was offered to learners in Music and English, which formed part of their programme. A major contribution of the chapter is to define teacher qualities that engage students from diverse backgrounds, including empathy, knowledge of the students' backgrounds and a broad interest in language as an essential part of learning, awareness of the importance of cognitive demand and a repertoire of pedagogical strategies for these learners. The implication is that pedagogy in such programmes offers important insights for broader educational contexts.

In her chapter on students with interrupted education and from an African refugee background who now reside in Australia, Dooley poses some difficult questions about the responsibility for learning language and content at school. Her study gives voice to African parents, the students themselves and to their teachers as they grapple with the options available when students do not understand mainstream vocabulary, content or classroom instructions. Dooley draws attention to the (im)possibilities for engagement in learning if the conditions for expressing incomprehension or seeking help are not in place. Contrasting the supportive environment of the intensive language school with the more confronting mainstream high school, the author shows that mainstream teacher talk often ignores the needs of students with interrupted schooling and limited literacy. Further, such students may face derision from peers if they constantly require help or ask questions. The study points to the need for increased awareness of the expectations and problems faced by these students as they struggle with school discourses and content.

Culturally and linguistically diverse students in immigrant-receiving countries are often concentrated in settings of educational disadvantage where bilingualism and cultural background can be quickly transformed into explanations of poor performance. Windle argues that it is essential for teachers, who seek to empower such students, to be able to identify the nature of the academic difficulties confronting them. This requires an appreciation both of the social contexts of students and of the operation of schooling as cultural institutions embedded in socially unequal power relations. The chapter discusses a study of migrant students in French and Australian secondary schools that are located in working-class and culturally diverse neighbourhoods. It presents extracts of student writing, as well as views from teachers and students, in order to demonstrate an apparent mismatch between perceptions of difficulty and sources of difficulty with written expression. The chapter suggests that teachers, and students themselves, often misrecognise both the source and the nature of the 'language difficulties' they encounter at school.

Part 2: Language Policy and Curriculum

Lo Bianco's chapter opens up the section on language policy and curriculum. It addresses political dilemmas of language education and links them to the workings of two contradictory political discourses – economic and cultural. Lo Bianco argues that these discourses do not take into account the communicative and educative needs of multicultural nation-states. The economic discourse of efficiency usually reduces language learning to a set of skills that the citizens of a nation-state need to acquire in order to participate in global market economies. While this discourse puts an emphasis on English as the language of globalisation and is considered by many as a threat to local languages and identities, cultural discourses are enacted in response to the perceived colonisation. This exposes nationalism and ethnic protectionism as movements that often engender a conservative backlash in language education with regard to differences. Lo Bianco addresses these contradictions in the politics of language education by developing an alternative concept of 'critical worldmindedness'. He presents an appealing argument for considering it as a new organising principle of curriculum and pedagogy in multicultural conditions.

Kostogriz engages further with the issues of difference, dialogical interdependence and power that Lo Bianco discusses in his chapter. His chapter situates English language and literacy education within current debates in Australia about teacher professional standards, national curriculum and their ability to respond to cultural and linguistic difference. It identifies blind spots and contradictions inherent in the curriculum frameworks and in the discourse of professional standards, emphasising the often neglected issues of professional ethics. Kostogriz re-evaluates the contribution of Derrida, Levinas and Bakhtin to English teaching and draws on their concepts of hospitality, responsibility and dialogism to provide an alternative perspective on curriculum and pedagogy. The chapter puts emphasis on dialogical ethics in pedagogical zones of contact with difference. It urges the reader to think about the possibilities of opening up English language education to the Other, making it more hospitable. Kostogriz discusses a pedagogical practice of transculturation in culturally and linguistically diverse classrooms. As an act of hospitality, transculturation can be a way of enabling students to understand and negotiate differences, their connectedness and meaning dynamics in dialogical encounters with the Other.

Addressing a similar set of concerns, Costley and Leung present a case study that highlights the mismatch between the English National Curriculum Policy and the specific needs of individual schools and the realities of their multilingual and multicultural classes. The English language support teacher in this study, herself from a non-English-speaking background, works with groups of students in withdrawal classes to develop not only their linguistic knowledge and skills, but also a sense of responsibility towards schooling and the behaviours, values and practices expected in a UK school. The study shows that judicious use of funding, which enables minority migrant students to be withdrawn from mainstream classes in order to meet their specific needs and, hence, narrow the gaps between the likelihood of low achievement and expected outcomes, can make difference more visible.

Raising the need to re-think and re-conceptualise the teaching of languages for the 21st century, especially in supposed monolingual anglophone countries such as the UK, Coyle argues the need for making language curriculum and pedagogical practices more responsive to the multicultural composition of society. This requires a change in the public perception of difference, in particular in representing linguistic diversity as an asset rather than a liability. The chapter outlines the concept of the borderless classroom as a way forward in languages teaching and learning in the post-method era. Languages in 21st century societies and economies, as Coyle argues, need to be taught as means for both learning and communication. This will enable language learners to participate in knowledge production and also to value languages as a part of the knowledge base for life-long learning. Such recognition of language learning would require language educators to move away from a focus on using a modified version of Savignon's (2004) concept of communicative language teaching, to an approach that favours language in use, such as that required in the Content Learning in Languages approach. It would also include the development of both cultural and intercultural awareness.

Gearon re-focuses the discussion of curriculum, professional ethics and practice in previous chapters, to language teacher preparation. She addresses the extent to which existing teacher education courses preparing novice teachers of languages other than English enable their graduates to cope with the scenarios and dilemmas they may face in multilingual and multicultural classrooms in Australia. Her chapter illustrates the lack of content specifically concerned with concepts of intercultural awareness and competence. It also points to the non-recognition of the diversity of languages and cultures among school students who may be learning yet another language and culture other than English, regardless of the one they use outside of school in their own ethnolinguistic communities.

Part 3: Research Directions in Diverse Contexts

Creese, Bhatt and Martin explore the research processes of a multi-lingual research team working in the multilingual sites of complementary schools in the UK. They describe two aspects of researcher-identity negotiation, the first focusing on relationships with research participants, and the second on researcher identity within a nine-member research team. They report on how researchers use their linguistic, social and cultural resources to negotiate access and build relationships with participants in the research process and with one another in the research team. In disclosing divergent researcher perspectives, they hope to produce a healthier, more contested and contradictory ethnography, which captures the complexities of research in linguistically and culturally diverse schools.

Dagenais, Moore and Sabatier open up a range of dilemmas and tensions in their chapter on a teacher-researcher collaboration in Canada. Their interview data with two teachers, drawn from a much larger interinstitutional project, honour the teachers as 'knowers', yet elegantly present the complexity of such collaboration in schools. Teachers have different levels of investment in projects, as well as many non-negotiable institutional constraints; researchers draw on research and theory that may well be challenged by classroom realities; the project becomes professional development for all concerned. The authors also highlight contradictions between policy rhetoric that privileges multiculturalism, and official languages policy that excludes the overt linguistic capital of vast numbers of children from diverse language backgrounds. Their project led to a deep consideration of what counts as knowledge in multilingual schools, as well as the potentially transforming multiple roles available to those who embark on teacher-researcher collaboration.

In their chapter on foreign language education in Finland, Dufva and Salo draw theoretically on the work of the Bakhtin Circle and contemporary authors who have discussed dialogism in relation to language learning and teaching research. The chapter focuses on the everyday conceptualisations of language. It suggests that different, open-ended ways of studying the experienced aspects of the language learning process are important research tools. The authors argue that tasks and activities that elicit learners' beliefs are important also as pedagogical tools. They briefly survey research on beliefs about languages and discuss the diversity of students' perspectives on and attitudes to foreign languages. The chapter points out that every classroom is a multivoiced ensemble where different notions of language exist. It argues that it is highly probable that both learners and teachers do not have one single conceptualisation, but several. Making these conceptualisations audible – or visible by such means as drawings or photographs – creates an opportunity for increasing the learners' language awareness, thereby making language learning more meaningful.

Smythe and Toohey, in their chapter, make a compelling case for re-thinking how migrant and refugee children engage with literacies. The New Literacy Studies and a sociocultural perspective on learning inform the research project presented in the chapter. It focuses, in particular, on culturally and semiotically rich practices that these students participate in, and are socialised to, outside school. It is argued that migrant and refugee children are immersed in culturally and linguistically rich communal environments where they learn how to navigate and negotiate multiple ways of meaning- and identity-making. Their everyday literacy events represent a sophisticated set of practices that can be understood, as Smythe and Toohey illustrate, as a mixture of school literacy and home literacies, dominant culture/language and 'heritage' cultures/languages, youth culture and technoliteracies. As such, the authors are careful not to essentialise the urban community itself, for this is not a community of sameness. The photo-project described in this chapter reveals the work of multiple identities and funds of knowledge in becoming literate.

References

Anderson, A., Hamilton, R., Moore, D., Loewen, S. and Frater-Mathieson, K. (2004) Education of refugee children: Theoretical perspectives and best practice. In R. Hamilton and D. Moore (eds) *Educational Interventions for Refugee Children: Theoretical Perspectives and Implementing Best Practice* (pp. 1–11). London and New York: Routledge Falmer.

Brown, J., Miller, J. and Mitchell, J. (2006) Interrupted schooling and the acquisition of literacy: Experiences of Sudanese refugees in Victorian secondary schools. *Australian Journal of Language and Literacy* 29 (2), 150–162.

Collier, V. (1995) Acquiring a second language for school. *Reading Rockets*. US Dept. of Education: Office of Special Programs. On WWW at http://www.readingrockets.org/article.php?ID = 185. Accessed 21.6.05.

Commins, N. and Miramontes, O. (2005) *Linguistic Diversity and Teaching*. Mahwah, NJ: Erlbaum.

Cummins, J. (1991) Interdependence of first- and second-language proficiency in bilingual children. In E. Bialystok (ed.) *Language Processing in Bilingual Children* (pp. 70–89). Cambridge: Cambridge University Press.

Cummins, J. (1997) Cultural and linguistic diversity in education: A mainstream issue? *Educational Review* 49 (2), 105–114.

Cummins, J. (2000) *Language, Power and Pedagogy: Bilingual Children in the Crossfire*. Clevedon: Multilingual Matters.

Cummins, J. (2003) Challenging the construction of difference as deficit: Where are identity, intellect, imagination, and power in the new regime of truth? In P. Trifonas (ed.) *Pedagogies of Difference* (pp. 41–60). New York: Routledge Falmer.

European Commission (2008) On WWW at http://europa.eu/scadplus/leg/en/cha/c11068.htm. Accessed January 2008.

Kostogriz, A. (2005) (Trans)cultural spaces of writing. In B. Doecke and G. Parr (eds) *Writing = learning* (pp. 104–119). Adelaide: AATE/Wakefield Press.

Kostogriz, A. (2007) Spaces of professional learning. In M. Berry, A. Clemans and A. Kostogriz (eds) *Dimensions of Professional Learning: Professionalism, Identities and Practice* (pp. 23–36). Rotterdam: Sense Publishers.

Kramsch, C. (2008) Ecological perspectives on foreign language education. *Language Teaching* 4 (3), 389–408.

Labov, W. (2007) Reading: The imperative challenge to applied linguistics. Plenary address at AAAL Annual Conference, Costa Mesa, April 21–24.

McBrien, J.L. (2005) Educational needs and barriers for refugee students in the United States: A review of the literature. *Review of Educational Research* 75 (3), 329–364.

Nieto, S. (2000) *Affirming Diversity: The Sociopolitical Context of Multicultural Education* (3rd edn). New York: Longman.

Nieto, S. (2006) Solidarity, courage and heart: What teacher educators can learn from a new generation of teachers. *Intercultural Education* 17 (5), 457–473.

Rutter, J. (2006) *Refugee Children in the UK*. Maidenhead, UK: Open University Press.

Savignon, S. (2004) Language, identity, and curriculum design: Communicative language teaching in the 21st century. In C. Van Esch and O. Saint John (eds) *New Insights in Foreign Language Learning and Teaching* (pp. 71–88). Frankfurt Am Main: Peter Lang Verlag.

Thomas, W.P. and Collier, V.P. (1997) Language Minority Student Achievement and Program Effectiveness. NCBE Resource Collection Series, No. 9. ED436087.

Chapter 2

Multilingual Educational Systems: An Added Challenge for Immigrant Students

DAVID LASAGABASTER

Introduction

In the 1996–1997 academic year, the Spanish educational system had only 60,000 students of immigrant origin, whereas 10 years later this figure had increased to 600,000. The Basque Autonomous Community (BAC henceforth), as one of the 17 autonomous communities that make up Spain, has also experienced a remarkable increase in the number of immigrants attending its schools. This new situation has had an obvious impact on the Basque educational system, in which three languages co-exist in the curriculum: Basque, Spanish (the two co-official languages in the BAC) and English, which is taught as a foreign language from the age of four onwards. Unlike Catalan and Galician (also co-official in other Spanish bilingual communities), Basque is not typologically related to Spanish, which makes its learning more of a challenge. This chapter analyses the linguistically complex situation regarding immigrant pupils and the challenges it creates, both from the teachers' and students' perspectives.

Europe aspires to conserve and promote linguistic diversity, an area considered as an integral part of the European ideal. With this in mind, the European Commission set up the Group of Intellectuals for Intercultural Dialogue (chaired by the writer Amin Maalouf), which was entrusted with the task of defining the contribution of multilingualism to intercultural dialogue, and whose reflections were set out in a report entitled *A Rewarding Challenge: How the Multiplicity of Languages Could Strengthen Europe* (Maalouf, 2008).

This group proposed that the European Union should advocate the idea of a *personal adoptive language*, according to which every European should choose a language different from both their language of identity and their language of international communication, in an attempt to overcome the overwhelming hegemony of the English language. In fact, as the number of official languages in the European Union increases with the incorporation of new member states, the predominance of English as the main *lingua franca* becomes more and more remarkable (Coleman, 2006).

The personal adoptive language would give an enormous boost to minority languages, and native speakers of these languages might feel less excluded and disillusioned with the European project. This could result in more favourable attitudes towards their surroundings and neighbours. The objective would be to make European citizens and leaders fully aware of the important role that multilingualism has to play in the construction of a linguistically diverse but socially cohesive European Union.

According to this proposal, the personal adoptive language should become a sort of second mother tongue and would be included in the school and university syllabus of every European citizen. The selection of the personal adoptive language would not be limited to the official languages of the European Union, but would also include languages from other continents (due to a desire to strengthen economic ties, for example) and the languages of the migrant population, European and non-European alike. In the latter option, the group makes the following considerations:

> Just as immigrants would be encouraged to fully adopt the language of the host country and the culture it carries, it would be fair and useful for the immigrants' languages of identity to also be part of the languages which Europeans themselves would be encouraged to adopt. We have to gradually get out of this one-way relationship in which people from elsewhere are getting better and better at learning European languages, while very few Europeans take the trouble to learn the languages of the immigrants. The latter need to feel that their languages, their literature, their cultures are known and appreciated by the societies in which they live, and we feel that the approach based on the *personal adoptive language* could help to dispel this *malaise*. (Maalouf, 2008: 21; emphasis in the original)

The *personal adoptive language* proposal therefore embraces the assumption that immigrants will adopt the language(s) of the host country and that locals will learn the languages of the immigrants. This is precisely what is going to be assessed in this chapter: how both teachers and students perceive multilingualism in the BAC in Spain, a bilingual context where the presence of several languages at school is the norm, as the three compulsory languages of the curriculum co-exist with the languages spoken by an ever-increasing number of students of immigrant origin. In Europe, linguistic diversity comprises both official and non-national languages, the latter including both regional and immigrant languages (Barni & Extra, 2008).

It has to be highlighted that Spain is a newcomer to the main group of immigration-receiver European member states: Germany, the UK and France have much higher numbers and a longer tradition, but in the last few years Spain has become one of the most attractive targets for migratory movements, basically due to the buoyant economic situation of the late 1990s and the early 2000s, and to the Spanish language (a large proportion of the immigrants come from Latin American Spanish-speaking countries). In fact, in 2005, Spain took in more immigrants than any other European country.

The Basque Context

Bilingual areas where a minority language and a majority one co-exist are far from uncommon. In the case of Spain, the statutes of six (Catalonia, the Valencian Community, the Balearic islands, Galicia, the BAC, and Navarre) out of a total of 17 autonomous communities proclaim the existence of a language of their own, which together with Spanish – the majority language – is the official language in their territory (for further information, see Huguet *et al.*, 2008). In the context under analysis in this chapter, the BAC, Basque and Spanish are both taught throughout primary, secondary and tertiary education. To make linguistic matters more complex, the teaching of English from an early age has spread to almost every single school, which is why all students enrolled in the Basque educational system have to tackle three languages from the age of four onwards. If the students are of immigrant origin and their first language (L1) does not coincide with any of the aforementioned three languages, then their linguistic background is made up of at least four languages from this early age. This obviously presents quite a challenge, especially if the three languages used at school are different from the one(s) spoken at home.

This is the linguistic reality that immigrant students have to face in the BAC. As for the general sociolinguistic situation, the entire population speaks Spanish, whereas Basque is spoken fluently by 35% and an additional 10% are considered passive bilinguals (they understand the

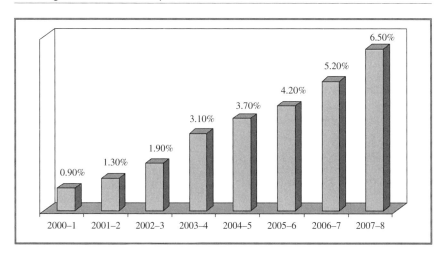

Figure 2.1 Percentage of immigrant students in primary and secondary education (BAC)

language but have difficulties speaking it). That is why Basque is usually referred to as the minority language in this autonomous community.

The evolution of immigrant students can be observed in Figure 2.1. In just eight years the percentage of immigrant students has gone up steadily from 0.9% to the current 6.5%, and seems unlikely to recede. However, it has to be pointed out that this percentage is below that in Spain (around 9%) and far from the percentages of other Spanish autonomous communities such as Catalonia or Madrid (well above 12%).

As is the case in Europe and the rest of Spain, the rapid increase in the number of immigrants and the subsequent linguistic and cultural diversity are not only a source of enrichment, but also a source of strain and friction.

As for the Basque educational system, it has to be underlined that currently there are three linguistic models in which children can complete their studies:

- *Model A*: this is a regular programme in which Spanish is the vehicle language and Basque is taught only as a subject (four to five hours per week). The L1 of the students is Spanish. Although it was originally designed to include some subjects in Basque in the last years of compulsory education, this original resolution has been discarded. Students' command of Basque and their attitudes towards it are very poor.

- *Model B*: this is an early partial immersion programme in which both Basque and Spanish are used as means of instruction. These students' L1 is usually Spanish, although there may be some rare exceptions with Basque as their L1. In this model, the first three years (kindergarten) are generally taught through Basque. At the age of six – the first year of primary education – students start on the reading-writing process and mathematics in Spanish. Some schools have evolved towards a more *intensive* model B, in which the reading-writing process and part of or the whole subject of Maths is carried out in Basque. Without any doubt, this is the most heterogeneous model, and depending on different factors such as the sociolinguistic setting in which the school is located or the availability of Basque teaching staff, the time allotted to each of the languages varies considerably, and so does students' command of Basque.
- *Model D*: a total immersion programme for those students whose L1 is Spanish and a maintenance programme for those with Basque as their L1 (unlike Finland or Canada, where total immersion programmes are used only with students who have no knowledge of the vehicle language). Spanish is only taught as a subject (four to five hours per week). Of the three approaches, model D students attain the greatest fluency in Basque and their attitudes are the most favourable.

Currently, approximately half of immigrant students enrolled in primary and secondary education choose model A (43%), while models B (28.9%) and D (27.9%) are less popular. These percentages contrast starkly with those of local students, among whom model D is the most widely selected: model A (26.4%), model B (21.4%) and model D (52%).

The Study

The sample consisted of 151 teachers and immigrant students who were divided into three groups: 76 students of immigrant origin who completed a questionnaire, 66 in-service teachers who also filled out a questionnaire and 9 in-service teachers who were invited to take part in two group discussions. All the participants in the study worked or studied in Vitoria-Gasteiz, the capital of the BAC.

The students came from 17 different countries of origin. These newcomers had spent an average of four and a half years in the BAC, although half of them had lived in the BAC for two years or less. Of their families, three out of four might be considered lower class. All of them were enrolled in model A and had very little knowledge (if any) of

Basque. They completed a questionnaire in which they were asked about the three languages of the curriculum and their own language(s) (see Ibarraran *et al.*, 2008, for further details).

The 66 in-service teachers were invited to fill in a questionnaire. In one part of the questionnaire, they were invited to freely express their opinions about the immigrant students' own languages. Some of the respondents worked in schools with a high percentage of immigrants, whereas others had few (or none) in their classes. Their mean age was 43 years, 44.6% were male and 55.4% female.

Two discussion groups in which nine teachers participated complemented the data from the questionnaires. They taught at two schools where the percentage of immigrant students was very high (40 and 18%, respectively), and had an average of 14 and 5.2 years' teaching experience. The objective was to analyse their opinions about immigrant students' language competence and attitudes.

Results

First of all, the attitudes held by immigrant students will be examined. Their attitudes towards the different languages in contact were divided into three categories: unfavourable attitudes, neutral attitudes and favourable attitudes. Figure 2.2 contains the percentage of students who showed positive attitudes towards each language.

The results reflect that immigrant students held very favourable attitudes towards their own language; it is important to remember that, in the case of their own languages, only those students whose mother tongue was not Spanish were included in the analysis. In fact, the

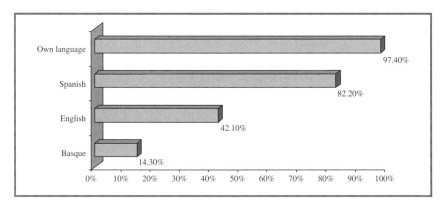

Figure 2.2 Immigrant students' favourable attitudes towards each language

percentage of favourable attitudes (just one student did not show positive attitudes) is higher than that of Spanish, the majority language in the community where they live and the language of the school. Curiously enough, more held a favourable attitude towards English (42.10%) than towards Basque (14.30%). Thus, the results clearly demonstrate that immigrant students overwhelmingly support their own languages (above all when these are different from Spanish) and remain loyal to them, whereas they turn their backs on Basque.

In the open questionnaire, the immigrant students were given the option of expressing their opinions about their own languages and the vast majority of them pointed out that their languages should have some presence in their schools: 'I would love to study my mother tongue at school, because now I speak most of the time Spanish and I am forgetting my mother tongue, Romanian'; 'I love my language, its writing and the way we speak it. It is really attractive. Yes, I would definitely like to study it at high school, so that we could learn more about my culture'. Their comments regarding the Basque language, however, were rather negative (even derogatory on many occasions) and they complained that there was no need to learn a language that was hardly present in their context and which was only spoken in this small part of Spain: 'I do not like it and I think it should be obliterated from the curriculum'; 'I don't like it at all. It is boring, and it is useless'; 'I don't like learning it. It is not important. It is only spoken in the Basque Country but not in other areas. Moreover, I don't intend to live here for ever'.

The teachers also completed closed and open items in their questionnaire. They were first asked to rate the importance/necessity of a list of languages on a four-point scale: very important/necessary, quite important/necessary, not very important/necessary and not important/ necessary at all. Figure 2.3 provides the percentage of teachers who regarded each language as very or rather important/necessary.

Both Spanish and English were highly rated by all the participants, the Basque language lagging slightly behind (87.7%). Two European languages, French (79.7%) and German (69.8%) came next; however, there was a wide gulf between these and all the other languages, which were considered important by less than half of the participants. Chinese and Arabic, the two more international languages spoken by immigrant students, gathered exactly the same support (both regarded as important/necessary by 40.7% of the respondents), followed by Latin, a subject included in the curriculum of those students who choose Humanities instead of Science before entering university. Catalan (34.5%) and Portuguese (27.6%) were not highly rated, whereas the remaining

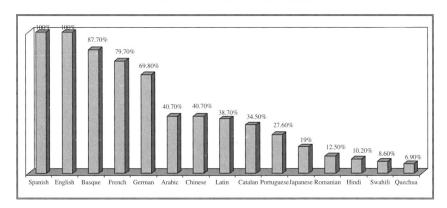

Figure 2.3 Percentage of teachers who regarded each language as very/quite important/necessary

languages were not considered to be important/necessary: Japanese (19%), Romanian (12.5%), Hindi (10.2%), Swahili (8.6%) and Quechua (6.9%).

The three compulsory languages in the curriculum are the most highly valued, followed by French and German. Therefore, the European languages are well ahead of the immigrants' languages in the teachers' preferences. Arabic and Chinese are supported by around 40% of the participants, but the remaining immigrant languages find little favour.

Besides the part of the closed questionnaire considered above, teachers could also express their opinions about the immigrant students' languages through the open questionnaire. Despite the results summarised in Figure 2.3, the majority of the teachers' comments showed the importance attached to the maintenance of the immigrants' own languages. As a matter of fact, one of the most recurrent terms present in their comments is *respect*. Basque teachers affirmed that immigrant students' own languages must be respected and that efforts should be made so that they are not eventually lost: 'I have a feeling of absolute respect. These languages are part of their cultures and they should therefore be maintained'. This idea of respect is closely linked with the term *integration*, in the sense that the respondents stated that the integration process would be boosted if their languages were respected. One of the teachers put it this way:

Their own languages are of the utmost importance for their family structure and for students to be aware of who they are in the world. Integration must go hand in hand with respect to their family, folk, language and culture, if the feeling of having been separated from their roots is to be avoided. If there is a rupture with their language, this will lead to a feeling of having been uprooted from their family and cultural surroundings and this will make integration in our social, cultural and educational context unfeasible.

Another wrote the following:

In my opinion it is very important for immigrant students to have the possibility of establishing relationships and of expressing themselves in their own language. To impede this option would mean to destroy their links with their origins.

The idea of respect relates not only to pupils learning more about themselves, but also to their classmates getting to know them. Some of the respondents went even further and proposed that their classmates should be provided with some rudimentary instruction regarding these other languages in order to become acquainted with these cultures. The immigrant students' languages are therefore highly regarded as a bridge to their integration.

However, some of the respondents were more critical. Fourteen (out of 66) of their statements were quite candid, indicating that helping the students conserve their own language may not only be rather complex, but could even hinder their integration. These comments can be divided into three main categories.

The first category encompasses those comments in which the teachers showed their concern because they considered that immigrant students should direct all their efforts towards learning the languages of the community they live in. They see the immigrant languages as a hurdle to social integration, and that the official languages of the BAC deserve to be the main targets of students' linguistic endeavours. The following three quotations are a very good case in point:

I respect their own languages, but in my opinion they have to integrate and this is basically carried out by means of the language spoken where they live.

Their languages are important, as ours are. The thing is that if they intend to integrate here then learning our language or languages must be compulsory; they have no other possible way to achieve it.

I have no knowledge and no relationship with their languages, but I think they have to be helped to be able to express themselves in both Basque and Spanish. The maintenance of their own languages may bring about the creation of ghettos.

The second main reason put forward by those against the maintenance option had to do with the difficulties to be faced if their own languages were encouraged. The lack of human and material resources, the difficulties involved in learning the different languages as well as the lack of time, were highlighted as insurmountable obstacles: 'These languages are only used in their family environment. They have no future in our context and, moreover, the learning of these languages is very complicated and tough'. Even among those teachers who were more positive about supporting the immigrant languages, some voices acknowledged that, despite their interest in learning them, a lack of time was the definitive barrier.

The third category consisted of comments in which support was limited to the international languages that are also frequently spoken by immigrant students who come from former European colonies. The presence of students from African countries such as Morocco or Senegal was observed as a possibility to foster the use of French, an international language that is more prestigious and useful in some teachers' eyes than Arabic or Wolof, to name but two of the languages spoken in the aforementioned countries.

In an attempt to complement the data gathered through the open and closed items included in the questionnaire, two discussion groups were organised (Ibarraran *et al.*, 2008). Discussion groups can become a powerful tool if the participants are actively engaged with the questions raised by the researcher/prompter and if the discussion allows the participants to develop their own views based on sound critical thinking. Bearing in mind that a good group discussion depends on the following four factors, the researcher tried to comply with all four of them: (1) the discussion must have a purpose: the analysis of what is going on in multilingual and multicultural classes; (2) the participants must have something to say: all the teachers had wide experience in the teaching world and were practised at handling diverse classroom situations; (3) the participants must feel comfortable participating: the researcher/prompter endeavoured to let the teachers be the main protagonists and limited his role to prompting different issues; and (4) meaningful questions should be raised: all the issues dealt with were focused on their teaching experience and their everyday work.

Of the different issues raised during these discussions, we will concentrate here on the teachers' opinions about their immigrant students' language competence and attitudes. All the participants agreed that immigrant students' command of everyday language was rather good, however they had more than a few problems when it came to using the language in an academic context. And this was the case, even among pupils from Latin America for whom Spanish was their mother tongue. One of the teachers put it this way:

> They can learn the language for daily life purposes... but when it comes to command of the school language – reading textbooks, understanding teachers' explanations, dealing with the complex terminology of different subjects – they are completely lost.

These difficulties emerge in their learning process due to their limited knowledge of the academic language. Problems arise in school subjects such as history, which require a better command of the language when compared to others where their lack of academic language proficiency is not such a hindrance, as the following quotation from one of the discussants shows:

> They are students, for example, who have no problems in maths or physics, because they understand the international symbolic language... and also in English as they have studied it before in their home countries. But in subjects such as history and philosophy... they lack the necessary language competence to tackle the required level of abstraction and subsequently to deal with them successfully.

These teachers were aware that their immigrant students can fare successfully – or will manage in the short run in the case of those more recently arrived – in the first of these language dimensions, but they also emphatically expressed their students' deficit in the second dimension. And this was so, even among those students from Spanish-speaking countries.

Although the participants in the study did not make reference to any theoretical framework, this dichotomy corresponds to Cummins' (1984, 2000) well-known distinction between Basic Interpersonal Communicative Skills (BICS) and Cognitive Academic Language Proficiency (CALP). Cummins posited that a great many classroom activities are cognitively demanding and frequently have to be independently completed by the student without any help from the context. The ability to perform such tasks in a second language is known as CALP. This kind of language proficiency contrasts with BICS, which refers to the language proficiency needed to carry out other sorts of tasks more related to interpersonal communication. This interpersonal communication is not so cognitively demanding as CALP and relies heavily on context in order to clarify meaning; a face-to-face speaking activity for instance, or even a listening activity wherein intonation, stress or the speaker's mood is usually helpful when trying to decode the intended message. Although migrant children attain the proficiency level of their monolingual peers in simple communication skills quite quickly, this may hide their inadequacy to cope with the cognitive and academic demands of the classroom activities, which need much more time.

Regarding the linguistic issue, the teachers participating in the discussion groups can be divided into two groups. The first group is made up of those who stated that the observed differences among immigrant students are due to their linguistic aptitude and the similarity between their L1 and Spanish: 'We find that some students, for instance, Romanian, Portuguese or Brazilian students, learn the language more easily, they understand the spoken language much better'. These teachers, however, also acknowledged the BICS/CALP distinction even among those students who speak languages that are typologically related to Spanish. The second group consisted of those for whom the immigrant students' level of literacy and sociocultural variables exerted a much greater influence on language learning than the (dis)similarity between the learning language and the students' L1. This viewpoint was expressed in the following consideration:

The linguistic structures of the mother tongue can facilitate or not the acquisition of another language... but our experience indicates that in the long run the general processes of adaptation, achievement or acquisition have much more to do with the socio-cultural back-ground of the immigrant students' family, whether their families have academic qualifications or not (...) In my opinion it is risky to characterise them according to ethnic origin, or try to find, let's say, homogeneous behaviours, although I am aware that some common traits can be found.

The teachers were unanimous and regarded Spanish as the language immigrant students need in order to understand their new surroundings and perform successfully, to succeed at school and to get a job. The following comment serves to illustrate this point:

Their families do not know anything about our educational system, which they find abstruse. And then they tell their child: as Spanish is the language we will need in our business, this is the language you have to learn well. You have to become my support in front of the customer, and that is the reason why you have to learn good Spanish at the local school.

In the case of Basque, all teachers considered that this language was not a priority for immigrant students, as both teachers and students concurred that Spanish is the language they need for their integration. At this stage, it has to be remembered that all the discussants were model A teachers, that is to say, teachers who lack the necessary language profile to teach in Basque:

> Spanish is the language they need for... for everyday life. As for Basque, although they are initially interested, it is obvious that as the level of difficulty increases, more often than not they feel frustrated, they are not motivated any more; it happens to be very difficult, or they simply say that there is no point in learning it if they are not going to speak it out on the street.

This quotation raises two points. Firstly, that Basque is a non-Indo-European language that has no typological relatedness to Spanish or English. In these teachers' opinion, this makes its learning very complex, therefore students need to make an additional effort to learn it. Curiously enough, these teachers do not take into account that for many pupils from Africa, Basque is as typologically distant as Spanish, as their diverse mother tongues bear little connection with these European languages. Secondly, Vitoria-Gasteiz, the capital city of the BAC (where this study was undertaken), is one of the Basque areas in which Basque is least spoken and this may be the reason why students may have the impression that there is no need to learn it. Although immigrant students tend to enrol in models B and D in areas where Basque is more widely spoken, this is not the case in this city.

As far as English as a foreign language is concerned, the teachers highlighted the differences among students, depending on the language background with which they enter high school. Brazilian and Arabic students, for example, find learning English very hard because foreign language teaching starts much later in their country of origin than in the Basque educational system (in the BAC, English teaching starts at the age of four):

> Brazilian students are not usually very competent in English because in their home country they start learning it from the age of twelve/ thirteen onwards. Similarly, students of Arabic origin usually speak French and have had very little contact (or none at all) with the English language.

Curiously enough, immigrant students held significantly more positive attitudes towards English than their local counterparts, and this despite their English proficiency being lower (Ibarraran *et al.*, 2008). In the case of English, and as shown in the open question of the questionnaire, the immigrant students are led by an instrumental orientation, due to its role as the lingua franca and to how useful it is to obtain a job.

When the teachers were asked about the purported benefits of the presence of the immigrant students' own languages in the school, two different viewpoints stood out. Although the vast majority of these experienced teachers were in favour of including these languages in school life, some believed that the students' motivation was not good enough to assure some degree of success, despite their families' interest in maintaining their home languages. Others stated that all the speakers of a language should be gathered in a single school outside the regular timetable. In this way, their motivation would increase and the speakers of the same language would not feel so isolated. In any case, the right option does not seem to be straightforward and they were well aware that there are no simplistic solutions. Moreover, the very recent arrival of large numbers of immigrant students into the Basque educational system gives teachers the impression that the authorities are implementing makeshift measures on too many occasions. In fact, one of their main complaints had to do with the lack of material and human resources to tackle this new situation.

Discussion and Conclusion

From the 1996/1997 to the 2006/2007 academic year, the number of immigrant students in Spanish schools increased 767.46%. In the case of the BAC, it went up 23% between 2006/2007 and 2007/2008, that is to say, in just one year. This data clearly confirms that the increasing presence of immigrant students is a question that deserves to be analysed in detail in Spain in general (see Pérez-Vidal *et al.*, 2008) and in the Basque context in particular.

Students of immigrant origin need to learn the two official languages of the BAC, namely Basque and Spanish, as this is not only a linguistic right, but also a must if they are to become members of the community and help their integration, both in the social sphere in general and in the labour market in particular. For the time being, the majority of them are choosing a linguistic model (model A) that does not allow them to become sufficiently proficient in Basque and fosters negative attitudes towards it, as research studies recurrently demonstrate (Lasagabaster, 2007). These results tally with those obtained by Bernaus *et al.* (2004) among immigrant students in Catalonia with regard to the Catalan language. Immigrant students need to be more positive about Basque and realise how important this language is in their attempt to integrate into Basque society. However, it is also a fact that those students who arrive in the BAC at a late age, for example at the age of 12 or older, will have to choose between the two languages (due to lack of time, as they leave compulsory education at 16) and will probably choose Spanish, this being the majority language. Despite this choice, the school system must endeavour to foster positive attitudes towards Basque also among these late arrivals. If we are realistic, late arrivals will be forced to select Spanish most of the time, but this does not mean that they can leave the school system without being fully aware of the importance and the role played by the Basque language. The main task of education is to provide every single child with the skills required to be able to function as members of society (a bilingual society in the case of the BAC). Education must accomplish this task by empowering students through the acquisition of the necessary knowledge, skills and attitudes. This is the emancipatory function of education for all children (Van Avermaet, 2006), irrespective of their origin or when they join the educational system.

There is no doubt that learning three languages requires a big effort, but it is also true that youngsters can manage if they are provided with the right atmosphere and adequate methodology. And this is especially true in the case of those students of immigrant origin who are born in the BAC, who have the right to learn the two official languages and the foreign one. If they leave compulsory education without these trilingual skills, they will be in a weak position with respect to their classmates, and this will impede social cohesion.

Immigrant students who start with fewer opportunities seem to have major difficulties catching up with their peers at school. More often than not, the gap actually increases during schooling instead of decreasing, and this may seem the case in bilingual areas, such as the BAC, where even at nursery school there are three languages present in the curriculum. The ever-increasing multicultural diversity found in Basque schools demands appropriate action. Thus, Basque schools will have to adapt their teaching methods to this diversity so that they can compensate for the student's differences. If academic and social failure are to be avoided, the school system should adapt to the students rather than the students to the school (Van Avermaet, 2006); that is to say, the school system should endeavour to organise teaching so that all students acquire the school languages needed to function not only at school, but also in society.

Moreover, there is another important linguistic issue that also has to be considered, namely immigrant students' right to learn their own language(s). In the BAC, they have not asked for this right yet, unlike in Canada (Coelho, 1998) or Australia (Clyne & Kipp, 2006), but the educational system must be ready for this prospective situation. The loss of their own languages should be avoided, as their maintenance has positive effects at three different levels:

(1)   At the cognitive level: the development of their L1 will help them to learn the other languages present in the curriculum and to succeed at school (Cummins, 2002). However, Martín Rojo and Mijares (2007) assert that most Spanish schools follow an *only Spanish* language policy, according to which all previous knowledge, including the immigrant students' own languages and cultures, is simply disregarded.

(2)   At the personal level: their own languages may help immigrant students both from an instrumental perspective (i.e. to get a job in the future) and from an integrative perspective (i.e. to reinforce their identity).

(3)   At the social level: their languages may become a very useful tool when it comes to the development of trade and industry (Clyne & Kipp, 2006). If we invest in immigrant children's languages, there will be an economic return in the short run.

However, our results demonstrate that teachers rate European languages much higher than those spoken by the immigrant students. These results are in accord with those obtained by Kouritzin *et al.* (2007), who examined pre-service teachers' attitudes towards foreign language teaching and learning in Canada. Despite the fact that the perceived collective social value of multilingualism was very high, the respondents did not attach an important personal value to it. When asked to rate the languages, English was overwhelmingly chosen as most important, followed by French, Spanish, Japanese, German, Cantonese and Mandarin, whereas very few chose Tagalog, Ukrainian or an Aboriginal language, despite the fact that these languages were present in their communities. Kouritzin, Piquemal and Nakagawa state that those interested in the teaching profession should become committed to cultural and linguistic diversity and be aware of the important limitations entailed by monolingualism, both in the personal and the social spheres.

In Spain, little attention has been paid so far to the languages spoken by immigrant students, who are obliged to mimic the cultural behaviour of the host community. And this same trend can be found in most contexts where immigration has had an impact on the different educational systems (Corbett, 2003). The immigrant cultures receive little or no attention at all, despite interesting initiatives such as the one put forward by the European Union through the *personal adoptive language*, which we referred to in the introduction. This is probably a very feasible way to bridge this gap between *local* and *immigrant* languages. There are many different ways in which immigrant languages can be included in the curriculum. Being able to speak English will not be such an asset in a few years' time, when many students will be reasonably fluent. The inclusion of the personal adoptive language would not only help to diminish the overwhelming hegemony held by English, but it would also help to increase social cohesion as speakers of other languages will perceive that their language and culture are also appreciated.

Last but not least, there is an urgent need to redesign teacher training degrees so that future teachers are fully aware of the paramount importance of linguistic diversity, and are able to promote this linguistic and cultural diversity. The incorporation of a multilingual and multi-cultural dimension into teacher training is an imperative. Only in this way can the policy recommendations made by the European Commission's Directorate-General for Education and Culture be carried out, especially concerning the need to ensure that mainstream education and training policies include provision for teaching regional, minority, migrant and neighbouring languages. School systems require open-minded teachers who are ready to open their classroom doors to different languages and cultures and to capitalise on the diversity pupils bring with them when they come to school (Dooly & Eastment, 2008). Diversity has to be seen not as a problem, but rather as richness. Once diversity is properly understood, everybody will become aware that monolingual-ism is the *privilege* of the rich.

References

Barni, M. and Extra, G. (2008) *Mapping Linguistic Diversity in Multicultural Contexts*. Berlin and New York: Mouton de Gruyter.

Bernaus, M., Masgoret, A-M., Gardner, R.C. and Reyes, E. (2004) Motivation and attitudes toward learning languages in multicultural classrooms. *International Journal of Multilingualism* 1 (2), 75–89.

Clyne, M. and Kipp, S. (2006) *Tiles in a Multilingual Mosaic: Macedonian, Filipino and Somali in Melbourne*. Canberra, Australia: Pacific Linguistics.

Coelho, E. (1998) *Teaching and Learning in Multicultural Schools*. Clevedon: Multilingual Matters.

Coleman, J.A. (2006) English-medium teaching in European higher education. *Language Teaching* 39 (1), 1–14.

Corbett, J. (2003) *An Intercultural Approach to English Language Teaching.* Clevedon: Multilingual Matters.

Cummins, J. (1984) Wanted: A theoretical framework for relating language proficiency to academic achievement among bilingual students. In C. Rivera (ed.) *Language Proficiency and Academic Achievement* (pp. 2–19). Clevedon: Multilingual Matters.

Cummins, J. (2000) Putting language proficiency in its place: Responding to critiques of the conversational/academic language distinction. In J. Cenoz and U. Jessner (eds) *English in Europe: The Acquisition of a Third Language* (pp. 54–83). Clevedon: Multilingual Matters.

Cummins, J. (2002) *Negotiating Identities: Education for Empowerment in a Diverse Society.* Los Angeles, CA: California Association for Bilingual Education.

Dooly, M. and Eastment, D. (eds) (2008) *"How We're Going about It." Teachers' Voices on Innovative Approaches to Teaching and Learning Languages.* Newcastle: Cambridge Scholars Publishing.

Huguet, Á., Lasagabaster, D. and Vila, I. (2008) Bilingual education in Spain: Present realities and future challenges. In J. Cummins and N.H. Hornberger (eds) *Encyclopedia of Language and Education,* 2nd Edition Volume 5: *Bilingual Education* (pp. 225–235). New York: Springer Science + Business Media LLC.

Ibarraran, A., Lasagabaster, D. and Sierra, J.M. (2008) Multilingualism and language attitudes: Local versus immigrant students' perceptions. *Language Awareness* 17 (4), 326–341.

Kouritzin, S.G., Piquemal, N.A.C. and Nakagawa, S. (2007) Pre-service teacher beliefs about foreign language teaching and learning. *Journal of Multilingual and Multicultural Development* 28 (3), 220–237.

Lasagabaster, D. (2007) Language use and language attitudes in the Basque Country. In D. Lasagabaster and Á. Huguet (eds) *Multilingualism in European Bilingual Contexts: Language Use and Attitudes* (pp. 65–89). Clevedon: Multilingual Matters.

Maalouf, A. (ed.) (2008) *A Rewarding Challenge. How the Multiplicity of Languages Could Strengthen Europe.* Brussels: European Commission.

Martín Rojo, L. and Mijares, L. (2007) "Sólo en español." Una reflexión sobre la norma monolingüe y la realidad multilingüe de los centros escolares. *Revista de Educación* 343, 93–112.

Pérez-Vidal, C., Juan-Garau, M. and Bel, A. (eds) (2008) *A Portrait of the Young in the New Multilingual Spain.* Clevedon: Multilingual Matters.

Van Avermaet, P. (2006) Socially disadvantaged learners and languages of education. On WWW at http//www.coe.int/t/dg4/linguistic/Source/Va n_Avermaet_final_EN.doc. Accessed 1.6.08.

Chapter 3

Teaching with an Accent: Linguistically Diverse Preservice Teachers in Australian Classrooms

JENNIFER MILLER

Introduction

As globalisation increasingly impacts on all education institutions and sectors, teachers and preservice education students in many countries grapple with extremely diverse classrooms and pedagogical complexities. Many studies, including several reported in this volume, have looked at how language teachers' work has been changed by dramatic increases in the number of students from culturally and linguistically diverse (CALD) backgrounds, including immigrants and refugee learners (Leung, 2002; McBrien, 2005; Miller *et al.*, 2005; Norton & Toohey, 2004). But there is limited research on the similarly increasing numbers of teachers from CALD backgrounds. Australia, like Canada and the UK, already has an immensely diverse population, with 25% of people born overseas, but international students are adding to the mix in preservice teacher education courses. Further, at a time of severe teacher shortages in several key areas, Australia now relies heavily on developing an international teaching force. This is particularly the case in second and foreign language programmes. In one study of 35 preservice teachers of English as a Second Language (ESL) at an Australian university, it was found that 13 of the students (35%) did not speak English as a first language, 24 students (64%) had parents for whom English was not the first language, and 16 students (43%) were born outside Australia in 14 different countries (Brown & Miller, 2006). As part of a global trend towards the internationalisation of tertiary education, Australian universities now have extremely diverse classrooms in language teacher education, with huge growth in international enrolments from Asian and European countries in the past five years.

This chapter reports on a recent study of five preservice education students completing a postgraduate Diploma of Education in a large Australian university. The course included two five-week practicum teaching blocks. All spoke English as a second or additional language and were from a range of countries, including China, Egypt, Sri Lanka, Germany and Italy. Although only two of the five were language teachers, all encountered issues powerfully related to the use of English and their identities as non-native speakers in their practicum schools. Using data from focus group (FG) interviews and written reflections on the practicum, this chapter explores two issues related to language use and professional identity for this group of CALD teachers. It addresses the following questions:

- What cultural and linguistic challenges confront preservice teachers from linguistically diverse backgrounds?
- What is the role of English in developing a professional identity?
- How can preservice teacher education programmes better support teachers from diverse backgrounds?

In this chapter, I present the context of the study, followed by an overview of theory and research on the key themes of identity and language use. I then briefly outline the methodology of the study, before addressing the questions above using data from interviews and reflections. In the final section, I look at the implications of the study for teacher education in plurilingual times.

Globalised Education and Teaching

In 2008, there were 150,000 international fee-paying students in higher education in Australia. International students come to Australia because of a range of university entry pathways, including university preparatory courses, schools and English language courses. Student recruitment is also linked to a favourable policy of migration or permanent residency under the general skilled migration category, whereby successful students can apply for residency (Healy, 2008). In addition to international students in education programmes, as in the ESL curriculum class described in the opening paragraph, many local students are from diverse linguistic and cultural backgrounds, and may or may not speak English at home.

What are the pressures faced by beginning teachers who have an accent, who may use non-standard language forms occasionally, or who look and sound different as they enter Australian classrooms, which can also be highly diverse? Santoro (1999) suggests that while all preservice teachers may struggle with the diversity of students and programmes currently in schools, preservice teachers from diverse language and cultural backgrounds may face additional cultural issues, including racism, during the practicum. For these teachers, language variety and use may implicate professional identity in crucial ways. For over a decade, many researchers in the language education field have continuously highlighted the role of language use in the construction of identity (Cummins, 2000; Gee, 1996, 2004; Goldstein, 2003; Hawkins, 2004; Miller, 2003; Norton & Toohey, 2004). It is, therefore, important to frame identity theory as central to this study.

Teaching and Identity

The critical sociocultural framing of recent research into language use tends to demonstrate that identity is a core concept, along with agency, discourse, culture, diversity, social interaction, local context and lived experience (Miller, 2009). Within this frame, identity is viewed as relational, negotiated, discursively constructed and socially enacted. It has been variously described as 'how a person understands his or her relationship to the world' (Norton, 2000: 5); 'a constant ongoing negotiation of how we relate to the world' (Pennycook, 2001: 149); 'relational, constructed and altered by how I see others and how they see me in our shared experiences and negotiated interactions' (Johnson, 2003: 788); or 'Being recognized as a certain "kind of person" ... connected not to internal states but to performances in society' (Gee, 2000–2001: 99).

If one accepts the theoretical view that identity is relational, interactional and constructed in social contexts, it cannot be viewed as an *entity*, but rather it needs to be seen in relation to discursive, social, cultural and institutional elements. Regarding preservice teacher education, we can say that language teaching cannot be separated from social language use in classrooms, or from situated meanings within social practices, involving specific social and institutional contexts and memberships. What does this mean for linguistically diverse students in preservice teacher education? Duff and Uchida (1997) stress some of the elements that are key to understanding issues of identity, language, culture and social context. They write:

> Language teachers and students in any setting naturally represent a wide array of social and cultural roles and identities: as teachers or students, as gendered and cultured individuals, as expatriates or nationals, as native speakers or non-native speakers, as content-area

or TESL/English language specialists, as individuals with political convictions, and as members of families, organizations, and society at large. (Duff & Uchida, 1997: 451)

This statement highlights the multidimensional nature of identity and also the inappropriateness of stereotyping or essentialising students for whom English is not a first language. However, the alternatives laid out by Duff and Ushida may not be equally valued in mainstream school contexts. Ideological and institutional processes also impact on the ways in which linguistic minority teachers are viewed and heard.

Being Heard

Preservice teachers who are users of English as an additional language have to cope with the ways they are heard or represented by others. Their experiences in classrooms may vary widely, depending on their personal resources such as language proficiency, social capital, personal biography, interactional skills, knowledge and attitudes (Miller, 2009). Gee (1996, 2004) makes the point that in any teacher's communication to their students, the 'what', the 'how', the 'who', the 'who to' and the 'what's happening' will all come into play. Identity in these terms is 'enacted', but it is also ascribed by the hearer, who has the power to accept or to deny both the message and the identity of the speaker. It is important to keep this two-way process in mind, namely, that identity is a way of doing things, but is critically related to what is legitimated by others in any social context. All teachers have their 'ways of being' in language classrooms, yet most would attest to the power of their students to grant or refuse a hearing. Preservice teachers on the practicum must also be legitimated as speakers and as teachers by their supervisors, students and the school administration, adding another layer of power to the mix.

In his introduction to Bourdieu's (1991: 18) *Language and Symbolic Power*, Thompson reminds us that in Bourdieu's terms,

> differences in terms of accent, grammar and vocabulary – the very differences overlooked by formal linguistics – are indices of the social positions of speakers and reflections of the quantities of linguistic capital (and other capital) which they possess.

These differences are indices to the listener about the speaker. Just as accent can function as 'the last back door to discrimination' (Lippi-Green, 1997: 73), in an English-speaking country, with an English-medium education system, the manner of speaking may be part of legitimising and/or discriminatory processes and practices. Bourdieu (1993: 66) states, 'One of the political effects of the dominant language is this: "He says it so well it must be true"'. Clearly, the reverse may also be applied to those subjected to the dominant discourse. If teachers don't 'say it well', what are the consequences? Accents, intelligibility and written and spoken language proficiency all become salient to understanding the experience of preservice teachers operating in an additional language.

Identity and the Non-native English-speaking Teacher

Part of the difficulty of writing about the teachers in this study is a question of nomenclature. I continue to struggle with a descriptor for these teachers, as does a literature that refers to native and non-native speakers; linguistic minorities; CALD background speakers; users of English as a second or additional language; bilingual, multilingual or plurilingual cohorts, multicultural groups and so on. If we take the example of the highly diverse cohort described in the introduction, how inadequate the term 'non-native English speaker' seems. The binary of native-speaker versus non-native speaker and assumptions about native speaker competence have been contested for some years (Davies, 2003; Higgins, 2003; Leung *et al.*, 1997; Lippi-Green, 1997; McKay, 2003), yet institutions are remarkably resistant to what is perceived as a change in standards of English language use. Although varieties of English are a fact of life in Australia, teachers are subject to certain institutional constraints and expectations, many of them entirely appropriate.

In most Western universities, international students usually have to demonstrate high levels of performance on International English Language Testing System (IELTS) or Test of English as a Foreign Language (TOEFL) tests, particularly for preservice teacher education courses (an overall IELTS score of 7 in my university). For obvious reasons, teachers in English medium classrooms are expected to have advanced levels of English language competence in all areas. However, due to the multiple pathways of entry to such courses (e.g. via high school or citizenship), some students circumvent language-testing requirements. If they do have English language difficulties, as indeed some do, issues usually arise during the practicum. The issues and data presented below throw light on the complex, multidimensional linguistic and identity issues that arise for the teachers involved. Hall (1996: 4) suggests that identities are about the process of 'becoming rather than being: not "who we are" or "where we came from", so much as what we might become, how we have been represented and how that bears on how we might represent ourselves'. This process is critical for beginning teachers who are perceived as being 'from elsewhere', but who are struggling to become Australian teachers. I turn now to the study and its findings.

The Study

The research reported here was part of a wider project on English language proficiency of non-native-speaking preservice teachers and teacher readiness, and the role of English in the development of a professional teacher identity. In Australia, all preservice teachers require two teaching subject areas. For the purposes of this chapter, I use data from written reflections and two one-hour audiorecorded focus groups (FGs) with five participants, focusing on the role of English in the development of a professional identity for these student teachers (Table 3.1). All were Graduate Diploma of Education students who had completed their undergraduate degrees in their countries of origin, and had just done the second five-week teaching practicum. They were near the end of their one-year course at the time of the study. Names are pseudonyms. Note that all were mature-age students.

Table 3.1 Participants

Name	*Age*	*Country of origin*	*LOR (years)*	*Specialist teaching areas*	*Languages spoken at home*	*Years studying English*
Andrea	39	China	10	Maths and Mandarin	Cantonese and English	25
Lorine	34	Sri Lanka	2.5	Maths and IT	English and Sinhalese	8
Mike	35	Egypt	2.5	Economics, Social Studies	Arabic	10
Tina	40+	Germany	11	ESL, German	English	19
Nick	40	Italy	2	Maths, Physics	English	4

Note: LOR: length of residence

There were some similarities, but also clear differences between the students. Andrea and Tina had been in Australia for many years and were permanent residents. Both Andrea and Nick had married Australian partners, and Nick said he had learned English largely through interactions with his wife. Tina's English was close to an Australian variety with a very slight German accent, whereas Andrea referred to her fluent but often grammatically inaccurate English as her 'Chinglish'. Although she had studied English for longest, her oral and written English were problematic, as will be seen in the data. Nick and Mike spoke fluently and confidently in the FG, while Lorine was perhaps the quietest and least confident of the five. Note that the language of the data has not been 'corrected' and is presented as spoken or written.

Two Themes of Teacher Diversity in Australian Classrooms

An earlier study of ESL preservice teachers at the same university found that although an overwhelming majority of students dismissed the claim that native speakers of English made the best ESL teachers, there was an implicit positioning of native speaker as the 'ideal' (Brown & Miller, 2006). 'Near native fluency' was identified as a desirable language level for a teacher, and indeed no-one would argue that any teacher should be less than competent in their skills in, and knowledge of, the language that they teach. This study sought to further understand the implications of such an assumption. How do beginning teachers who are, in most cases, not heard as native English speakers represent their identities in Australian classrooms? What linguistic and cultural challenges do they face? The data from the FGs and reflections revealed two key themes relevant to these questions. In brief, they are first, the relationship between identity and accent in teaching, and second, the perceived cultural gaps in knowledge and experience, some of which relate to Australian English. These are elaborated below.

English, Identity and Accent

For CALD teachers, accent is salient in several ways, and all participants mentioned it as a problematic issue for them. As speakers in schools, they faced being misheard or even unheard at times, and they also had to grapple with the diversity of their students' accents in English. Furthermore, in their preservice course, the Australian accents of their peers were also sometimes a challenge in tutorials, as these comments by Nick and Andrea indicate.

When there is a tutorial, I find it very hard to follow the Australian accent and especially when there is some interruption from someone to say something about the situation in his school and the other one in the other corner of the room says something – it's very hard! (Nick, FG 2)

In terms of the tutorial group you need to hide, you can't say your problem – you maybe look idiot, or you maybe look uninformed, stupid, or something. You don't bring out your problem, so you are scared to ask any question. (Andrea, FG 1)

The struggle to understand Australian English spoken at speed, often with colloquialisms and assumed cultural understandings was difficult for all of these students. Andrea pinpoints the problem of sounding 'stupid', a comment that implicates identity. As Lippi-Green (1997) stresses, the negative assessment of accented or occasionally halting English is also a rejection of the speaker's identity. The fear of 'looking or sounding like an idiot' is the fear that keeps many international students silent. Nick reinforced this as follows,

I feel frustrated because in my native language, I can be very sophisticated and academic with my language and here instead in English, I must keep very simple no, all the time because I don't have all this skill with the English language. So sometime I perceive that other people, the people in front of me, think that I'm a little stupid no, I mean but not so educated. (Nick, FG 2)

Nick also highlighted the inequity that can occur in the tutorials, where Anglo-Australian speakers make little effort to hear and include their international peers. He stated, 'sometimes I find that the Australians have not the patience to hear us, to stay and listen, to put some attention, while we must do this for them' (FG 1).

It should be added that lecturers and tutors who took no account of the presence of international students were also criticised by the participants. Tina said:

If Australian students talk too quickly or like with an accent, there's nothing to complain about. But I think at least the tutor or the lecturer should have an awareness of like – oh there are international students there, they may not understand, and do some explanation. ...Actually maybe it is out of like good intentions, like don't want you to feel awkward, but sometimes we need help, we need extra help. (Tina, FG 2)

Other students added that some lecturers' use of colloquialisms and slang, as well as fast delivery, indicated a similar lack of awareness, and assumptions about the homogeneity of the cohort that were both inappropriate and inaccurate in an Australian plurilingual and multicultural context. It was significant that the participants all contrasted regular lectures and tutorials with study groups held specifically to support international preservice teachers, where they found a community, a voice and did not feel judged. Andrea stated she never felt 'language threatened' in these study groups, while Tina and Andrea highlighted the supportive relationships that developed with international peers.

Teaching with an accent

S1: Miss, you have an accent!
T: Of course I do. Everyone has an accent!
(too smart a reply, won't get away with this)
S1: Yeah, right, but I mean, your's [*sic*] isn't Aussie, like, it is different.
S2: Where are you from, Miss?
T: (oh dear, they found out, can't get away with this, better fess [*sic*] up)
Well, I am originally from Germany.
(Tina, written reflection)

The lines above were the opening to Tina's emailed reflection, and pinpoint the sense of being discovered and brought to account as an outsider. The practicum experience, where these preservice teachers faced supervisors, other teachers and their students, provided them with another arena in which their accents and sense of competence in English became salient. Lorine, like Nick above, contrasted her subject knowledge with her capacity to express herself clearly in English. She taught in an elite, mostly 'white' school, and this seemed to heighten her sense of anxiety. She stated:

> With my English speaking, I really haven't got many, uh, problems but all the time I feel it because it was uh, this school is mainly dominated by Anglo-Australian students. So, I didn't, I was very confident with my content knowledge but all the time I was nervous because of my speaking. I think my English is not good enough. With time I feel it. (Lorine, FG 2)

Largely because she was in a privileged private school, Lorine was not actually challenged by the behaviour of her students, or their reaction to her. This was not the case for others, who felt their 'non-nativeness' as a limitation to their classroom management. Here are two excerpts that reveal this.

And not being a native speaker I think left me less authority and sometimes they used slang and I couldn't quite understand what they were doing and I had to spot them. I said ok these are the rules and be, uh, much stricter a teacher than I would be. So, that made my limitation, showed me my limitation as a non-native speaker, both for ESL and English language speaking students, and I have to grapple with it. (Tina, FG 2)

One of my biggest worries to go into classroom was not to, ah, to pick up what they're saying or not to fully understand the jargon no?, the Australian jargon. So, also sometime if I think if they do some, they say something strange or some kind of swear things that I don't pick up, ah, they will feel authorised to say again, – "this fellow is not saying anything so we we are authorised to continue like this". Speaking with the others or things we are more worried, ah, to try to do some active listening or I don't know, to try to understand each other. But students are not really worried to make them(selves) understood. (Nick, FG 2)

It is no accident that, here, Tina and Nick are using terminology that would be familiar to readers of Bourdieu and to the notion of linguistic capital. The sense of being granted authority by the hearer, who has the legitimating role of 'believing listener' is critical for teachers. I am not suggesting that only non-native teachers struggle to get a hearing or to be authorised to speak in classrooms by their students (as thousands of unheard native-speaking teachers would attest), but that for these preservice teachers at least, their sense of control over their classrooms was partially linked to their sense of control over English. Nick's final point is that that students' lack of accommodation to an international variety of English was a real challenge for him. Mike had a similar experience. He said of the students:

They don't have tolerance in pronunciation – they don't have tolerance at all. Even during my teaching round the bishop of our church attended one of my classes. He liked very much the way I teach, but I didn't feel this from the students themselves. But from him he is very pleased from my way of teaching and even he asked the priest how long he has been in Australia because he speaks English very well. But in the students' eyes, I didn't feel this approval at all. They give me the impression that they feel that "you don't know how to speak like us".

It is to be hoped that the bishop did not ask the question in the presence of Mike, who could clearly have answered it himself! On one occasion, and under stress, Mike pronounced the word 'hemisphere' as 'hemisfire'. Instantly, a knowing student asked him what 'hemisfire' meant. He said it meant 'hemisphere', but this simple challenge by a student made an indelible impression on Mike, who raised it in both FGs and in his reflection. Having authority, being authorised to speak, student tolerance to variations in pronunciation and student approval were issues that bound language use to professional identity for these teachers, and to what I have elsewhere called 'audible difference' (Miller, 2003).

Before leaving the topic of accent, it is worth raising the problem of language use that is clearly non-standard, even problematic (see also Miller, forthcoming). This was the case for Andrea, whose 'Chinglish' was characterised by many grammatical and phonological errors. As a local resident living in Australia for a decade, she had not been required to do an English proficiency test for the course. She said she knew her science content in Chinese and was already an experienced teacher, but she struggled with content sometimes, depending on the topic, and with language consistently. Here is an excerpt from her written reflection on one topic, where she did not feel secure and her classroom behaviour management suffered accordingly.

> Because I am not very familiar with my Science topic so I try to avoid explain too much to the students—I do more Parcs [pracs] and experiments instead of chalk and talk—the students love the parc and activity—but they do still need the instructions and ex-planations—especially the weak ones. But the weak class is so noisy that I don't want to talk over them so I end up not explain or can't explain—at the end they complain I am not explain enough—which I am conscious too. So language ability do place an important part in our teaching and learning—I feel sorry for all the parties—for the teacher who struggle to deliver her messages, also for the students who struggle to understand that teacher. As a learner all my life, I will prefer a teacher who can speak pleasure English or Chinese too. I am very confident at my intelligent and knowledge but has doubt at

the abilities to communicate effetely to the students. (Andrea, emailed reflection, as received)

The trade-off for her lack of ability to explain clearly was to engage students in hands-on practical work, but this compromised the students' understanding, especially the weak ones who needed even clearer explanations. Unruly behaviour was a predictable outcome. By 'pleasure English', Andrea meant standard English, as she shows in the following comments.

> But, as a teacher myself, I don't want that the kids can't say the terminology, or the content is incorrect, because as a teacher that is my duty of job, to give them the correct pronunciation, so it is a lot of pressure for me to catch up with this language. So I wonder, is there anyway can help me to do my pronunciation more accurately in terms of the term, and in terms of not much accent. I hate my accent myself too, but for some reason you just have it. Because I don't want to listen to people speaking in accent, honestly. I want to listen to standard English. I want to have a precious experience when you are talking to people or listening, you want to have a nice sound. People with accent – it is awful! I understand kids don't like it or other people don't like it either. (Andrea, FG 2)

Here is a huge dilemma for Andrea, someone who hates her own accent in English, realises the students need to understand to learn, but is unsure what to do about it. She tends to conflate all aspects of proficiency as 'pronunciation', but the broader problem stands, for both teacher and student. How are students to achieve when the teacher is not always intelligible, or able to give precise and meaningful explanations? Unfortunately, I have no easy answer. Andrea was an outlier in this regard. None of the other four participants had this level of dysfluency in their use of English. Yet, irrespective of this, all experienced a level of negative assessment of their language competence. All struggled to get a hearing as it were, as the many interview excerpts above attest. Nick also struggled with a teaching supervisor whom he described as 'that kind of Australian that does not like non-Anglo-Saxon people'. Nick was, in my view, a highly articulate and communicative speaker, but his supervisor wrote on his report, 'his thick accent and relative inexperience with English has hampered his ability to communicate' (Nick, email reflection). In other words, the way he was heard positioned Nick as incompetent. He did not have this problem with his other supervisor or the students. I turn now to another related issue in language use, that of culture and cultural understandings.

Cultural Gaps: The Case of the Missing Childhood

The role of culture in communication was raised in several contexts in the data. The teachers were aware that their students lived in a different world, drew on resources that were unknown to them (the teachers), 'from what they watch on TV, from the way they live', as Nick put it. His fear that the students' use of Australian jargon might mean he could not understand them was, as he stated above, one of his 'biggest worries'. In his reflection, he wrote that he felt nervous communicating with teachers and students in terms of the demands of 'non-verbal communication and cultural knowledge'. In fact, the cultural knowledge and background that these cross-cultural teachers brought to the classroom was explicated by them as both a strength and a weakness. I'll begin with the latter.

In the FG, Tina commented that she felt she 'couldn't give them (her ESL students) so much of the cultural background and childhood experience in Australia as they wanted to know'. She later expanded on this in a written reflection:

> When I teach German I am happy to let the students know my country of birth as this seems to make it more natural for the students if I talk German in the classroom most of the time. In an ESL classroom, however, it seems to somewhat reduce my authenticity, especially since I noticed that the kids are as eager to learn about "the Australian way" as new words and expressions in English. Sometimes I seem to fail the students in that respect, especially when it comes to questions of childhood memories. Since I did not grow up in Australia, I cannot tell my students (about) Christmas days with 40 degree Christmas days, long summers by the beach, up country Victoria, riding horses through the paddocks or camping trips with parents to the outback. I feel I deprive the students, as I love to hear these stories from my friends who grew up in Australia. The "missing childhood" seems to matter less when I teach international students at university. (Tina, FG 2, reflection)

Here, Tina queries her right to the identity of an Australian teacher, even though many Australians were not privy to the stereotypical images she evokes of an Australian childhood. Tina belongs to the 25% of Australians who were born overseas, whose childhoods were elsewhere rather than 'missing', and who have enriched the country in many material and symbolic ways. Note the only context where she feels her culture as a 'lack' is the ESL classroom, where students are understandably curious about their new home country. It may be that students newly arrived from elsewhere want Australian language and cultural insights in order to locate themselves in a new place. Although very secure in her use of English, Tina wanted more cultural stories to relate to them. A slightly different problem was experienced by Lorine, who felt unable to relate to the culture of the staffroom in her school. She commented on lunchtimes in the staffroom as follows:

> So, I couldn't sometimes I couldn't get it, you know. I have been here for two years, nearly three years, two and a half years. So, I'm not really familiar with the culture. Probably that's why sometimes I cannot understand what they, what they were talking. I didn't know what I had to say. And the culture, I didn't know what was appropriate to tell, so, yes I, I feel very excluded at that time, yeah, because I didn't, I didn't, I didn't know what to do. So, I was just quiet, I just quietly listened to them. That's what I do. (Lorine, FG 1)

Here, the interpretation of culture and language is multilayered – it means being 'familiar', understanding the talk and topics of other teachers, knowing how to join in and what to say, knowing what is 'appropriate to tell' and knowing what to do. It is reminiscent of Gee's (1996: 7) notion of Discourses as 'ways of being in the world'. Tina feels outside of the staffroom discourse, and remains a quiet listener. Andrea provided a counterpoint to this position.

Andrea had lived in Australia for over 10 years, and realised it could be hard to fit into a school. She had an assertive strategy to overcome this:

> In my second teaching round [the practicum] right, umm, we, all the student teachers been assigned in one room. So if you don't actively involve with other staff, then basically you're not exist. So for doing that I go to the staffroom, I have lunch there and I have lunch with my supervisor, I have lunch with other staff. So I took, took a active role to get into the staff um, you know, uh conversation and stuff like that, but um maybe it's because um I got um thick skin, so [*Andrea laughter, group laughter*] I, I just don't care [*Andrea laughter*]. So, I whatever they say, I say too, you know, sometimes just bluffing, you just need to do it. (Andrea, FG 1)

Here is a preservice teacher who literally went beyond her assigned 'place', the room for practicum students, to join in the lunchroom discourse with the school staff. This initiative was required for her to be recognised as a colleague, and even for her to be seen 'to exist'. Furthermore, she was prepared to 'fake it' – to join in, laugh along, even when unsure of the meanings. This can be risky and I said so. Here is the exchange.

> **Jenny:** I mean, I think Andrea, you say you have thick skin, I don't know about that, but you take risks, and taking risks with a new group is um, it takes courage.
> **Andrea:** And also I, I understand that you are the new person there and you come and go, but they stay together. So we need to do something first other wise you can't get in.

This is a remarkable insight into becoming a social insider in a cultural context. She had also said of the teachers, 'they know each other but they don't know you'. The need to 'get in' and to be known, led her to leave the safer location and membership of the preservice teacher room and launch herself into the mainstream and its social and cultural practices.

Diverse cultural background as an asset

In contrast to the limitations expressed above regarding culture, several participants commented that their diverse cultural backgrounds constituted a strength for teaching, as shown in these three excerpts:

> Having the understanding of cross-cultural understanding, all the students in the class are the same for me whether they're Anglo-Australian or they came from Asia or European country. They're all the same to me. . . . in my classroom, they are all the same to me, because I, I also came from another country. I cater for them in the same way and if there are some, if there is some kids came from another country I know how they feel, and the, the difficulties they may have. (Lorine, FG 1)

> I believe that teachers don't teach only their method, no?, they don't teach only Maths, Physics or English or, we teach uh, also life skills or general uh, I think of even our different cultural background. I don't know we, we bring in the class some broad experience about uh I don't know, in general no?, not only the content of the methods. (Nick, FG 1)

> They [Australia] have to compete with the rest of the world first, yeah in the world and economics as well, so I think in term of we come from other country, we know other culture, we have different

um way of looking at the world, instead of one set of um thinking we got two set of thinking, one in English, one in our own language. Yeah, we need to give the other perspective and see the world in a broad way in the broad range and also we have many years of experience because we migrate from here and then there. We can teach them some skill which is other than always live in the same village, same house, same room, never, never go away. And they, there is not much chance like this in the future, so we prepare them for it, so we can tell them. Our strength is this. (Andrea, FG 1)

Lorine's point in the first excerpt highlights that teachers with cross-cultural backgrounds may tend towards accepting and non-discriminatory attitudes to CALD students (see also Brown & Miller, 2006). She also expresses solidarity with students from other countries, and the empathy that her own background allows. Nick's view is that broader knowledge of the outside world is the value-adding that CALD teachers can offer. Others agreed with him that they had more to offer than their teaching disciplines, as argued quite strenuously by Andrea. This excerpt was from a longer 'historical overview' of the Australian economy, in which she described the way Australians just 'pulled money from the ground' in the past. These times were gone, she argued, and global competition had arrived. She and her peers were evidence of the mass global movements of people and ideas. Having looked at the past, she turned to the future, in which her students would not have easy options. Being a cross-cultural teacher was part of her identity, and her 'strength' was to prepare students for the multiple perspectives needed to live in the future.

Conclusion and Implications for Teacher Education

Researchers have drawn attention to the disconnection between teacher education programmes and the realities of classroom language teaching (Flores, 2001; Johnson, 1996). Recent research also emphasises that issues of identity, discourse and power are mostly positioned outside the core business of teacher education (Morgan, 2004). How are we to reinvigorate teacher education in a context of the cultural and linguistic diversity that characterises the highly mobile, globalised populations and institutions of the 21st century? In schools and classrooms in many countries now, the cultural and linguistic diversity of both students and teachers is a fact of life, entailing the multiple dimensions of culture, ethnicity, language varieties and plurilingualism, and shifting identities in ever-changing social conditions. For preservice teachers about to embark on careers in these diverse places, the process of 'becoming rather than being', referred to by Hall (1996: 4), is a key notion. Pennycook (2004: 329) calls on researchers to problematise teaching practice and specifically the practicum, including 'the categories we employ to understand the social world', while maintaining issues of power, identity and discourse as central to practice.

The challenges faced by the preservice teachers in this study require a rethinking of a number of such categories, including standard language, the native-non-native binary, teacher knowledge and cultural and linguistic diversity itself. Although designed to address questions about linguistic and professional identity, the study also raises several questions. What kind of capital is ascribed to teachers from diverse language backgrounds? What is the role of individual difference as opposed to institutional practice and discrimination in legitimated language use? How are we to understand and to validate the nexus between professional identity and pedagogy? As with any small-scale qualitative study, there are no easy solutions. Rather, the data indicate a need for teacher educators to recalibrate aspects of their programmes to cater for the diversity within both their courses and in the practicum.

The two primary themes presented in this chapter centred on 'accent' and 'culture'. It was shown that linguistically diverse preservice teachers find that both their lecturers and local students are insensitive to linguistic and cultural challenges faced by international and other students, and that inappropriate assumptions are made about the ease of participation in lectures and tutorials. These students did not want to 'sound like an idiot', and felt they had substantial knowledge and experience that went untapped. While broad generalisations cannot be made, there are a number of implications for teacher education from this study. In a linguistically and culturally diverse world, teacher education programmes need to do more than pay lip service to the value of diversity. They need to:

- Ensure lecturers interrogate their own assumptions about language use and cultural expressions.
- Value alternative knowledge and languages in material ways.
- Have *all* students engage critically with the nexus between identity and language use, both theoretically and in practical terms before and after the practicum.
- Problematise the role of language in discrimination.

- Have an explicit focus on the language in the specialist content areas (needed by both international student teachers and the many students from non-English-speaking backgrounds in their classes).
- Build in language support for ESL teachers who need it, including work on Australian accents and cultural references.

- Promote systematic collaboration between local and international students in tutorials and assignments.

At the same time, the onus is also on teachers from diverse language backgrounds to take responsibility for their own language development in general communication and in their specialist teaching area. There will always be individual differences – Andrea's English made it difficult for her to teach effectively; Nick encountered one racist teaching supervisor. However, in a globalised world, all teachers have to maximise their linguistic repertoires and intercultural skills. Luke and Goldstein (2006) argue that 'the question of how to teach around and across difference has become probably the single most pressing issue facing teacher education and preparation programs' (Luke & Goldstein, 2006: 2). They suggest that programmes often attempt to diversify their readings and discourses, yet still end up 'broadcasting from the centre, from the cloister of monoculture' (Luke & Goldstein, 2006: 3). Historically, the differences among students have been widely addressed in research literature – far more work is needed on the 'differences' of their teachers.

References

Brown, J. and Miller, J. (2006) Dilemmas of identity in teacher education: Reflections on one preservice ESL teacher cohort. In K. Cadman and K. O'Regan (eds) *Tales out of School* (pp. 118–128). Special edition of *TESOL in Context*.

Bourdieu, P. (1991) *Language and Symbolic Power*. Oxford: Polity Press.

Bourdieu, P. (1993) *Sociology in Question*. London: Sage.

Cummins, J. (2000) *Language, Power and Pedagogy: Bilingual Children in the Crossfire*. Clevedon: Multilingual Matters.

Davies, A. (2003) *The Native Speaker: Myth and Reality* (2nd edn). Clevedon: Multilingual Matters.

Duff, P. and Uchida, Y. (1997) The negotiation of teachers' sociocultural identities and practices in postsecondary EFL classrooms. *TESOL Quarterly* 31 (3), 451–461.

Flores, M. (2001) Person and context in becoming a new teacher. *Journal of Education for Teaching* 27 (2), 135–148.

Gee, J. (1996) *Social Linguistics and Literacies: Ideology in Discourses*. London: Falmer Press.

Gee, J. (2000–2001) Identity as an analytic lens for research in education. In W. Secada (ed.) *Review of Research in Education 25* (pp. 99–126). Washington, DC: American Educational Research Association.

Gee, J. (2004) Learning language as a matter of learning social languages within discourses. In M. Hawkins (ed.) *Language Learning and Teacher Education: A Sociocultural Approach* (pp. 13–32). Clevedon: Multilingual Matters.

Goldstein, T. (2003) *Teaching and Learning in a Multilingual School: Choices, Risks and Dilemmas.* Mahwah, NJ: Lawrence Erlbaum Associates.

Hall, S. (1996) Introduction: Who needs identity? In S. Hall and P. du Gay (eds) *Questions of Cultural Identity* (pp. 1–17). London: Sage.

Hawkins, M. (2004) *Language Learning and Teacher Education: A Sociocultural Approach.* Clevedon: Multilingual Matters.

Healy, G. (2008, June 4) Pathways lure more foreigners. *The Australian Higher Education Supplement.* On WWW at http://www.theaustralian.news.com.au/story/0,,23805532-12332,00.html?from = public_rss. Accessed 22.12.08.

Higgins, C. (2003) Ownership of English in the Outer Circle: An alternative to the NS-NNS dichotomy. *TESOL Quarterly* 37 (4), 615–644.

Johnson, K. (1996) The vision vs the reality: The tensions of the TESOL practicum. In D. Freeman and J. Richards (eds) *Teacher Learning in Language Teaching* (pp. 30–49). New York: Cambridge University Press.

Johnson, K. (2003) "Every experience is a moving force": Identity and growth through mentoring. *Teaching and Teacher Education* 19, 787–800.

Leung, C. (2002) Privileged opinion and local reality: Possibilities of teacher professionalism. In C. Leung (ed.) *Language and Additional/Second Language Issues for School Education: A Reader for Teachers* (pp. 116–127). Watford: National Association for Language Development in the Curriculum (NALDIC).

Leung, C., Harris, R. and Rampton, B. (1997) The idealised native speaker, reified ethnicities, and classroom realities. *TESOL Quarterly* 31 (3), 543–560.

Lippi-Green, R. (1997) *English with an Accent: Language, Ideology and Discrimination in the United States.* London: Routledge.

Luke, A. and Goldstein, T. (2006) Building intercultural capital: A response to Rogers, Marshall and Tyson. [Online-only Supplement to Rogers, T., Marshall, E. and Tyson, C. (2006) Dialogic narratives of literacy, teaching, and schooling.] On WWW at www.reading.org/Library/Retrieve.cfm?D=10.1598/RRQ.41.2.3 &F=RRQ-41-2-Rogers_Luke.pdf. Accessed 2.9.08.

McBrien, J.L. (2005) Educational needs and barriers for refugee students in the United States: A review of the literature. *Review of Educational Research* 75 (3), 329–364.

McKay, S. (2003) Toward an appropriate EIL pedagogy: Re-examining common ELT assumptions. *International Journal of Applied Linguistics* 13 (1), 1–22.

Miller, J. (2009) Teacher identity. In A. Burns and J. Richards (eds) *Cambridge Guide to Second Language Teacher Education* (pp. 172–181). Cambridge: Cambridge University Press.

Miller, J. (forthcoming) Chinese preservice teachers in Australia: Language, identity and practice. In G. Slethaug and J. Ryan (eds) *The Chinese Learner and International Education.* Hong Kong: HKU Press.

Miller, J. (2003) *Audible Difference: ESL and Social Identity.* Clevedon: Multilingual Matters.

Miller, J., Mitchell, J. and Brown, J. (2005) African refugees with interrupted schooling in the high school mainstream: Dilemmas for teachers and students. *Prospect: An Australian Journal of TESOL* 20 (2), 19–33.

Morgan, B. (2004) Teacher identity as pedagogy: Towards a field-internal conceptualization in bilingual and second language education. *Bilingual Education and Bilingualism* 7 (2 & 3), 172–188.

Norton, B. (2000) *Identity and Language Learning: Gender, Ethnicity and Educational Change*. London: Longman.

Norton, B. and Toohey, K. (eds) (2004) *Critical Pedagogies and Language Learning*. Cambridge: Cambridge University Press.

Pennycook, A. (2001) *Critical Applied Linguistics: A Critical Introduction*. Mahwah, NJ: Lawrence Erlbaum Associates.

Pennycook, A. (2004) Critical moments in a TESOL praxicum. In B. Norton and K. Toohey (eds) *Critical Pedagogies and Language Learning* (pp. 327–346). Cambridge: Cambridge University Press.

Santoro, N. (1999) Relationships of power: An analysis of school practicum discourse. *Journal of Intercultural Studies* 20 (1), 31–42.

Chapter 4

High Challenge, High Support Programmes with English as a Second Language Learners: A Teacher-Researcher Collaboration

JENNIFER HAMMOND

Introduction

In Australia, as in most western countries, student populations in many large urban schools are diverse. In cities such as Sydney, student profiles may include up to 80 or 90% of students for whom English is a second or additional language. These students may be drawn from 30 or more linguistic and cultural backgrounds and from diverse socio-economic backgrounds. Traditionally, the education of such students has been regarded as a minority issue, and as something that can be addressed by those who are specialist teachers. Yet, given the scale of diversity among student populations, especially in our city schools, there are strong grounds for arguing that English as a Second Language (ESL) education is a mainstream issue. Thus, there are also strong grounds for arguing that the needs of ESL students, and debates about the most effective ways of addressing those needs are mainstream issues.

Initial responses to the presence of linguistically and culturally diverse students, in Australia as elsewhere, were to establish separate English courses. However, the number of students and the limited availability of specialist ESL teachers in Australian schools soon made this response impractical. In addition, many teachers and educators recognised that, once beyond the initial stages of learning English, ESL students were generally better supported when working with other English-speaking students and when engaged in learning across the curriculum. The resulting emphasis on learning language in a content-based curriculum has been a major feature of pedagogical responses to the needs of ESL students in Australia for many years.

There are, in my view, at least three major intersecting domains of knowledge that need to be drawn upon when planning and implementing effective content-based, language-oriented ESL courses. These domains are relevant to ESL specialist teachers, but, I suggest, also equally relevant to teachers in mainstream classes with ESL and other diverse students, and to teacher educators in their work with pre-service teachers. These are:

- developing sufficient knowledge about language to undertake analysis of students' language abilities, and of the language and literacy demands of relevant curriculum content; the ability to draw on such analysis to plan and implement courses that explicitly and systematically teach language relevant to the curriculum content;
- identifying pedagogical strategies that provide sufficient levels of targeted support (scaffolding) to ensure students are able to participate fully and equitably in the curriculum;
- providing well-planned courses, characterised by high intellectual challenge, which investigate key curriculum knowledge structures in ways that both challenge and engage students.

These domains have been acknowledged by many educators working in a number of countries, and thus are not unique to ESL education in Australia. However, the particular ways in which they intersect and the educational programmes that result tend to vary somewhat between countries. For example, systemic functional linguistics has had a greater impact on language and literacy teaching in Australia than in some other countries, with the result that there has been more emphasis on a systematic approach to language teaching here. Such an approach has provided insights into the demands of academic language and literacy, and guidance into ways of teaching registers and genres relevant to curriculum content (e.g. Christie, 2005; Christie & Martin, 2007; Derewianka, 1990). Socio-cultural theories of learning that build on Vygotsky's notion of the Zone of Proximal Development and his arguments regarding the social nature of learning (Vygotsky, 1978) have impacted internationally and nationally on ways of understanding learning environments (Mercer, 1995; Miller, 2004; van Lier, 2000; Wells & Claxton, 2002). In Australia, as elsewhere, such work has built on the metaphor of 'scaffolding' to identify pedagogical strategies that provide high levels of targeted support for students in their engagement with curriculum content (Dufficy, 2005b; Gibbons, 2002, 2006; Hammond & Gibbons, 2005).

The emphasis on intellectual challenge represents a more recent, but in my view, very important dimension in debates about responses to the needs of ESL students. There is ongoing evidence that students from diverse linguistic and cultural backgrounds achieve lower levels of academic success than their English-speaking peers (Thompson & de Bortoli, 2006). There is also evidence that in many large, diverse urban schools pedagogical interactions between teachers and students are characterised by tasks that are minimal in scope and intellectually undemanding (Johnston & Hayes, 2008). Miller (2004) argues that schools have a moral obligation to provide conditions that challenge the marginalisation of minority groups. If schools are to meet this obligation, then a priority is to ensure that *all* students have access to courses that both challenge and engage.

In Australia, as in other countries, there has been recent broad emphasis on the quality of teaching as a key factor in students' educational success (Ramsey, 2000; Vinson *et al.*, 2002). A number of states in Australia have put in place educational initiatives that emphasise the importance of programmes characterised by high intellectual challenge as a way of improving the overall quality of teaching (New Basics Branch, 2002; NSW DET, 2003). These initiatives have drawn on research conducted by Newmann and colleagues in the USA (e.g. Newmann and Associates, 1996; Newmann *et al.*, 1996).

Although not specifically designed for ESL students, the Australian quality teaching initiatives are clearly relevant. In recent research, my colleagues and I investigated implications of the New South Wales state initiative in quality teaching for ESL students who were located within middle year mainstream classes (Hammond, 2008). Outcomes from the research indicated that while there was a need for more explicit focus on language teaching, the initiative had an overall positive impact for ESL students. Our conclusions from the research were that such initiatives offered an important way forward for planning and implementing courses for ESL students, which could be characterised both by *high challenge* and *high support*.

Investigating Intellectual Challenge: A Collaboration Between Teachers and Researchers

In follow-up research, my colleagues and I worked towards more focused interventions in a number of schools (Hammond *et al.*,

2005–2007). Our aim here was to work with teachers to plan and implement programmes that were characterised by high intellectual challenge, but also by the necessary support that would enable all students, including ESL students, to engage with high challenge curricula. Thus, we aimed to incorporate the three domains of knowledge referred to earlier, but with a particular emphasis on intellectual challenge. Teachers from five schools participated with researchers in an ongoing collaboration over a period of two years.

Building on the earlier research into teachers' responses to quality teaching initiatives (Hammond, 2008), we decided to begin with detailed work based around 'tools' associated with intellectual challenge. This was followed by in-school planning, data collection and analysis, then further professional input and reflection based on analysis of data.

The 'tools' of intellectual challenge were *Essential Questions*, *Rich Tasks*, and *Substantive Conversations*. Of these, *Rich Tasks* and *Substantive Conversations* were drawn from the literature supporting the Queensland and New South Wales initiatives of *Productive Pedagogies* and *Quality Teaching* (Education Queensland, 2000; New Basics Branch, 2002; NSW DET, 2003).

Rich Tasks, according to the literature, should be representative of an educational outcome of demonstrable and substantial intellectual and educational value; they should be problem based, with relevance beyond the school curriculum; and they should be recognisable by educators, parents and community stakeholders as being significant and important (Education Queensland, 2000: 55). *Substantive Conversations* are described in the literature as talk that regularly engages students in ongoing conversations about concepts and ideas that they are encountering, thereby supporting students in creating or negotiating understanding of curriculum content (New Basics Branch, 2002: 7). Thus, both *Rich Tasks* and *Substantive Conversations* are tools that support students' engagement with curriculum content at a deep level of understanding.

Essential Questions from the broader literature on curriculum development. They identify key areas of knowledge in the curriculum. They reflect high levels of generalisation and provide a way of framing inquiry and organising learning. They are related to programme goals, but whereas goals reflect desired learning outcomes, *Essential Questions* identify key knowledge constructs, or the 'big ideas' that are central to curriculum content. Thus, *Essential Questions* represent a higher level of generalisation or abstraction than programme goals.

In this chapter, I illustrate the outcomes of the collaborative research of this work by focusing on the programme in one of the schools that participated in our research – City School (pseudonym), a reception school for recently arrived migrants and refugees. Although City School was somewhat atypical of other participating schools, in that it was not a mainstream school, the work in this school, I suggest, is highly relevant to a broader understanding of ESL pedagogy. Programme features that emerged as significant with the first phase learners in City School were similar to those in the mainstream classes, but at City School they tended to be amplified. Key features of high challenge, high support programmes in the reception school thus highlight implications for other ESL students and other programmes. They also highlight the interwoven relationship between focused language teaching, pedagogical strategies that provide high levels of support, and implementation of intellectually challenging content-based ESL programmes.

City School

City School provides orientation, settlement and welfare programmes, as well as intensive English language tuition to newly arrived, secondary-aged students. The school has approximately 350 students, including migrants, refugees and long-term temporary resident students from over 30 countries. Depending on their level of English and on their academic progress, students spend between six and 12 months at the school. The school as a whole implemented a content-based approach to language teaching, and aimed to introduce students to the mainstream curriculum that they would encounter when they made the transition into high school. However, the idea of deliberately introducing high levels of intellectual challenge was new in the school.

With support from the school executive and from researchers in the project, the Music teacher and the English teacher developed and implemented programmes that prioritised high intellectual challenge. The majority of students who participated in the Music and English courses had been at the school for six to nine months and were in the final Transition class prior to making the move to local high schools. Although the students were beyond the initial stages of learning English, they could still be categorised as first phase learners. Music and English were taught as separate classes, but the same group of students attended both subjects. The teachers thus shared programme goals and built on each other's lessons in their attempt to achieve deeper levels of understanding in both curriculum areas. They also worked together on the culminating task of their programmes – a major performance around the theme of identity and belonging.

In their processes of planning, the teachers identified themes of *belonging* and *conformity* as being relevant to the curriculum content of both the Music and English courses and as being especially relevant to the students at City School. The teachers developed shared *Essential Questions* that aimed to identify the 'big ideas' that were central to their curricula and that guided the more detailed planning and implementation of sequences of lessons within units of work. These *Essential Questions* were:

- Why do we study the arts?
- How can the arts help us understand pressure to conform and the desire to belong?
- How do the arts reflect the time and culture in which they are written?
- To what extent do you have to compromise to belong?

In Music, the *Essential Questions* were addressed through the study of specific songs and the lyrics of these songs, through identification of themes within these songs, and through discussion of the relevance of these themes to the lives of students and to the concepts of *belonging* and pressure for *conformity*. In English, the essential questions were addressed through a comparative study of selected literary texts and modern films based on similar narratives and themes. In both subjects, the curriculum content was based on state curriculum documents that were compulsory for mainstream schools. Since these students would soon exit the reception school, the teachers were concerned to prepare students for the kind of work that they would encounter when they made the transition into a mainstream high school.

Approximately half way through the units of work, the teachers introduced the *Rich Task* – preparation for, and presentation of, a concert organised around the theme of belonging. The concert required students to draw on their understanding of the concept of *belonging*, but it allowed them considerable creative latitude in how they did this.

In our work on planning and implementing high challenge programmes, a number of features emerged as particularly significant. Although evident in all research schools, these features were especially evident at City School. They included:

- Working with 'big ideas' and working between levels of abstraction.
- Providing high levels of linguistic, multimodal and multilingual support.

- Acknowledging the importance of the affective dimension of learning.
- Providing space for students' multiple identities.

Working with Big Ideas: Working Between Levels of Abstraction

As indicated, the central theme of the Music and English courses at City School was that of *belonging* and *conformity*. Although the focus on these abstract themes was new, both Music and English teachers had previously taught units of work based on similar curriculum content.

As a result of their participation in the research on intellectual challenge, lessons were framed around the *Essential Questions* and the abstract concepts that were identified in those *Questions*. The curriculum content in the new programme also became the means whereby 'big ideas' (of *conformity* and *belonging*) could be introduced and explored. In their planning, teachers needed first to ask themselves such questions to clarify what they regarded as key knowledge structures that were central to their disciplines and to the specific units that they were planning. These 'Why?' questions also provided the context in which the design and implementation of the *Rich Task* became meaningful. Teachers then encouraged students to consider why these 'big' ideas were important, why they were worth studying, why they were relevant.

By framing curriculum content in relation to abstract ideas and key knowledge structures, teachers were able to talk to students at more abstract levels than had previously been the case. This talk provided opportunities for the students to begin to engage in *Substantive Conversations*. At City School, where students were still very much in the process of learning English, discussions about abstract concepts, such as *belonging* and *conformity*, presented challenges. A characteristic feature here, and in other schools, was that teachers' talk ranged between the very concrete and more abstract understandings of these concepts. The following short excerpt from the Music class provides an illustration of this feature:

> **Teacher:** And the topic that we're working with is *belonging*. This is the easiest reading of it. Okay, this is *my* bag, these are *my* keys. That's the simplest meaning for *belonging*. ...So *belonging* is about more than my keys, your pencil case. What are some of the wider meanings, what are some of the other meanings of *belonging*. What about language, culture, family?
> **Student:** Friends

Teacher: Friends. What's yours Tom?
Student: Relations
Teacher: Relations, yes, very important
Students: Country, planet
Teacher: Planet, absolutely. The planet is very important. OK, Janet Jackson [referring to a song that students are familiar with] says that we need to belong. It's not something like chocolate that we want. Or new red shoes. She says that we need it, like water or air.

I just want to show you the work of a man called Maslow (shows a summary of Maslow's hierarchy of needs). He said that we need food, somewhere to live, we need to be warm, very important in winter. He said that if we have this we can feel safe. He says, I need to feel safe and protected. And most of us, not everybody, but most of us get that feeling of safety from our family. Not everybody has a safe family. If I have this (pointing to hierarchy of needs in the list) I can go to belonging. He says you need relationships with people and you need to feel that you are important to other people. He says it [belonging] is a need. It's not something that doesn't matter.

It was clear from the limited nature of contributions here, and elsewhere, that the students were indeed first phase ESL learners. In this exchange, they were able to respond to the teacher in English, but they did so minimally. However, as with many other ESL students, such limited classroom responses did not necessarily imply limited participation. Students' body language, evident in the classroom videos, suggested that they understood and were actively involved in such discussions.

Of relevance here is the range of ways in which the teacher discussed the meaning of *belonging*. She began by revising the simplest and most concrete meaning of the term (*this is my bag, these are my keys*), before inviting students to contribute 'wider meanings' (*friends, relations, country, planet*). She then introduced a more abstract way of thinking about *belonging* by referring to Maslow's hierarchy of needs, and the place of *belonging* within this hierarchy. With these first phase learners, the shifts were small. Nevertheless, within this short excerpt, the teacher introduced three progressively more abstract ways of understanding and talking about the notion of *belonging*. The shift between levels of abstraction, evident in this short extract, was typical of many other exchanges that occurred in City School lessons. Such shifts were also characteristic of exchanges between teachers and students in other research schools. In the above extract, the teacher worked from concrete to more abstract meanings, although this was not always the case. Quite frequently, in this and other programmes, shifts occurred in the opposite direction, where teachers would illustrate abstract meanings by providing concrete examples that were familiar to the everyday world of the students. The importance of such exchanges lay in the way in which they built on students' concrete understandings to introduce new and more abstract ways of thinking about key concepts.

The introduction of more abstract ways of thinking and talking about concepts such as *belonging* provided opportunities for students to begin to participate in *Substantive Conversations*. At various points in the sequence of lessons in the City School Music programme, for example, understandings of the meaning of *belonging* were revisited and students discussed the meaning and relevance of this concept to specific songs, to the lives of students themselves and to the broader society in which we all live.

Support as well as Challenge: Linguistic, Multimodal and Multilingual Scaffolding

In order to engage with key concepts and abstract ideas, students need considerable support. First phase ESL learners, in particular, need support to learn the English that will enable them to participate in discussions of such concepts. At City School, as in the other research schools, high levels of support were provided in a range of ways.

Linguistic support

With first phase learners at City School, explicit and systematic teaching of the English language was a major feature. In the Music and English units, language teaching included teaching of pronunciation, vocabulary and grammatical features. It also included teaching of, and about, specific oral and written genres, their rhetorical structures, organisation of paragraphs and aspects of cohesion. Decisions about the foci of language lessons were based on specific demands of curriculum content. Thus, the language teaching component of the programmes was driven by the nature of the curriculum content.

Support for students' learning of language was both designed-in and contingent (Hammond & Gibbons, 2005). That is, when planning their programmes, teachers deliberately planned for the teaching of specific genres, grammatical features, key vocabulary and specific features of cohesion. In addition, they used the contingent 'teachable moment' to emphasise relevant aspects of English language as they arose in the unfolding of lessons. At times, students' attention was incidentally drawn to a relevant aspect of language, often the meaning of specific vocabulary, or an aspect of grammar. At other times, specific aspects of language were explicitly taught. At such points, there was a switch from curriculum content to a focus on the relevant language feature, followed by a switch back to the curriculum content. This occurred, for example, when a specific genre or features of the genre were being taught.

In a programme with first phase students, we would certainly expect careful and focused teaching of English. Of note in the Music and English lessons, however, was the amount of time devoted to language teaching, the small steps that were necessary to ensure students learned relevant features of English, and the care with which such teaching was interwoven with curriculum content. Also of note was the combination of this language teaching with multimodal and multilingual support.

Multimodal and multilingual support

In both the Music and English course, concepts that were introduced through talk between teacher and students, were reinforced through a range of multimodal, meaning-making systems in the classrooms. Students learned orally and aurally through interactions between teacher and students, and through group interactions between students. Such learning was then reinforced through the multimodal support that was available within their classrooms. Such support was a feature of programmes in all research schools, but was particularly marked at City School.

Use of the internet was incorporated into classes, and students were encouraged to follow up class work through further use of the internet. Walls in both classrooms were covered in charts and pictures. These visual prompts provided reminders of previous lessons and on-going support for students in subsequent tasks. Students also learned through physical activity: in Music through the playing of musical instruments; in English through classroom performances based on the films and texts that students were studying; and in both programmes through the physical representation of meaning in performances in the final concert.

The multimodal nature of both programmes meant that they were rich in 'message abundancy' (Gibbons, 2003). That is, they were rich in the ways that they deployed diverse meaning-making systems in the teaching and learning of concepts. As Gibbons and I have argued previously (Hammond & Gibbons, 2005), message abundancy is of central importance in the education of ESL students. The use of multiple meaning-making systems, or semiotic systems, provides students with access to similar messages and information from a variety of sources. In City School, as in other schools, message abundancy played an important role in support of the development of *Substantive Conversations* within the classes. It provided students with diverse ways in which to take and make meaning in regard to the complex concepts introduced in their programmes.

Importantly, programmes at City School were also multilingual. Both Music and English teachers encouraged students to work in their first languages to enable them to support developing understandings of concepts. This typically occurred during group work where students discussed complex concepts in their first languages before talking about the same concepts in English. Thus, students could initially concentrate on clarifying understandings of concepts through discussions in the language that they were most familiar with, before grappling with the demands of expressing their understandings in English.

An incident that occurred during one of the Music lessons provides some illustration both of the value of working with multiple languages, and of the challenge and frustration faced by students as they struggled to debate complex concepts in their limited English. In this Music lesson, students had been working with the lyrics of the song *Numb*, by Linkin Park. These lyrics included *I'm tired of being what you want me to be, feeling so faithless, lost under the surface, don't know what you're expecting of me, put under the pressure of walking in your shoes*. These lyrics were clearly relevant to the broad themes of *belonging* and *conformity*. The students were given a worksheet that asked them to discuss the following questions in first language groups before regrouping to discuss the same questions in English:

- What is the feeling/tone in the song *Numb*? Have you ever felt like this since you came to Australia?
- What is the name of a song from your country that has the same feeling as *Numb*?
- Do you think it is helpful to study a song like *Numb*? Why/why not?

The students engaged in quite animated discussion of the questions in their first language groups; however, discussion of the same questions in English presented a greater challenge. The teacher joined groups in turn to support discussion between students. In one group, while discussing whether or not it was helpful to study songs like *Numb*, she asked a student if there were 'angry' songs like this in Korea. The girl replied no. While discussing the same question with another group, the teacher referred to the Korean student's response. This sparked an intense and animated exchange of some minutes in Korean between students in the two groups. It was summarised by the student in the second group as 'We have angry song in Korea'. The linguistic and conceptual richness, the complexity and emotion that appeared to be evident in the first language discussion in the Music lesson was lost in the translation into English. Despite evidence that the students struggled to engage in discussion of abstract concepts in English, the space within the programmes to work in their familiar first language provided opportunities for them to continue to develop conceptually while at the same time grappling with English.

Acknowledging the Importance of the Affective Dimension of Learning

At City School, both the Music and English teachers stressed the importance of learning environments where students could feel safe, cared for, respected and understood as individuals, and where there was predictability in the organisation of classes and programmes. The teachers explained this as follows:

> Their [the students'] greatest need is structure. They need to know what to expect when they walk into the classroom. With so much changing around them, they need to know that some things will be the same. (English teacher)

> They [the students] need that feeling of safety in the room... They also need structure, they need to know where they're going. They need repetition of stuff. (Music teacher)

Our observations of teachers across the research project suggest that there were two major ways in which the affective dimension was acknowledged:

> Respect for students as people and as individuals
> Respect for students as capable learners

At City School, it was clear that both teachers genuinely liked the students. They were interested in their well-being, enjoyed talking to them both in and out of class, and were familiar with the (sometimes traumatic) backgrounds and life stories of individual students. Additionally, they were interested in different cultures and languages. They had extensive knowledge of the socio-economic and political circumstances of students' first cultures. Although they were not fluent in the many languages represented by students in their classes, they had a broad interest in, and quite an extensive knowledge about, these languages. Thus, they were able to predict some of the challenges that students from specific language groups would face while learning English. They were also able to talk explicitly to the students about first and second languages and about language learning, and did so frequently.

The teachers' affection for their students, their knowledge and respect for the students' linguistic and cultural backgrounds contributed to an environment where students felt respected and valued as people and as individuals. While positive and supportive learning environments are generally a feature of reception schools (Miller, 2004), we found the classroom environments in other research schools were also characterised by attitudes of affection and respect for students as individuals.

Equally importantly, the teachers had high expectations of their students' abilities as learners: they believed their students were capable of intellectual engagement. The City School English teacher explained the importance of intellectual challenge for first phase learners as follows:

> Another of their (students') needs is to feel challenged. Often material is watered down far too much for the ESL students, and this does not challenge their intellect.

Thus, the teachers expected their students to engage with mainstream curricula as part of their preparation for mainstream high school. They pushed their students to work with 'big ideas' and they expected their students to take innovative and creative roles in planning and performing the final concert (the *Rich Task*). The teachers' participation in the research on intellectual challenge served to reinforce their high expectations of students' capabilities.

Previous research has highlighted the importance of teachers' expectations on students' academic success and on their beliefs in their own abilities (e.g. Mehan, 1992). At City School, teachers' expectations served to raise students' own expectations of what was possible for them to achieve. Since these students were soon to make the transition into mainstream high schools, this ability to project forward and imagine themselves as successful learners (van Lier, 2004) was especially important.

As Dufficy (2005a) has argued, the importance of the affective dimension in learning is frequently underestimated. An emphasis on affect in all the research schools contributed to safe, supportive and friendly learning environments for students. At City School, this emphasis had a further consequence. It provided space for these first phase students to be recognised, and to recognise themselves, as more than struggling learners.

Providing Space for Multiple Identities: More than just Struggling Learners

As indicated, City School students were beyond the initial stages of learning English, and could understand class instructions and engage in conversational English. However, they were still very much in the process of learning academic English. In class, a number of the students were quiet; some were reluctant to respond to teachers' questions or engage in class discussion as they lacked confidence in their abilities with English. Even students, who were personally outgoing and obviously enjoyed engaging in repartee with teachers and fellow students, clearly struggled with academic English.

Yet, as illustrated in the Music class incident, described previously, when given an opportunity to talk about concepts in their first languages, students revealed quite different abilities and levels of confidence. In such contexts, they engaged in rapid, fluent and intense discussions. Their body language changed: they leaned forward, hand gestures punctuated their comments and their facial expressions were animated. They looked and sounded like different people. The comparisons between students as struggling English learners and the same students as fluent interlocutors in their first languages were even more marked in students' contributions to planning and performance in the final concert – the *Rich Task* of the English and Music courses.

The nature of the *Rich Task* was such that it enabled students and teachers to explore the themes of *belonging* and *conformity* in ways that were creative and multimodal. The concert combined Greek choruses with individual and group performances from the students. The initial Greek choruses were performed multilingually – students spoke in first languages, while the English translation was projected behind the performers. The final Greek chorus, which involved all students, was performed in English. Many of the individual performances, while performed in the students' first languages, were also supported bilingually with projected English translations. These translations were prepared collaboratively by teachers and students. At times, photographs were projected behind the performers. Some performances consisted of students playing musical instruments. Students' vocal performances were accompanied by other students or by members of staff playing musical instruments or by recorded music. Thus, performances were supported aurally, multimodally and bilingually. The final concert was well organised, tightly choreographed, fast paced and dramatic.

Students' individual performances were quite diverse. One boy elected to play a traditional Chinese violin, a difficult instrument, and one that was unfamiliar to many of the other students. There was a cowboy song written by a Chinese boy, performed on guitar and sung in Chinese, with English translation projected on screen behind him. A young Korean girl, who had a history of truanting from school, performed a popular Korean song with great panache, and two Korean boys, who worked quietly in class as they struggled with English, performed like pop stars with the accompaniment of karaoke music to great applause.

In addition to the quality of performances, the processes of planning for the concert revealed an emotional maturity that would not otherwise have been obvious. An example serves to illustrate this point. One of the musical performances consisted of a Korean girl (the same one who frequently truanted from school) and a Chinese boy singing a romantic duet. The performance began with each performer standing some way apart and singing separate sections of the song. They then walked towards each other on stage, joined hands (to the cheers of the audience) and sang together. On the surface this appeared to be a performance of a rather sweet and innocuous song. However, it had a deeper significance. There had previously been racial tension at the school between Chinese and Korean students. The young boy and girl had suggested that they perform this song together as a way of making a statement about friendship transcending ethnic boundaries. It was, thus, part of a broader school agenda that emphasised interracial and interethnic harmony and the need for mutual respect and tolerance of difference.

What emerged very clearly in the concert were the talents, the emotional sensitivity, the maturity, the humour and the intelligence of the students. What also emerged was the depth of students' understanding of the concepts of *belonging* and *conformity*. Significantly, the concert provided space for very different student identities to become visible and audible to staff and to fellow students. By providing space for multiple languages, multimodal learning environments and programmes that challenged and supported students' learning, the school also provided the space for students' diverse identities to be recognised. In these programmes, students were able to draw on different linguistic resources to invoke different representations of identity (Miller, 2004: 128), thereby enabling them to *be* much more than struggling learners.

Conclusion: The Broader Relevance of City School Programmes

I began this chapter by arguing that, because of the diversity of student populations in so many of our schools, the needs of ESL students and debates about effective ways of addressing these needs are mainstream, rather than minority, educational issues. I also argued that there are at least three intersecting domains of knowledge that are relevant to the planning and implementing of programmes that address the needs of ESL and other diverse students.

While most obviously relevant for ESL teachers, I have suggested that these domains are also relevant to mainstream teachers working with ESL and other students in their classrooms.

My overall purpose in the chapter has been to highlight the dimension of intellectual challenge as an important component in response to the educational needs of ESL and other students, but also to point to ways in which its implementation is necessarily interwoven with explicit and systematic teaching of language, and with strategies that provide necessary and targeted high levels of support (scaffolding) for students.

In my discussion of intellectual challenge, and of the 'intellectual practices' (Gibbons, 2008) of enacted classroom, I have drawn on recent collaborative research undertaken by teachers and researchers. I have focused in particular on one of the participating schools, City School, and the ways in which the teachers at this school worked with the tools of intellectual challenge to identify key concepts that transcended specific curriculum disciplines. My discussion of the work in this school has highlighted key features that emerged from the research into the implementation of high challenge programmes. These were:

- The challenge for students provided by the introduction of 'big ideas' and the need for teachers to work between concrete and abstract representations to support students' engagement with those ideas.

- The high levels of linguistic and multimodal support necessary for students in their engagement with curriculum content, and especially with big ideas.
- The importance of the affective dimension of learning in terms of providing warm, supportive and respectful learning environments, but also in terms of respect for learners and high teacher expectations of what is possible for students to achieve.
- The importance of recognising students' multiple identities and of providing space for those identities to be acknowledged within school programmes.

As I have noted, these features were not exclusive to City School. They were evident in all schools that participated in the research, although in City School they were especially evident.

Importantly, the work in all schools provided evidence that it is possible and practical to implement programmes with ESL learners where the level of intellectual challenge is deliberately raised (Gibbons, 2009). The work at City School provided evidence that first phase learners are capable of intellectual engagement, even if their English language development is not quite at the level of their conceptual understanding. The value of focusing on this programme, I suggest, is that it amplifies issues that are relevant to other programmes, and highlights their relevance to a broader understanding of pedagogies that support culturally and linguistically diverse students.

References

Christie, F. (2005) *Language Education in the Primary Years*. Sydney: University of NSW Press.

Christie, F. and Martin, J.R. (eds) (2007) *Language, Knowledge and Pedagogy: Functional Linguistics and Sociological Perspectives*. London: Continuum.

Derewianka, B. (1990) *Exploring How Texts Work*. Sydney: Primary English Teaching Association.

Dufficy, P. (2005a) 'Becoming' in classroom talk. *Prospect* 20 (1), 59–81.

Dufficy, P. (2005b) *Designing Learning for Diverse Classrooms*. Sydney: Primary English Teaching Association.

Education Queensland (2000) *New Basics Project Technical Paper*. Version: 3 April 2000.

Gibbons, P. (2002) *Scaffolding Language, Scaffolding Learning: Teaching Second Language Learners in the Mainstream Classroom*. Portsmouth, NH: Heinemann.

Gibbons, P. (2003) Mediating language learning: Teacher interactions with ESL students in a content-based classroom. *TESOL Quarterly* 37 (2), 247–273.

Gibbons, P. (2006) *Bridging Discourses in the ESL Classroom.* London: Continuum.

Gibbons, P. (2008) "It was taught good and I learned a lot": Intellectual practices and ESL learners in the middle years. *Australian Journal of Language and Literacy* 31 (2), 155–173.

Gibbons, P. (2009) *Challenging Expectations, Challenging Curriculum: English Language Learners, Content Literacy, and Intellectual Engagement in the Middle Grades.* Portsmouth NH: Heinemann.

Hammond, J. (2008) Intellectual challenge and ESL students: Implications of quality teaching initiatives. *Australian Journal of Language and Literacy* 31 (2), 128–154.

Hammond, J. and Gibbons, P. (2005) Putting scaffolding to work: The contribution of scaffolding in articulating ESL education. *Prospect* 20 (1), 6–30.

Hammond, J., Gibbons, P., Michell, M., Dufficy, P., Cruickshank, K. and Sharpe, M. (2005–2007) Challenging pedagogies: Engaging ESL students in intellectual quality. Linkage grant jointly funded by Australian Research Council and Multicultural Programs Unit, NSW Department of Education and Training.

Johnston, K. and Hayes, D. (2008) "This is as good as it gets": Classroom lessons and learning in challenging circumstances. *Australian Journal of Language and Literacy* 31 (2), 109–127.

Mehan, H. (1992) Understanding inequality in school: The contribution of interpretive studies. *Sociology of Education* 65 (1), 1–20.

Mercer, N. (1995) *The Guided Construction of Knowledge: Talk Amongst Teachers and Learners.* Clevedon: Multilingual Matters.

Miller, J. (2004) Social languages and schooling: The uptake of sociolinguistic perspectives in school. In M. Hawkins (ed.) *Language Learning and Teacher Education* (pp. 113–146). Clevedon: Multilingual Matters.

New Basics Branch (2002) *Productive Pedagogies: Classroom Observation Manual.* Brisbane: Education Queensland.

Newmann, F.M. and Associates (1996) *Authentic Achievement: Restructuring Schools for Intellectual Quality.* San Francisco, CA: Jossey-Bass.

Newmann, F.M., Marks, H. and Gamoran, A. (1996) Authentic pedagogy and student performance. *American Journal of Education* 104 (4), 280–312.

NSW DET Curriculum Support Directorate (ed.) (2003) *Quality Teaching in NSW Public Schools: Discussion Paper.* Sydney: NSW Department of Education and Training.

Ramsey, G. (2000) *Quality Matters – Revitalising Teaching: Critical Times, Critical Choices.* Report of the Review of Teacher Education. Sydney: NSW Department of Education and Training.

Thompson, S. and de Bortoli, L. (2006) *Exploring Scientific Literacy: How Australia Measures Up. The PISA Survey of Students' Scientific, Reading and Mathematical Literacy Skills.* Melbourne: Australian Council for Educational Research.

van Lier, L. (2000) From input to affordance: Social-interactive learning from an ecological perspective. In J. Lantolf (ed.) *Sociocultural Theory and Second Language Learning* (pp. 245–259). Oxford: Oxford University Press.

van Lier, L. (2004) *The Ecology and Semiotics of Language Learning: A Sociocultural Perspective.* Dordrecht: Springer.

Vinson, A., Johnston, K. and Esson, K. (2002) *Inquiry into the Provision of Public Education in NSW*. Sydney: NSW Teachers Federation and the Federation of P&C Associations of NSW.

Vygotsky, L. (1978) *Mind in Society: The Development of Higher Psychological Processes* (M. Cole, V. John-Steiner, S. Scribner and E. Souberman, trans. and eds). Cambridge, MA: Harvard University Press.

Wells, G. and Claxton, G. (eds) (2002) *Learning for Life in the 21st Century*. Oxford: Blackwell.

Chapter 5

Language and Inclusion in Mainstream Classrooms

KAREN DOOLEY

Learning in English

Understanding what the teacher says or what is written in texts used in class is a key to academic engagement. Yet, for students who are learning the medium of instruction as an additional language, understanding is often elusive. What causes this? And whose responsibility is it to resolve it? These are perennial questions asked by teachers of English language learners. Answers are complex. What is fitting for Taiwanese professional migrants with continuous, high quality schooling is unlikely to be so for Burundians who started school at a later age and did so in a refugee camp. It is the experiences of refugees from Africa that I focus on in this chapter.

Currently, there is concern about the incompatibility of conceptions of education held by Western educators and African students and their families. It is inadequate, it has been asserted, for teachers to assume that 'their explaining "the way we teach here" will bridge expectations' (Romaniw, 2007). Informed and research-validated awareness is required. In this chapter, my aim is to make a contribution in this regard by looking at what African middle school students and their parents and educators in Australia say about what causes difficulties of understanding in an English language school system, and the responsibilities of students and teachers to resolve these difficulties.

The chapter reports an interview study that followed eight students from an intensive English language school through transition into mainstream high schools. The study is being conducted as teachers in Australia and in other countries of resettlement, including the UK (Rutter, 2006), the USA (McBrien, 2005), New Zealand (Hamilton, 2004) and Canada (Dachyshyn, 2008), are grappling with the needs of refugees from Africa. Most of the new arrivals in Australia have had little, no or severely interrupted schooling. Some are preliterate and many have low-level literacy skills. Academic development is often incommensurate with that of age peers (Ollif & Couch, 2005; Miller *et al.*, 2005; Brown *et al.*, 2006; Refugee Health Research Centre, 2007a). This learner profile became more common in Australia in the years leading up to this study and is challenging even experienced teachers of language learners and refugees (e.g. Community Relations Commission, 2006; Refugee Education Partnership Project, 2007).

The study was funded in a context where school engagement is seen as a key to successful resettlement of young Africans (Queensland Government, 2008). The focus is on middle school students' transition from intensive language school into high school because the risk of disengagement in this moment is heightened, even when students have done well in language studies (e.g. Olliff & Couch, 2005; Cassity & Gow, 2006; Community Relations Commission, 2006; Refugee Education Partners Project, 2007; Refugee Health Research Centre, 2007a).

Research indicates that the pre-arrival experience is implicated in academic engagement after resettlement. A comparative study of Congolese, Sudanese and Somali refugees (Rutter, 2006) found that students from homes where fluent English was spoken, and who had enjoyed continuity of schooling, were most successful in the UK. At risk were limited bilinguals with high-level competence in no language, a finding explained in terms of Cummins' interdependence hypothesis about the transfer of competence between a learner's languages. Also at risk were students who had strong first language and English oral skills, but little exposure to the written word in any language outside of school. Complementary findings and explanations are emerging from research in Australia (e.g. Ollif & Couch, 2005; Miller *et al.*, 2005; Brown *et al.*, 2006; Refugee Education Partnership Project, 2007; Refugee Health Research Centre, 2007b).

Post-arrival experiences in Western schools, including adequacy of English language support, are also implicated in academic engagement. To this end, strategies for helping refugees learn English and literacy for content area study are being made available to mainstream teachers (Luizzi & Saker, 2008), and are subject to research (Miller, 2009). Of particular interest for this chapter is research that looks at student understanding of spoken and written language in the mainstream content area classroom. One study concluded that 'teachers talked too much, yet didn't explain things clearly' for Sudanese students in science classes (Miller, 2009: 582). Student responses to difficulties of understanding in this situation included asking the teacher for clarification and looking up a dictionary. This latter strategy is a source of difficulty for

African students in some Australian classrooms, as is the use of worksheets rather than a coherent textbook (Brown *et al.*, 2006; Cassity & Gow, 2006; Ahmed, 2007).

There is some tension over the question of who is responsible for resolving student problems of understanding. It has been suggested that some African students do not want to lose face by asking for help (Burgoyne & Hull, 2007). Yet, there is evidence that such requests do not always meet with friendly responses. An ethnographic study conducted in Canada with 41 refugee parents from countries that included the Democratic Republic of the Congo, Rwanda, Burundi, Djibouti, Eritrea, Somalia and Sudan, reported racism: 'When she [my daughter] asks questions she does not get answers, she does not get any attention. Now it is already recorded in her mind that there is discrimination' (Dachyshyn, 2008: 257). Similar findings emerged from an interview study conducted with 14- to 19-year-olds attending schools and colleges in London:

> Some teachers when they finished explaining to the class, they came to give you help. But others didn't. The geography teacher – he was very horrible to me – when I don't understand he used to get angry because he has to explain again and waste time. (McDonald, 1998: 165)

It is worth noting that these experiences are not limited to African students. They resonate with the stories of other refugees in Australian schools (Federation of Vietnamese Women's Associations in Australia, 1999).

In the data produced for this study there were many comments about difficulties of understanding instruction in English. My aim in this chapter is to look closely at these data, drawing conclusions and implications for practices that might enable teachers in Australia and other Western countries to better support African young people learning the language of instruction in school. The chapter has three sections. In the first, I provide a brief overview of the study. The eight focal students are introduced, and the design and methods of the study are described. In the second section of the chapter, I present analyses of data illustrating the students' difficulties of understanding in the classroom, highlighting both causes of and responses to these. In the final section, I draw conclusions and implications for practice to better support African students' understanding of instruction in English. I hope that the suggestions are useful to teachers of other learners with profiles akin to those of this study's participants.

From the Great Lakes and The Horn of Africa to Australia

The study reported here began at an intensive language school for adolescents in a metropolitan Australian city and continued after the students transitioned into three suburban high schools. Participants included Rwandans and Burundians who had taken refuge in Tanzania after violence broke out in the Great Lakes region in the 1990s, Eritreans who had fled to Sudan to escape the conflict with Ethiopia, and Sudanese who had sought refuge in Egypt from civil strife.

The students arrived in Australia with histories of severely interrupted and/or low quality schooling. One of the students had spent six years in a regular school in Sudan, which she described as poorly resourced but 'nice'. Four of the students had a year or so of regular schooling before spending four or more years in camp or refugee schools while in transit in Tanzania, Sudan and Egypt, sometimes after breaks of months and years. Three of the students had about four years of camp or refugee schooling only, in one case after starting at age nine and in two cases having to repeat both first and second grades due to lack of progress. The quality of camp and refugee schooling varied considerably. While some participants described very poorly resourced but well-organised provision in Tanzania and Sudan, others described arrangements in Egypt that they thought were more about keeping children occupied than academic learning.

Administrators at the intensive language school selected the participating students. The intent was to work with both high- and low-achieving students from the major cohorts at the school, although it was recognised that relative performance might shift during the course of the project. Despite individual differences in experience, three general patterns of language and literacy history were evident in the school population and the study participants.

The Sudanese students, Shusu and Caroline (all names are pseudonyms), had been schooled in Arabic in Sudan and Egypt, although neither could write the language. They had both started learning English at school in Egypt, and Shusu showed some knowledge of Roman script on arrival in Australia. At the intensive language school, both students were placed in the Beginners class where no English is assumed.

The Eritrean students, Sophia and Mohammad, had been schooled in Arabic in Sudan and both had some reading and writing skill in that language. Sophia was placed in Beginners, and Mohammad in Foundation, a class that teaches 'learning to learn' skills and has been set up since refugees with little, no or severely interrupted schooling began arriving from Africa. Both students speak Tigrinya, and Sophia also speaks some Blin. Neither student spoke English prior to arrival in Australia, although the language is widely used by educated Eritreans.

The Rwandan and Burundian students had been schooled in Kirundi and French in Tanzania. English and Swahili are languages of instruction in that country, but refugees were schooled for repatriation. Nonetheless, three of the students, Jenny, John and Michael, had begun learning English while in Tanzania. These students spoke four or five languages and dialects, including Swahili, French, English, Kinyarwanda, and Burundian and Tanzanian dialects of Kirundi, and were literate in some of these languages and dialects prior to arrival in Australia. Oral and written proficiency levels were not known. Jenny attended an Australian primary school for a few months before entering the intensive language school at Beginners level. Michael was also placed in Beginners, and John in Post-beginners. The other student, George, an indigenous Burundian, spoke Kirundi and Swahili prior to arrival in Australia. Unable to read and write in any language, he was placed in Foundation.

The research team consisted of three Education academics and a research assistant. The project began when the research assistant and I spent a week immersed in lessons, support activities and meetings at the intensive language school. A first round of interviews took place with teachers, administrators and African educators at the school, then focal groups with students and parents followed. The research assistant and I conducted all of the interviews, sometimes in collaboration with another researcher from the team. Interpreters assisted with student and parent interviews, though it should be noted that students sometimes re-sponded in English. Questions addressed the students' school histories, including opportunities for social, linguistic and academic development. All interviews were audio-recorded digitally. A second round of inter-views was conducted 18 months to two years later with seven of the students and their parents (George had withdrawn from school), and English as a Second Language (ESL) personnel in the three suburban high schools to which the students had transitioned. All the students and one of the parents used English for this interview. Another parent asked for an interpreter, but chose to begin the interview in English before the interpreter arrived.

After the audio-recordings were fully transcribed by professional transcribers and accuracy checked by an interviewer, detailed qualitative analyses using Gee's (2005) tools for critically analysing language data were undertaken on the transcripts. A conceptual model of student confusion (Plaut, 2006) informed the findings reported here. The model describes conceptions of the causes of and proper responses to confusion, as facets of student and teacher thought. Student questions are viewed as one of several sources of information about confusion available to teachers in the classroom. Research, using the model conducted in a US high school serving White, Hispanic, African American and Asian populations, found both matches and mismatches between student and teacher conceptions of confusion. It pointed to problems arising when students do not signal confusion or when they view resolving their confusion as the teacher's responsibility, and when teachers misinterpret whether or not a student is confused and what they are confused about.

Difficulties of Understanding in the English Language Classroom

To begin, data relating to the causes of problems of understanding are presented. The analysis will then turn to the interviewees' models of teacher and student responsibility for resolving difficulties of understanding.

'They find it very hard, especially because of the English level'

Interviewees nominated English as the cause of students' lack of understanding. Problems included the pace of teacher talk, unfamiliar content area language and inadequate oral explanations and instructions.

John, who was schooled for six years in a Tanzanian camp after his family fled Burundi, anticipated some of these difficulties while still at intensive language school. In response to a question in his first interview about what he knew of high school, John spoke directly to the researcher in English, bypassing the interpreter. He repeated what his friends who had already made the transition from the intensive language school had told him:

> **R:**   Do you know anybody who's gone from here? Finished at [intensive language school] and they're at high school now?
> **John:** Yes.
> **R:**   What do they tell you about high school?
> **John:** They tell me if you're going, to speak English... if the teacher, if 'you', say, 'you can do like this' and he gives the sheets, the work, he is not help.

In this comment, John repeats teacher talk relayed to him by his friends: 'The teacher say "You can do like this"'. He describes what happens next, as told to him by his friends: 'he gives the sheets, the work, he is not help'. Two interpretations of John's comments are possible. On the one hand, he might be describing a teacher assigning homework; and on the other, he might be describing 'seatwork', a lesson structure in which the teacher gives the class directions and then the students work independently, usually with teacher help (Lemke, 1990). In either case, there is potential for students to not understand the task or the content written on 'the sheets'.

Jenny's mother made similar comments about difficulties of under-standing. This woman, whose own mother was a teacher in Burundi, and who had herself worked as a teacher in a refugee camp, made the comments in the course of explaining why she exhorted her daughter to ask questions in class. The comments arose in the second interview when clarification was being sought on points made in the first interview. The following exchange occurred after the interview was interrupted by a knock at the door. The interview was conducted in English.

> **R:** Sorry, you were saying that you get a lot of notes from school and you don't understand
>
> **JM:** Yes, when I get, when I was study, the teacher give us the lot of paper, and when I don't understand I was very sad, 'Why have this?'....
>
> **R:** So this was in [adult education setting]?
>
> **JM:** Yes.
>
> **R:** So when the [adult education teacher] gave you lots of paper?
>
> **JM:** Yes, but I was very sad because I did not understand.
>
> **R:** And the teacher said?
>
> **JM:** He said sometimes, he'd tell me and help me, 'this means this'. I asked my teacher, 'I want in this, I want examples, maybe in three words'. If she gives me in three words I understand.

Like John's friends at high school, Jenny's mother struggled to understand 'the lot of paper' given to her. She wanted comprehensible oral explanations of what was written on worksheets: 'If she gives me in three words I understand'.

It was not only the lack of explanation of written English that caused problems of understanding for participants in this study. Oral English itself was also identified as a barrier to participation in the classroom. Several students commented on this when asked about the ease of transitioning from intensive language school into high school. The following comments were made by Caroline, a Sudanese, who had one year of regular schooling before her family fled from Egypt where she had four years of refugee schooling. Asked whether high school was difficult or not, Caroline said it was 'hard'. The interviewer then probed the reasons for this:

R: Ok, what's hard?
Caroline: Sometimes the teacher talk too fast.

Sophia, the Eritrean student who had enjoyed six years of stable schooling in Sudan, responded similarly to the same question. A child of parents with qualifications in pharmacy and nutrition, Sophia was awarded first prize for academic achievement in her Sudanese school six years in succession. She said she did not find the mainstream content hard at high school, but struggled with English use in the classroom:

R: ...So do you find it difficult in the mainstream classes or not?
S: I don't find it difficult [in the mainstream subjects] but, yeah, sometimes I find it difficult to quickly understand from the teacher and that... too many new, like new words to me... a little bit fast for me...

It was the pace at which new English words were introduced in content area classes that caused problems for Sophia. Teachers and African educators working as paraprofessionals in the study schools made similar observations. The following excerpt is taken from an interview with the head of the ESL unit in the high school to which George transitioned.

T8: ...my [ESL] teacher aides go to the classes... so they are there with... the academic support, what the teachers are saying. If the kids don't understand, you know how the Australian accent, it's too, they can speak very fast and it's very difficult for students to understand, some of these teacher aides will actually help them with the, to understand what the assignments are... Unfortunately there are not enough [ESL] teachers to go and support them in the mainstream. With maths the language might be difficult, SOSE [Studies of Society and Environment], again the content will be very difficult and the instructions are very limited and the kids don't understand what the teachers are saying. So the [ESL] teachers and the [ESL] teacher aides... help with the content and the, academically, you know, help them with the assignments and explain what the ah, expectations are, the task is...

The pace of mainstream teacher talk, the difficulty of content area language and the inadequacy of instructions are all identified as causes of problems of understanding by this ESL teacher. The point is that there was broad agreement among the study participants that written and oral English presented barriers to students' academic achievement at high school. In the words of a Rwandan teacher who was working in a paraprofessional role in one of the study schools: 'Sometimes some subjects are not well understood so they can't do well. It will take a long time to improve their English level and to be able to follow what is being taught'. The analysis turns now to the participants' beliefs about where the responsibility for redressing difficulties of understanding rests during the lengthy period of English language learning faced by the students at high school.

'If I don't understand something I can ask them and they'll help me'

Most of the participants held both teacher and student responsible for addressing problems of understanding. They stated that it was the students' responsibility to signal a lack of understanding, although there was some dissent on this point. They also stated that it was the teacher's responsibility to fix the problem, and students and parents evaluated teachers positively and negatively in this regard.

Some of the parents spoke approvingly of their children being encouraged to signal to teachers at the intensive language school when they did not understand. In doing so, they repeated teacher talk relayed to them by their children. The mother of Shusu, one of the Sudanese students, made the following indicative statements in response to a question eliciting comment on 'the best thing' about the intensive language school.

Shusu's mother: the best thing Shusu was talking of is that the teachers who are at [intensive language school], whether they were from the mainstream Australians or the Sudanese background, he used to tell Shusu 'that as you are working hard, if you don't get anything or you can't understand anything here in the class, don't hesitate to see us at any time at any place or outside of the office' and that was a good thing for Shusu and she was following that one very well and it helped her a lot.

Several of the students made similar comments, noting that they were encouraged to seek teacher help either in class or outside class at the intensive language school. Shusu's comments are indicative.

R: So, how does the teacher help you [to learn English]?

S: ...there is difficult words, something difficult to us, we ask the teacher and the teacher solve it to us.

Teachers at the intensive language school indicated that they prepared students for transition to high school by teaching them to signal when they needed help. A science teacher stated that content area language was taught to this end: 'So, at least, if they need to ask a question they have enough language in those two subjects, maths and science, they could ask a question'. The same teacher spoke also of more generic training. His comments were made in response to my question about what the school can do to prepare the students for transition. The question was prompted by his statement that the students 'go into their shell' during transition, and so must be able to 'express... what their needs are'.

T2: ...we do prepare them. We do tell them, what are the, we create scenarios, what they face there [at high school], and what is the best for them to do, you know, like always put your hand up and express, even if you don't know anything, don't feel you know, that you don't know anything, and you can't ask questions, you can always ask questions. You can ask for help either before school or after school.

Two parents stated that they encouraged their children to ask questions in class. When asked what parents can do to help their children succeed at school, John's mother said that she could not help him with 'academics', but she could advise him: 'whenever you have the trouble ask the teacher'. Asked why she gave this advice, she said that a teacher from the intensive language school had telephoned her and told her that John was ready for high school, but needed to signal when he did not understand.

John's mother: ...he, he does not ask the teachers anything, you know, asking questions, and in that way the teachers say if he does not ask any questions the teacher assume that he understands. That's the only weakness that are found in [], otherwise [] is doing fine.

By contrast, Jenny's mother, who had taught in a refugee camp, explained that it was her own experience as a student in Australia that prompted her to encourage her daughter to ask questions in class. In her first interview, she had said that she told Jenny to ask questions in class:

Jenny's
mother: ...the problem Jenny had before is to be too quiet and even is, she didn't understand anything, she couldn't ask the teachers to explain again, but we parents knew that, we advised her and showed her the importance of asking a question in the class.

In response to my question in the second interview asking why she gave this advice, Jenny's mother invoked her own difficulties, cited earlier in this chapter, understanding the sheets handed out in her English class. She concluded by repeating what she had told Jenny.

Jenny's
mother: ...I wanted to know all those things [on the sheet]. I told Jenny "you can ask your teacher, if you don't understand you can ask your teacher, 'I don't understand'."

Some of the students and parents spoke of positive responses to the students' requests for help from high school teachers. They said that the teachers 'always' helped when students signalled that they did not understand. Jenny's comments are indicative:

R: What do you do if there's a problem and you can't understand in a lesson?
Jenny: Ask the teacher about it.
R: And do the teachers always help?
Jenny: Yes.

By contrast, some students recounted negative experiences. Caroline, a Sudanese student whose exit report from the intensive language school noted literacy problems, thought she was made to wait too long for help.

Caroline: ...when you put your hands up, they don't come quickly and you just get angry, yeah, and you say that you don't need help anymore.

Most of the students assumed that they should put their hands up in class to signal that they needed help. Sophia was the exception. After explaining that the pace of oral English made it difficult to understand in class, she said she did not want to put her hand up, preferring instead to ask outside of class. I probed the comment.

Sophia: ...I find it difficult to quickly understand from the teacher and that, I don't want to put my hand up and ask so I ask the teacher after the class.

. . . .

R: Why don't you want to put your hand up in class?
Sophia: I don't know.
R: Do the teachers want you to put your hand up in class?
Sophia: Yeah. They say, 'If you don't understand, put your hand up', but, yeah
R: Do other kids put their hands up?
Sophia: No, they've got the same feeling as me.

The next time I met Sophia, I probed her comments further. This meeting was an incidental one that occurred when Sophia arrived home from school while I was still interviewing her mother. After her mother had left the room, Sophia came in to chat with me and clarified points from her interview.

R: I think you said it [teacher talk] was too fast
Sophia: Yeah, something like that, and then when you ask, like, 'you don't even know what's going on in the class'
R: Yeah
Sophia: You ask and then everyone go like, 'well, she was talking all the time'
R: Yeah.

There are multiple ways to interpret the comment 'and then everyone go like...'. Sophia might be relaying criticism of her for talking while she should have been listening to the teacher, or for taking up too much of the lesson talking to the teacher, or for not understanding despite the teacher having talked a lot. In any case, the point that matters is that Sophia was fearful of being criticised by peers for asking questions in class. Asked at the end of her second interview to suggest something that teachers could do to better help African students, Sophia returned to this issue, and proposed an alternative strategy.

Sophia: Um, like, like when you say something, you need to explain more and more because even if you, don't understand with our hand up, but we need them to say more.

Like Sophia, Caroline commented in her second interview on the negative responses of peers to requests for help in class. She observed that some students 'laugh at you and say you don't know things'. Jenny likewise indicated that she had been 'scared' to ask questions when she entered primary school in Australia. The reason she gave was that she did not know anyone in the class. By contrast, John thought some African students were unnecessarily afraid of asking questions in class.

R: Before you said your teachers are one of the good things about the [high] school. What's good about the teachers?

John: Yeah, because sometimes if I don't understand something I can ask them, and they'll help me. Yeah, they help me to understand it, yeah.

R: When do you ask them? Do you ask them during the lesson or after the lesson?

John: Oh, yeah, I ask them like during the lesson before I forget it because sometimes I can forget it and don't ask so I'll go home without understanding it, yeah, so I better ask during the lesson.

Questioned about why some African students are afraid to ask questions in class, John said that 'sometimes they think like the other students will laugh at them'. Asked whether this is the case, John said that students were laughed at for asking 'silly questions', and that some students thought this meant they would be laughed at for asking any question: 'So they think like any question, they laugh at the other student'. In any case, John emphasised that it was more important 'to know what it says' than to worry about being ridiculed.

Conclusions and Implications

The study reported in this chapter was conducted amid concerns about the incompatibility of concepts of education held by Africans arriving in the West as refugees and by Western teachers. It looked specifically at how African middle school students and parents, and educators in Australian schools – African and otherwise – talked about causes of the students' problems of understanding, and responsibility for redressing these, at intensive language school and in transition to high school.

Participants were unanimous in identifying English as a cause of problems of understanding at high school, specifically, the pace of talk, the heavy load of new technical vocabulary and inadequate explanation. This is not surprising given long-established evidence, cited repeatedly in research on school experiences of African students in the West, that it takes up to 10 years for refugees and others with little, no or severely interrupted schooling to attain the academic language required for average achievement levels (Collier, 1989). While English is often a particular challenge for students transitioning to high school (Miller, 1999), many are arguing that the brief period of intensive language education to which students are entitled in Australia is particularly inadequate for students now arriving as refugees from Africa (Nega, 2007; Refugee Education Partnership Project, 2007). This is an issue for the attention of governments and school systems.

Some of the educators who participated in this study raised questions about whether the form of multilinguality of some students was prolonging their English language learning. They described the Burundian and Rwandan cohorts as the most multilingual of all in the intensive language school's 30-year history. A school administrator and a paraprofessional, who had taught language for many years in regular Rwandan schools and a Tanzanian refugee camp, both expressed concern that partial mastery of multiple languages might be constraining the English language learning of some students (for a UK example, see Rutter, 2006). This issue was beyond the parameters of the study, but warrants future research.

For teachers and teacher educators, the study's findings raise pedagogic issues. Contra existing literature on student confusion (Plaut, 2006), there was considerable similarity in the participants' models of responsibility for resolving student confusion. In general, participants assumed students should signal confusion and teachers should resolve it. This seems to reflect teachers' deliberate efforts to socialise students into learning-to-learn behaviours valued in Australian schools, but as the case of Jenny and her parents shows, other influences are also at work.

Students' talk of current and past anxiety about signalling confusion and asking for help in class warrants attention. At the least, teachers need to be aware of this possibility. Further, they can consider whether a more receptive peer environment for asking questions can be created (Dooley, 2009). It is also important to identify the limits of reliance on students signalling confusion. While conducting this study, I spent a stint as the least proficient student in a university class in China. My teachers welcomed and responded kindly to any question, but like some of this study's participants, I did not want to ask all the questions I 'should' have asked. I hated being 'the one who never understands and always holds the class up with her questions'. There was a constant trade-off between understanding and face or self-image that caused the teacher in me to reflect on the proper balance between student and teacher responsibility for resolving student confusion. When is 'the way we teach here' (Romaniw, 2007) inadequate for certain students? When does it become imperative for teachers to pre-empt student confusion? For teachers of English language learners, when is it necessary to change established pedagogy through use of ESL in the mainstream techniques or systematic and explicit teaching of content area language (Miller, 2009)? When is seatwork and reliance on worksheets inadequate? These are some of the questions that might be asked by teachers of English language learners with little, no or severely interrupted schooling.

Acknowledgements

This chapter reports on Australian Research Council funded project, LP0561597. I thank the editors of this volume for their thought-provoking response to the first draft. I also thank the generosity of the participating students, parents and teachers in four schools, and Jen Tan and Sean O'Callaghan for research assistance.

References

Ahmed, B. (2007) Introduction. Proceedings of the Conference of the African Think Tank Inc., *African Resettlement in Australia: The Way Forward.* University of Melbourne, 11–13 April. On WWW at http://209.85.173.132/search?q=ca che:oxB8eOWxapkJ:www.att.org.au/documents/African%2520Resettlement% 2520Report.pdf+African+reselttlement+in+australia&hl=en&ct=clnk& cd=1&gl=au. Accessed 19.12.08.

Brown, J., Miller, J. and Mitchell, J. (2006) Interrupted schooling and the acquisition of literacy: Experiences of Sudanese refugees in Victorian secondary schools. *Australian Journal of Language and Literacy* 29 (2), 150–162.

Burgoyne, U. and Hull, O. (2007) *Classroom Management Strategies to Address the Needs of Sudanese Refugee Learners.* Adelaide: Australian Government, NCVER.

Cassity, E. and Gow, G. (2006) Shifting space and cultural place: The transition experiences of African young people in Western Sydney high schools. In P.L. Jeffery (ed.) *AARE 2005 International Education Research Conference. Creative Dissent, Constructive Solutions* (Vol. 1, pp. 1–15). Melbourne: AARE.

Collier, V.P. (1989) How long? A synthesis of research on academic achievement in a second language. *TESOL Quarterly* 23 (3), 509–531.

Community Relations Commission for a multicultural NSW (2006) *Investigation into African humanitarian settlement in NSW: Report of the Community Relations Commission for a multicultural NSW.* Sydney: New South Wales Government. On WWW at http://www.crc.nsw.gov.au/publications/documents/african_ humanitarian_settlement. Accessed 19.12.08.

Dachyshyn, D.M. (2008) Refugee families with preschool children: Adjustment to life in Canada. In L. Adams and A. Kirova (eds) *Global Migration and Education: Schools, Children and Families* (pp. 251–262). Mahwah, NJ: Lawrence Erlbaum Associates.

Dooley, K. (2009) Intercultural conversation: Building understanding together. *Journal of Adolescent and Adult Literacy* 52 (6), 497–506.

Federation of Vietnamese Women's Associations in Australia (1999) *Journey to Freedom.* Sydney: Federation of Vietnamese Women's Associations in Australia.

Gee, J. (2005) *An Introduction to Discourse Analysis: Theory and Method* (2nd edn). New York: Routledge.

Hamilton, R. (2004) Schools, teachers and the education of refugee children. In R. Hamilton and D. Moore (eds) *Educational Interventions for Refugee Children: Theoretical Perspectives and Implementing Best Practice* (pp. 83–96). London and New York: RoutledgeFalmer.

Lemke, J.L. (1990) *Talking Science: Language, Learning and Values.* Norwood, NJ: Ablex Publishing Corporation.

Luizzi, P. and Saker, J. (2008) Planning the learning environment for refugee background students. *Pen,* 162. Marrickville, NSW: Primary English Teaching Association.

McBrien, J.L. (2005) Educational needs and barriers for refugee students in the United States: A review of literature. *Review of Educational Research* 75 (3), 329–365.

McDonald, J. (1998) Refugee students' experiences of the UK education system. In J. Rutter and C. Jones (eds) *Refugee Education: Mapping the Field* (pp. 149–170). London: Trentham Books.

Miller, J. (1999) Becoming audible: Social identity and second language use. *Journal of Intercultural Studies* 20 (2), 149–165.

Miller, J. (2009) Teaching refugee learners with interrupted education in science: Vocabulary, literacy and pedagogy. *International Journal of Science Education* 31 (4), 571–592.

Miller, J., Mitchell, J. and Brown, J. (2005) African refugees with interrupted schooling in the high school mainstream: Dilemmas for teachers. *Prospect* 20 (2), 19–33.

Nega, A. (2007) Day Three: Plenary presentation. Proceedings of the Conference of the African Think Tank Inc., *African Resettlement in Australia: The Way Forward.* University of Melbourne, 11–13 April. On WWW at http://209.85.173.132/search?q = cache:oxB8eOWxapkJ:www.att.org.au/documents/African%2520Resettlement%2520Report.pdf + African + reselttlement + in + australia&hl = en&ct = clnk&cd = 1&gl = au. Accessed 19.12.08.

Olliff, L. and Couch, J. (2005) Pathways and pitfalls: The journey of refugee young people in and around the education system in Greater Dandenong, Victoria. *Youth Studies Australia* 24 (3), 42–46.

Plaut, S. (2006) "I just don't get it": Teachers' and students' conceptions of confusion and implications for teaching and learning in the high school English classroom. *Curriculum Inquiry* 36 (4), 391–421.

Queensland Government, Department of Communities (2008) *New Futures: The Queensland Government's Engagement with African Refugees* (August). On WWW at http://www.multicultural.qld.gov.au/publications/reports/new-futures.pdf. Accessed 3.11.08.

Refugee Education Partnership Project (2007) *The Education Needs of Young Refugees in Victoria.* Brunswick, Vic.: Victorian Foundation for Survivors of Torture Inc.

Refugee Health Research Centre (2007a) Refugee youth and the school environment. *Good Starts for Refugee Youth, Broadsheet #5.* On WWW at http://www.latrobe. edu.au/rhrc/refugee_youth.html#broadsheets. Accessed 18.12.08.

Refugee Health Research Centre (2007b) What keeps refugee boys in school. *Good Starts for Refugee Youth, Broadsheet #1.* On WWW at http://www.latrobe. edu.au/rhrc/refugee_youth.html#broadsheets. Accessed 18.12.08.

Romaniw, S. (2007) Education Concurrent Workshop. Proceedings of the Conference of the African Think Tank Inc., *African Resettlement in Australia: The Way Forward.* University of Melbourne, 11–13 April. On WWW at http:// 209.85.173.132/search?q = cache:oxB8eOWxapkJ:www.att.org.au/documents/ African%2520Resettlement%2520Report.pdf+African+ reselttlement+ in + australia&hl = en&ct = clnk&cd = 1&gl = au. Accessed 19.12.08.

Rutter, J. (2006) *Refugee Children in the UK.* Maidenhead, UK: Open University Press.

Chapter 6

Influences on the Written Expression of Bilingual Students: Teacher Beliefs and Cultural Dissonance

JOEL WINDLE

In educational settings where bilingual students perform poorly, bilingualism and cultural background can be quickly transformed into explanations of poor performance. These explanations are not only found in the folk theories of teachers, and even students, as I will discuss further below, but are also present in academic work (Costa-Lascoux, 1989; Kagitçibasi, 1988; Peköz, 1993; Simkin & Gauci, 1992). Costa-Lascoux writes:

> Bilingualism acquired in a "lycée international" is not the same as that of an immigrant child. Composite, often impoverished and deformed, the languages spoken within families with little education, who emigrated several years previously, do not satisfy academic criteria. (Costa-Lascoux, 1989: 77)

This assertion suggests an element of social class judgement, identifying a cognitive or linguistic deficit among low socio-economic status migrant and second generation students. The claim of a negative influence from bilingualism *ipso facto* on academic development has been heavily criticised (Romaine, 1995), and the neutrality of the concept of linguistic competence has itself been called into question (Bourdieu *et al.*, 1994; Grenfell, 1998). Bourdieu identifies linguistic competence as a form of symbolic capital that is connected to and re-enforces the speaker's social status (Bourdieu, 1977). School, as an institution, helps to sanctify what counts as linguistic competence; what forms of speech are allowable and legitimate; and what forms are disqualified as 'impoverished and deformed'.

Rather than being impoverished or deformed in any objective sense, certain forms of language and communicative styles are merely misaligned with those officially and arbitrarily sanctioned by school, and are thus subordinated by them. This point is made by Labov, who showed that rather than being 'ungrammatical', the vernacular speech of African American youth in the USA indeed followed complex grammatical principles, but that these were different to the principles accepted by schools (Labov, 1972). The rich linguistic worlds of the home and the street (Brice Heath, 1982; Labov, 1972) are excluded from the world of school in these instances through a *social*, rather than a linguistic or cognitive process. This is important to bear in mind when considering the challenges confronting bilingual students who live and communicate within those linguistic communities whose spoken versions of the language of school are disqualified in academic speech and text production. Despite negative evaluation of their second language (L2) use by teachers, in working-class neighbourhoods bilingual students often only identify viable identities (identities that are validated by peers) that operate within this officially devalued speech community. The middle-class speech styles that align most closely with teacher expectations are either absent or rejected by peers. As Pavlenko notes, the issue of identity can cut both ways:

> L2 users' subject positions, in particular race, ethnicity, class and gender, mediate their access to linguistic resources available in the L2. On the other hand ... their agencies and investments in language learning and use are shaped by the range of identities available to them in the L1. (Pavlenko, 2002: 285)

My research in French and Australian secondary schools located in working-class and culturally diverse neighbourhoods suggests that teachers, and bilingual students themselves, often misrecognise both the source and the nature of the 'language difficulties' they encounter at school. In this chapter, I present extracts of student writing, as well as views from teachers and students, in order to demonstrate an apparent mismatch between perceptions of difficulty and sources of difficulty with written expression.

The Study

The data analysed below come from eight Australian secondary schools and four French secondary schools, where Year 11 students were surveyed and interviewed ($n = 924$).[1] In addition to the survey, interviews were conducted with teachers and students. I will begin by discussing teacher responses, before turning to responses to a single open-ended question on the student survey.

The schools participating in the study record academic performances, which are among the lowest in their respective systems, and were selected for the purposes of comparing the experiences of Turkish-background students in Australia and France from neighbourhoods with significant Turkish populations. Four out of five students are the children of blue collar or unemployed parents, and a majority is of migrant background. Of these, 80% in both samples are second generation migrants from Turkey, Lebanon and North Africa (the Maghreb). Virtually all first and second generation migrant students participating in the study use a language other than the national language at home and with friends – most often Turkish or Arabic. The data discussed here relate, therefore, to a particular type of school, rather than to French and Australian schools more generally.

Folk Theories of Bilingual Linguistic Deficit in Australia and France

The influence of teacher expectations and their expression in educational practices and cues on students' self-esteem, confidence, interest, persistence and cognitive outcomes has been long established (Persell, 1977: 123–134). In the secondary years, students are particularly sensitive to what they see as hostility and lack of respect from teachers (Centre for Applied Educational Research, 2002; Dubet, 1991; Felouzis, 1994). Even teachers who have no conscious bias interpret student behaviour and performance by reference to norms that may be foreign to students themselves, and which, in fact, refer only to a constructed 'fictive student' (Bourdieu *et al.*, 1994). 'Real' students are disadvantaged through the operation of a system predicated on pedagogical approaches and competencies that assume a socially narrow set of lived experiences for those pedagogies to be effective.

The attribution of academic difficulty to bilingualism among migrant-background students is connected to wider discourses about migrant incorporation, assimilation and cultural difference. These connections work through the institutional responses to linguistic and cultural difference established within schools and through the understandings that individual teachers bring with them, both of which contribute to a school culture of shared assumptions and understandings. The nature of these connections, and therefore the forms that folk theories about bilingual linguistic deficit take, can be identified by contrasting settings with different political and institutional frameworks relating to migrant incorporation.

French schools have long held an important place in the national project of forming a unified nation of citizens who all share common, Republican values, notably through the enforcement of French as a national language (Berque & Centre national de documentation pédagogique (France), 1985; Jennings, 2000; Larkin, 1997; Mauviel, 1985; van Zanten, 1997). Schooling has also been a site for anxiety about the emergence of 'communautarianism' and attachments that threaten loyalty to the state among migrants. The controversy around the *hijab* and its subsequent banning are good examples of how schooling is used as a site to police difference, and how teachers are given a license to act as 'guardians' of the Republic (Gaspard & Khosrokhavar, 1995; Windle, 2004). The strong association of migrant-background students with 'difficult' schools, in part arising from the class composition of post-Second World War migration to France, further constitutes migrant-background students as a visible target of negative teacher assessments and punishments (Choquet & Héran, 1996; Payet, 1996). Ethnic-minority boys in particular often appear as a 'deviant' group in the eyes of teachers (Perroton, 1999; van Zanten, 2001).

In terms of educational performance, therefore, teachers are willing to identify migration attributes as the cause of student difficulties and as a legitimate area for their intervention. This identification also fits in with a wider narrative about the threat of migrants to French society, upon which the far right National Front has capitalised in recent years. For instance, in the present study, the school counsellor at Dumas vocational school (France) attributes reading comprehension difficulties to the handicap of an early 'lack of language' among migrant-background students. This leads to exasperation among teachers: 'We don't know how to handle them any more' he complains. Similarly, at Claudel comprehensive, a mathematics teacher in the academic part of the school considers that the students in greatest difficulty are migrant-background students due to their poor mastery of French and limited vocabulary. This 'language difficulty' is felt across the curriculum, from learning mathematical concepts to history and geography. According to this mathematics teacher, students have trouble learning lessons and grasping all of the 'nuances the teacher gives in classroom exchanges'. For the school counsellor at Molière vocational school (France), the kind of student most likely to experience academic failure is 'from a disadvantaged socio-cultural environment, second generation migrant, or newly arrived from Turkey'. Migrant languages and allegiances to an ethnic community are identified in France as a threat to 'integration'. Hearing Turkish or Arabic spoken on the streets or in the school-yard constitutes a concern for the teachers in France interviewed for this study and as a challenge to the universalist, rational, republican culture, which teachers try to preserve and transmit.

In Australia, by contrast, a policy of multiculturalism has been incorporated into the cultural politics of education and public discourse since the Galbally report of the late 1970s (Galbally, 1978). Although Australian teachers less often express concern with cultural threats to cohesion, labelling and anxiety about ethnic boundaries remains visible. Comments made by an English teacher at Kuzey College reveal both the unrealistic self-evaluation students make at that school and the central place of gender in constructing a relationship to the curriculum. Hanan, an English teacher, considers that Turkish- and Lebanese-background boys are not able to manage basic literacy, appreciation of poetry and prose, comprehension of newspaper articles, justifying an argument and public speaking. While boys from these ethnic backgrounds lack a 'strong work ethic', according to some teachers, girls are more willing to 'buckle down'. Academic judgement here is closely tied to gendered and ethnic stereotypes. Cultural stereotypes can cut both ways, however, with research in Australia showing negative consequences for students from Asian backgrounds who are assumed to be 'pro-school' (Matthews, 2002).

What, then, is the impact of the folk theories held by teachers on students? The heavy emphasis on assimilation in France, and its more muted expression in Australia, appears to result in at least some internalisation among students. In both settings, students tend to devalue their linguistic and cultural resources, rather than seeing them as resources for learning. For many of these students, bilingualism appears to be a burden rather than an advantage in their engagement with school. Many students comment that moving between one language at home and another at school is difficult. For example, Alev and Cemre (female, Özel College, Australia) observe that they find studying English hard because they always speak Turkish at home, and hence their Turkish is better than their English. The practice of Turkish reflects the strength of ethnic identity and community in the lives of students, but it is also a source of anxiety for them in the academic setting because it is perceived to be self-limiting. This perceived limitation also influences subject choices, with students avoiding 'language-based' subjects and confining themselves to lower level mathematics, technology and science options. Closely tied to both student and teacher anxiety about the prevalence of communication in community languages is concern about lack of high culture, particularly canonical literary culture among students.

Between Perceptions and Practices

Despite the concerns raised by Alev, Cemre and others about their 'home language' contaminating or limiting their English, the study identified little evidence of a limitation in their communicative competency or fluency. While the second generation students in the study speak in a 'broader' accent and use more non-standard forms than their teachers, the students' oral communication in the dominant language generally falls within the range of variations found in the local non-migrant population. In Australia, features of the style of speaking associated with the second generation, which has come to be called 'wogspeak' (Warren, 1999), may be found across the populations of the schools in the study, but are more marked in the migrant-background students. The predominantly Turkish- and Lebanese-background students in this study only very rarely use forms that would be considered unacceptable by all 'native' L1 speakers. Dünya (Livingston College), to provide one such rare example, puts homework in a plural form: 'We never had homeworks in years seven, eight, nine, ten'.

More common 'errors' are non-standard forms that are accepted in informal settings, but disqualified in formal settings, such as double negatives and use of the past participle in place of the simple past form. The following statement by an English monolingual student provides an illustration: 'I've never, like, *came* from school and went home and straight away *get* into stuff' (Sam). Teachers, and the students themselves negatively judge such forms, however non-standard usage does not indicate any lack of sophistication or grammatical knowledge. It does, however, point to the 'identity work' students must perform to make the transition to formal and academic registers. While I will not provide examples here, the situation in France regarding the adoption by the second generation of a speaking style that has little legitimacy at school, and counts as 'incorrect' when judged by the framework of academic standards, is similar to that in Australia.

Literacy, legitimate language and identity

The strains of formal or scholastic language are greatest when students move from speech to the written word. Regardless of the language used for speech with family and friends, the movement to writing for academic purposes and audiences is something that students in the setting of this study generally manage poorly. Students' writing sheds light on their discomfort with the conventions of written language, and suggests that differences between bilingual and dominant language monolingual students in the appreciation of their linguistic capabilities are not translated into distinctive writing practices.

As part of the study, students were asked to provide a written response to the question 'if you were asked to describe your idea of a successful life, what would you say?' The context of the question is that of a classroom writing task undertaken for an academic study, even though the formula references oral speech. Teachers did not prepare students for the task, which was undertaken in examination-style conditions.

Students conceive the task set for them in two distinctive ways. The vast majority of students interpret the task as merely supplying information and show little attention to academic conventions. A smaller group of students present their responses in a formal, scholastic style, with attention to impressing the reader with their skill as writers. I will first discuss the Australian responses before discussing the responses in France.

Students who provide the former style of response typically use non-standard forms such as 'gona' for 'going to'. Such mistakes are made by non-migrant-background and migrant-background students alike. In the following example, the student phonetically spells non-standard pronunciations and confuses homophones:

> To me being happy at what ever I *wont* is all that will matter. why *worrie* what's *gonna* happen in 20 or 30 years when you know in 60 years *your* dead. (Female, dominant language background 226.4)[2]

Homophones present a particular challenge in making the transition from spoken to written language, and result in many errors:

> I want to get into the *coarse* I want (which I dont *no* yet)... (Female, second generation bilingual, Turkish background 9.1)

Typically, such responses are in list form and do not seek to develop thoughts into a coherent structure or complete syntax, and demonstrate little care for rules of capitalisation or punctuation:

> Finish VCE, Get into Uni, Have a career and Be financialy stable. (Female, second generation, Arabic bilingual, Lebanese background 462.8)

Second language difficulties?

Beyond a non-academic interpretation of the task and difficulty with the transition from spoken to written forms, some responses do show features of incomplete English acquisition. The following example from a first generation student shows uncertain use of tenses and fails to construct an accurate sentence or clause. In addition, the conventions of punctuation and capitalisation are missing:

> earning money happy. have the job you liked. (Male, first generation, Turkish background 463.8)

Some spelling also comes from the first language transfers in both first and second generation writers (commonly, for example, '*Turkiye*' for Turkey). A small number of second generation students also show marked features of learners of English as a second language. One student is unable to approximate what appears to be 'concentrating' in her brief response, nor to co-ordinate the verbs in her phrase:

> Keep it real and concerating. (Female, second generation, Arabic bilingual, Lebanese background 464.8)

The following example from a second generation student similarly displays incorrect word order, a missing verb, lack of cohesion between clauses and an incorrect conjugation:

> I would say people that successful at School, at work, and I work hared at school my perent supports me my successful and my work at school. (Female, second generation, Turkish background 221.4)

A number of responses present errors that are less clearly the result of incomplete language acquisition, but which are sufficiently ambiguous to raise the possibility. The following student trips up grammatically in a fairly complex sentence:

> A successful life for a person is someone's life who has achieved it by hard work and is happy about their life. (Female, second generation, Turkish background 19.1)

One interpretation of such difficulties is that at least some errors come from a slow and interrupted recording of thoughts, with successive clauses being added onto incomplete fragments in the absence of re-reading. In the conversational context, meaning may not be adversely affected by such discontinuities; and, indeed, even in writing, the meaning is clear. However, such an approach to a written text severely limits its effectiveness and coherence as a piece of prose for academic purposes.

Stronger students

A small number of responses take up a formal written style, and make use of a topic-sentence-headed paragraph structure. This is the kind of response that is rewarded in the context of writing for academic purposes, and can be found among migrant- and non-migrant-background students alike on only rare occasions. The following response provides an example of a cohesively organised piece of discourse, albeit one with numerous errors:

> My idea of a successful life is to create a balance in the 3 components of life which are: the religious component, Physical component and Mental component. If you balance out these components then you will lead a successful life. And if you want to maintain your view on a successful life, it is important to keep in mind that it is not important whether or not you fail, it matters on how fast you get back up on your feet. This advice is coming from a student who has done bad on one of his tests at one stage but keeping my confidence I recovered in the other tests and moved on. (Male, second generation, Turkish background 29.1)

This student has recognised that open-ended questions presented in school tasks generally seek the fullest possible answer in the form of complete sentences. He has drawn together a framework of general principles, an example and a moral lesson learned from the example. These conventions are also recognised by some first generation students, who despite grammatical and syntactical errors, show greater comfort with academic forms than many of their peers.

Difficulties with written French

As in Australia, most students in France present a direct and fragmentary answer that satisfies the substance of the question, while a minority show attention to the stylistic and formal conventions of academic writing. Again, L2 acquisition does not appear to account for most difficulties.

Students providing a minimalist response, most common in vocational streams, distinguish themselves on the level of discourse through the brevity and fragmentary nature of their responses. The following example is typical (capitalisation retained):

TRAVAILLER, RÉUSSIR SA VIE PROFESSIONNELLE *(WORK, SUC-CEED IN PROFESSIONAL LIFE)*. (Male, BEP French monolingual 729.11)[3]

A second characteristic of this strategy is that students show their disregard for spelling conventions from the outset by ignoring the spelling of 'une vie réussie' (*a successful life*) in the question and spelling it differently in their responses. Around half the students in the sample misspell this phrase. They have either not thought to check the spelling used in the question – which they have nevertheless been able to decode – or have not thought it important enough to bother with one spelling rather than another. After all, the meaning is not affected by the way the word is written down.

In the following example, a student has realised that there is a silent ending of some form required to modify the adjective 'réussi' (success-ful), but mistakenly uses the noun form, and on a second occasion approximates a third person plural verb ending:

> une famille reussite, un bon boulot, une vie trepidante et epanouie et des relations amicales reussitent (*a *success*[4] family, a good job, a busy and fulfilled life and *succeed* friendships*). (Male, BEP, French/Alsatian speaker 725.11)

Such errors suggest that students are inattentive readers and unable to recognise patterns in text they read in order to apply them to their own writing. Of course they may not have been explicitly taught these skills by their teachers, whose own lack of attention is raised by such patterns. The greater number of silent morphemes in French than in English, and the system of diacritic accents, means that there is ample room for errors arising from the distance between spoken and written language. Some common errors, which resemble those in Australia, and which arise from lack of attention to written form are the confusion of homonyms and phonetic spelling:

> une vie stable un *travaille* qui me *plaie* un bon salire et ne pas avoir de difficulté d'argent (*A stable life a *work* which I *like* a good *salary* and not to have money *problems**). (Male, BEP student, French/Italian bilingual 719.11)

Such errors are common for students of all language backgrounds. A male BEP student, who speaks both French and Alsatian at home, confuses 'ce' and 'se', fails to make an adjective agree with the noun it describes and misspells an adverb:

C'est une vie où l'on sait faire se qu'on souhaite (proffessionnellement, vie social) *(It's a life where you know *what* you want (*professionally*, *social* life))*. (733.11)

This student does in fact make a gesture to a more formal register by using the construction *'l'on'*, a characteristic of an elegant literate style. However, on a second occasion, when *l'on* is more appropriate to avoid the contraction *'qu'on'*, he does not use this construction. This misplaced flourish suggests an attempt at a register distinct from informal conversation. As an audible sign of a formal register (characteristic not just of written text, but of formal speech), the flourish *'l'on'* is certainly more accessible than precise spelling. Most students do not show even this accommodation to the written style and stick to very informal language:

Une vie réussie c'est quand t'a terminé tes études... *(A successful life is when *ya've* finished your studies)*. (Female, second generation, Turkish background 581.9)

The real traps for students lie in those constructions that are silent and have no existence other than on the page. Many students do not recognise a system of morphemes that have no phonological existence in everyday speech. Thus, the response 'd'avoir fait de bon étude supérieure' *(having done good *tertiary study*)* (male, Turkish background, BEP student 171) omits markers of gender and number that are unvoiced, but grammatically necessary in the written version of this sentence. To give another example, voiced liaisons are sometimes mistaken for feminine forms of adjectives:

un *bonne* emploie bien renuméré *(a *good* *well-paid* job)*. (Male, BEP, dominant language background 727.11)

Gendered strategies

Most visibly in the French classrooms, girls appear to devote more effort to revising their work. However, most attention and revision is devoted to superficial elements of writing: neatness of presentation and well-formed handwriting, with almost obsessive use of white-out on every line for some. Thus, the efforts of their corrections, while they might have been rewarded at an earlier point in their school career, do not contribute greatly to the quality of their writing. Students who adopt this strategy commonly confuse infinitives and past participles, often mistakenly replacing one for the other in their revisions:

Une vie réussie pour moi, c'est tout d'abord d'être installer dans une maison, d'être bien payer *(A successful life for me, its firstly to be *set up* in a house, to be well *paid*).* (Female, BEP, dominant language background 571.9)

And,

Je veux vite terminé mes études *(I want to quickly *finished* my studies).* (Female, BEP, second generation, Ivorian background 562.9)

First generation students

It is striking that first generation students who do show clear signs of incomplete acquisition of French are often more attuned to written conventions. As with the Australian sample, only a few first or second generation students showed signs of incomplete acquisition of French. The grammatical errors in the following example are typical of a 'non-native' speaker:

D'avoir une famille vivante danse une ambiance heureux, avoir des amie aussi, d'avoir un travail avec paie qui nous correspond à nos tâches et à nos niveau scolaire. De pouvoir pratiquer du sport ou d'autre loisirs en dehors du temps de travail. De vivre dans la bonne santé (To have a family *living* *in* a *happy* atmosphere, to have *friends* too, to have a job with *salary* which matches our tasks and our *levels* of schooling. To be able to practice sport or other leisure activities outside of work hours. To live in good health). (Male, BEP, first generation, Cambodian background 693.11)

In this example, despite errors in syntax, which might be signs of incomplete language acquisition, the spelling and use of accents and punctuation is actually more advanced than is the case for many 'native' speakers. Unsurprisingly, perhaps, this response comes from one of the most avid readers in the sample.

Stronger students

In the academic streams, the written language of students predictably adheres more strongly to school norms and the discursive structure is more obviously tailored to the task. In academic streams, almost all students begin their response with a full sentence, demonstrating awareness of academic conventions for such tasks. Some come in the form of topic sentences indicating a structure for the remainder of the text:

Une vie réussie prend en compte plusieurs facteurs... (Male, Bac S, dominant language background 915.12)

Students in academic streams also demonstrate that they re-read their work for spelling and grammar through more frequent self-corrections. Self-corrections more often result in a correct final version, rather than the modified form of error produced when students from other streams attempt self-correction. The optimisation of the tools of rhetoric remains the preserve of the most confident of these students:

Mais qu'est-ce qu'une vie réussie? A quoi ça sert de réussir sa vie, il faut la vivre au jour le jour et advienne que pourra, je m'en fous. Chacun fait comme il veut et ça ne sert à rien de vouloir à tous prix réussir sa vie puisque je pense qu'une fois qu'on a tout pour avoir une vie réussie, on ne sera pas plus heureux qu'avant et souvent bien au contraire! *(But what is a successful life? What is the point of a successful life, one must live one day at a time, and come what may, I do not care. Each does as he wishes and I think that once one has everything for a successful life one will be no happier than before, and often quite the contrary!)* (Male, Bac S, dominant language background 905.12)

This student attempts an erudite style with rhetorical questions and the proverbial locution 'advienne que pourra', albeit followed by a return to an informal register with 'je m'en fous'. The student also shows more scrupulous attention to written conventions, which separate weaker from stronger students.

It is primarily in the written execution, rather than by virtue of a lack of fluency, that students fail in their responses to appear competent in French. In this execution, many responses further appear clumsy by ignoring modes of personal implication and distancing expected in written discourse. The distinction here hangs not merely on competence, but on 'the forms of subjectivity' invested in discourse (Felouzis, 1994: 67).

Accounting for Difficulties in Written Expression

The writing habits of students in the sample suggest that at least some of the difficulties they face are those tied to the distance between non-standard vernacular versions of the dominant language and the conventions of formal, written versions. Only a few students show signs in their writing of the type of error that would be considered unacceptable in the spoken vernacular and that might signal incomplete language acquisition. This type of error includes incorrect ordering of words in a sentence, and confusion of gender and number in pronouns. Nevertheless, it is possible that other, related difficulties have not been captured through this study by virtue of its limited focus.

What is most evident in student responses is their misunderstanding of the task presented to them as requiring no special or specialised display of the style, forms or structures specific to academic work. The technical failings of students' writing stem from the same source as their 'failings' in overall form – failure to recognise the distance between everyday communication and academic performance. Even if students were to overcome all spelling and grammatical errors, technical prowess alone would not make them acceptable as 'writers'. To meet the demands of academic writing, students must abandon (albeit temporarily) those parts of their identities that are embodied in familiar forms of communication. The role they must take on requires an important process of resocialisation, an act of identity transformation that schools see as beyond their means or fail to recognise as a key dynamic structuring pedagogical relations. The distance between identities formed through primary and peer socialisation, and the norms, values and perspectives embodied in the role of academic writer must be recognised and bridged.

The way in which this distance is managed, student interviews suggest, varies according to the way in which difficulties with written language are understood. Migrant-background students are more likely to interpret their difficulties as arising from their bilingualism, and, for some, this may be overcome through application to better mastering English/French. For dominant language-background students, this interpretation is not possible, and instead many see themselves as 'just no good' at writing or as 'dumb'. By Year 11, many do not see much room for improvement in their writing skills – they are stuck with them – and so a more fatalistic attitude develops.

Conclusion: Some Implications of Folk Theories and Dissonant Linguistic Practices

How, then, can we theorise the relationship between the language use of bilinguals and academic performance as it concerns migrant-background students? Cummins (2000) argues that cognitive academic language proficiency (CALP) is a useful concept for describing the linguistic skills demanded by school. Unlike basic interpersonal communication (BIC), CALP requires knowledge of discourse conventions and specialised vocabulary, syntax and concepts. The rival concept, second language instructional competence (SLIC), has emerged from a critique of Cummins that seeks to further capture the cultural dimensions of schooling (MacSwan & Rolstad, 2003). However, both CALP and SLIC have been conceived of for application in the context of first generation migrants who are undertaking explicit L2 instruction. These concepts do not account for sources of difficulty outside of the processes of L2 acquisition.

The way in which students attribute meaning and value to learning activities and knowledge has important consequences for their success (Bautier *et al.*, 2000). Students who 'misunderstand' the intellectual and cognitive nature of school learning are disadvantaged by directing their efforts to merely completing tasks, biding time until the moment of their release at the end of the school day. Similarly, teachers misdirect their efforts when their explanations for student difficulty result from 'misunderstanding'. Teachers need to recognise students' primary discourses and build upon them.

Recognition and execution of legitimate forms or codes is socially structured by what Bernstein terms 'recognition rules', which establish legitimate relations between different forms, and 'realisation rules', which control legitimate relations within given forms of interaction (Bernstein, 1996: 19). Students and teachers must be aware of and master these rules in order to be able to 'switch' between 'everyday' and specialised scholarly interactions if they are to perform the roles in ways that are accorded institutional legitimacy. As Bernstein has noted, the 'eliciting speech context' provokes different reactions according to social position. Scholastic situations elicit linguistic responses in middle-class students that are more linked to the demands of schooling for 'universalistic' expression (Bernstein, 1972: 168). Teachers need to be mindful of this, and to draw out tensions between their own and their students' understandings, rather than leaping quickly to correction of student views. Grenfell (1998) suggests that teacher attempts at scaffolding may not always work purely positively when such differences in worldview between teacher and pupil are not explored. For example, when a student makes an unexpected utterance during a mathematics problem, the teacher typically,

> does not investigate what thinking results in this utterance, rather she talks the pupil through (according to) her own (legitimate) method. Her intention to teach is more powerful than her intention to understand the pupil. (Grenfell, 1998: 84)

The challenge for teachers is twofold. In the first instance, they must re-evaluate and redress the weight accorded to the 'language burden' of bilingualism as a source of poor academic performance, even when they do not personally subscribe to the folk theories outlined above. They must also reflect on effective strategies for addressing the types of difficulties that students face in academic study. Students' written work should be read by teachers not merely as expressing a level of technical competency, but a particular understanding of the demands of the task and its classification either as an 'everyday' undertaking or a performance with specific and specialised requirements. Further, they must understand students' engagement with schooling in terms of the identities and frames for understanding that they bring with them, and these can provide the basis for a strengthened connection between students and teachers if they are accorded a greater place in the classroom.

Notes

1. This is the second to last year of secondary schooling in Victoria, Australia. French participants came from the equivalent level, which is divided into streams. In this chapter, students from France are identified by their enrolment as being in a BEP (Brevet d'études professionnelles – Vocational certificate) or in a Baccalauréat (academic matriculation stream). Schools and students have been de-identified.
2. Original spelling and punctuation has been retained. Italicised words indicate the errors discussed. 'Dominant language background' refers to monolingual speakers of the national language.
3. Students from France are identified by their enrolment as being in a BEP (Brevet d'études professionnelles – Vocational certificate) or in a Baccalauréat (academic matriculation stream).
4. Asterisks are used to indicate where errors occur in the original, as these cannot always be translated as errors in the English version.

References

Bautier, E., Charlot, B. and Rochex, J-Y. (2000) Entre apprentissages et métier d'élève: Le rapport au savoir. In A. Van Zanten (ed.) *L'école. L'état des savoirs* (pp. 179–188). Paris: La Découverte.

Bernstein, B. (1972) Social class, language and socialization. In P.P. Giglioli (ed.) *Language and Social Context: Selected Readings* (pp. 157–178). Harmondsworth: Penguin.

Bernstein, B. (1996) *Pedagogy, Symbolic Control, and Identity: Theory, Research, Critique*. London and Washington, DC: Taylor & Francis.

Berque, J. and Centre national de documentation pédagogique (France) (1985) *L'Immigration à l'École de la République: Rapport d'un groupe de réflexion*. Paris: Documentation française: Centre national de documentation pédagogique.

Bourdieu, P. (1977) The economics of linguistic exchanges. *Social Science Information* 16 (6), 645–668.

Bourdieu, P., Passeron, J-C. and de Saint Martin, M. (1994) *Academic Discourse: Linguistic Misunderstanding and Professorial Power*. Cambridge: Polity Press.

Brice Heath, S. (1982) What no bedtime story means: Narrative skills at home and school. *Language in Society* 2, 49–76.

Centre for Applied Educational Research (2002) *Middle Years Research and Development (MYRAD) Project*. Melbourne: University of Melbourne, Department of Education & Training.

Choquet, O. and Héran, F. (1996) Quand les élèves jugent les collèges et les lycées. *Économie et Statistique* 293, 107–124.

Costa-Lascoux, J. (1989) Immigrant children in French schools: Equality or discrimination. In L. Eldering and J. Kloprogge (eds) *Different Cultures, Same School: Ethnic Minority Children in Europe* (pp. 61–84). Amsterdam/Berwyn, PA: Swets & Zeitlinger; Swets North America.

Cummins, J. (2000) *Language, Power and Pedagogy: Bilingual Children in the Crossfire*. Clevedon: Multilingual Matters.

Dubet, F. (1991) *Les Lycéens*. Paris: Seuil.

Felouzis, G. (1993) Conceptions de la réussite et socialisation scolaire. *Revue Française de Pédagogie* 105, 45–58.

Felouzis, G. (1994) *Le Collège au Quotidien*. Paris: PUF.

Galbally, F. (1978) *Migrant Services and Programs: Report of the Review of Post-arrival Programs and Services for Migrants*. Canberra: AGPS.

Gaspard, F. and Khosrokhavar, F. (1995) *Le Foulard et la République*. Paris: La découverte.

Grenfell, M. (1998) Language and the classroom. In M. Grenfell and D. James (eds) *Bourdieu and Education: Acts of Practical Theory* (pp. 72–88). London and Bristol, PA: Falmer Press.

Jennings, J. (2000) Citizenship, republicanism and multiculturalism in contemporary France. *British Journal of Political Science* 30 (4), 575.

Kagitçibasi, Ç. (1988) Turkish migrants: Views from the sending country. In R. Akçelik and J. Elley (eds) *Turkish Community in Australia* (pp. 1–20). Melbourne: Australian-Turkish Friendship Society Publications.

Labov, W. (1972) *The Logic of Nonstandard English*. Harmondsworth: Penguin.

Larkin, M. (1997) *France since the Popular Front: Government and People, 1936–1996* (2nd edn). Oxford and New York: Clarendon Press.

MacSwan, J. and Rolstad, K. (2003) Linguistic diversity, schooling, and social class: Rethinking our conception of language proficiency in language minority education. In C.B. Paulston and G.R. Tucker (eds) *Sociolinguistics: The Essential Readings* (pp. 329–342). Malden, MA: Blackwell.

Matthews, J. (2002) Racialised schooling, 'ethnic success' and Asian-Australian students. *British Journal of Sociology of Education* 32 (2), 193–207.

Mauviel, M. (1985) Sur le pluralisme culturel. In J. Berque (ed.) *L'Immigration à l'École de la République: Rapport d'un groupe de réflexion* (pp. 87–90). Paris: Documentation française: Centre national de documentation pédagogique.

Pavlenko, A. (2002) Poststructuralist approaches to the study of social factors in second language learning and use. In V. Cook (ed.) *Portraits of the L2 User* (pp. 277–302). Clevedon: Multilingual Matters.

Payet, J-P. (1996) La scolarisation des enfants et des jeunes issus de l'immigration en France. *Revue Française de Pédagogie* 117, 89–116.

Peköz, N.B. (1993) Second-generation Turkish youth's bilingual experience and its effects on individuals. In R. Akçelik and Australian-Turkish Friendship

Society (eds) *Turkish Youth in Australia* (pp. 121–137). Melbourne: Australian-Turkish Friendship Society.

Perroton, J. (1999) Les dimensions ethniques de l'expérience scolaire. *L'Année Sociologique* 50 (2), 437–467.

Persell, C.H. (1977) *Education and Inequality: A Theoretical and Empirical Synthesis*. New York: Free Press.

Romaine, S. (1995) *Bilingualism* (2nd edn). Oxford and Cambridge, MA: Blackwell.

Simkin, K. and Gauci, E. (1992) Ethnic diversity and multicultural education. In R.J. Burns and A.R. Welch (eds) *Contemporary Perspectives in Comparative Education* (pp. 327–361). New York: Garland.

van Zanten, A. (1997) Schooling immigrants in France in the 1990s: Success or failure of the republican model of integration. *Anthropology and Education Quarterly* 28 (3), 351–374.

van Zanten, A. (2001) *L'École de la Périphérie*. Paris: Presses Universitaires Françaises.

Warren, J. (1999) Wogspeak: Transformations of Australian English. *Journal of Australian Studies* 62, 86–94.

Windle, J. (2004) Schooling, symbolism and social power: The Hijab in Republican France. *Australian Educational Researcher* 31 (1), 95–112.

Part 2

Language Policy and Curriculum

In Eds Miller et al, 'Culturally, ~
linguistically Diverse Classrooms.'
Bristol, Multilingual Matters. (2009)

Chapter 7

Dilemmas of Efficiency, Identity and Worldmindedness

JOSEPH LO BIANCO

Introduction

Perhaps the strongest indicator of the transformed realities of contemporary education in a globalised world is the depth of cultural, racial and linguistic diversity in schools. Traditional societies of emigration now struggle to integrate immigrants. The immigrant-receiving societies encounter intensifying diversity as all occupational strata and all age profiles are on the move, characterising the 'age of migration' (Castles & Miller, 2003). Population mobility is perhaps the salient marker of our times with direct implications for educating and empowering vast numbers of students who do not speak the majority or dominant language. This diversity poses an extraordinary challenge for teachers whose traditional modes of offering compulsory foreign language must cater for a highly heterogeneous learner population. There are also direct consequences for general teaching and for second language pedagogy from such galloping cultural and linguistic diversity.

Ironically, the reasoning that underlies language education policy statements in different parts of the world is looking less diverse as time progresses. Language education is increasingly recruited to serve two broad purposes: first, economic agendas of competitive preparation for global markets and second, cultural agendas of forging or retaining a distinctive national identity. The global and the local are often mediated also by concessions to minorities present today in all nations, but these are invariably tokenistic. Policies for minority and indigenous languages are also notorious for the great disparity between what is funded compared to what is promised or claimed. Governments claim, expect or imagine deeply visionary outcomes from investments in language education, but these ambitious policy remits usually have an inverse relationship with budgetary allocations: the greater the ambition the more florid the discourse and the more florid the discourse the lower the financial allocations.

In general, discourses of efficiency are more comfortably natural to the public policy of national states. Education systems have always served goals of language socialisation of regional and social minorities, forging linguistic homogeneity in the interests of national unity. These stress communicative ease, transparency and convergence of social relations. On the other hand, identity ideologies stress difference, negotiation and divergence, and these classically make governments promise more than they intend to deliver. Under conditions of globalisation there is an intensification of both a hyper-instrumentalism attached to English, standard modes of literacy and foreign languages associated with trade and perceived 'national interest'. The national language, and priority foreign languages, get unproblematically connected to dominant inter-ests of market-based trade liberalisation, while literacy, usually con-ceived in rigidly normalised ways, functions as an index of general education investments and standards. As a result, one of the character-istic ways of doing international comparative research is to contrast literacy rates, along with Gross Domestic Product and various indicators of health and morbidity. Both symbolically and rhetorically, therefore, efficiency discourses are the strongest legitimising rationales in public education outlays.

Efficiency tends to position discourses of identity as reactive or resistant modes of reasoning, or as assertions of the rights of minorities usually relying on oppositional language. Because English is far and away the first foreign language of choice at all education levels in most parts of the world (Cha & Ham, 2008), reaction against the privileging of English tends to get cast as excessively nationalistic, anti-competitive or backward looking. Those who oppose 'too much English' tend to assert non-western pathways to economic modernisation, greater education effectiveness for minority populations through use of local languages and literacies, and concerns about the identity loss from the reduction of linguistic and cultural diversity.

This chapter reflects, in a rather broad way, on a range of language and cultural programmes, mostly on foreign language teaching for 'mainstream' learners of the languages of Western-European 'prestige others', but also immersion and bilingual education. One of the justifications often made on behalf of foreign languages in education concerns the impact that such language study is claimed to have on intercultural insight and awareness. However, given the privileging of prestige languages in national education systems, which are taught mostly to advantaged learners and for the admiration of foreign others, can we expect any flow on effects in multicultural awareness, inter-cultural competence or positive attitudes towards difference in general? The dilemmas posed by efficiency and identity rationales for teachers, learners and schools inform, in the latter part of the chapter, an alternative mode of conceiving public education for difference, organised under the conceptual category of 'critical worldmindedness'.

Worldmindedness is a notion that seeks to overcome a persisting problem in foreign and second language teaching. The premise on which this claim for worldmindedness is made rests on the persistence of interests. Extending reflections offered by Freadman (2001) about foreign language education in post-colonial times, critical worldmindedness builds on the three modes she identifies that mark foreign language education as a non-neutral or interested practice. The first concerns representation. Teachers 'stand for' the language they teach and represent the culture/s associated with it in particular ways. Curriculum docu-ments and the asymmetrical relations between teacher knowledge and learner dependence compound the already selective nature of curriculum design and textbook content. These factors turn teachers into representa-tives and agents acting 'on behalf of' the target language culture and often of its national community as well. Second, teachers construct and enact the culture for learners, becoming its performative agents. In how teachers say the target language culture exists, and the genres through which this culture is made available to learners, teachers rhetorically mediate the target language culture. In the process of teaching, learners are introduced to cultural products, communicative activities, social practices and various problems of the target language community. These challenges demand that teachers supply interpretive activity 'on behalf of' the target culture for learners. Third, professional careers, personal standing and various rewards conspire to make teachers, directly and indirectly, advocates for the target language culture, or make them engage in acts of serving interests.

Discourses of Identity

Issues of identity permeate all languages, most education systems, and the majority of societies, profoundly. Most societies are composed of diverse communities whose sense of common pasts, and anticipated common futures, are defined by shared communication. In effect, what we call *ethnic groups* are often communities of communication (Wright, 2000). For these communities of communication, globalisation and digitisation (Castells, 1996) provoke expansion in the possible forms of identity. This occurs at both the national and the sub-national levels. As a result, what counts as identity becomes so diverse and multiplying that when reading identity theory textbooks of the 1960s and 1970s, one is struck by the deep change that has occurred. To the old classics of race, nation, language and religion has been attached a multiplicity of additional identities, some temporary and fading, others stable and enduring. Some are resurgent versions of dormant past identities, while others are unique originals and hybrids, such as spontaneous expressions of more ancient impulses adapting to new circumstances.

New sources of identity

The sources of identity include recreational pursuits and sexual preferences, professional communities and bodies of knowledge, what we have read and what we do, our activities and stocks of information, dress and style, aesthetics and opinion, moral judgement and political commitment. For most of the 20th century, we operated with a view of identity and the self that was stable and enduring, permanent and fixed. The literature on identity in applied linguistics, western critical sociology and education research is today mostly convinced that identity is situated, contingent, multiple and shifting. The rapid spread of the idea of an impermanent self is astonishing when we reflect on what an important assumption it makes about the source of human self-consciousness.

The locomotive of information and communication technologies fuel many forms of sentiment and the new opportunities to display identity (in clothing, musical taste and practice, belief, and participation in real-time internet simulation), so that horizontal links are ubiquitous as the temporal and spatial axes of psychological orientation. It hardly surprises us anymore that a 16-year-old from Syracuse Sicily attests to more revealing and personally meaningful connections with largely anonymous peers in Bangkok and Santiago de Chile than with their age peers, much less blood relatives, in the next village. However, because such relations produce new member categories that are to us dynamic and horizontal, fresh and remarkable, we risk exaggerating their extent and neglecting the persistence of their opposite.

Old sources of identity

Traditional sources and modalities of identity have not been exterminated, not even the classical primordial groupings for whom 'one would willingly die or kill for' (Anderson, 1991). It is worth remembering that in the early years of the 20th century, the persuasive analysis of future identity formations relied on formulations cast by German sociologist Max Weber, predicting either the erosion or complete disappearance of the classical sentiments of nation, religion, state and race. Perhaps it would shock them today to observe how *un-eroded* these 'old' attachments are, and how the deployment of one of today's predicted instruments of blunting the old, i.e. digital communications, actually serves to reinforce, diffuse and intensify the identity classics. These persisting, *un-eroded* identity formations are manifested, as always, in conflict over territory, ideology, symbols, contested history and exclusive associations of categories of people to particular geo-political spaces.

This resurgence of aggressive claiming of place undermines the forecasts of high modernity, which imagined an ever more rational and enlightened future unencumbered by what it saw as atavistic identities. But these aggressive tendencies of nationalism and faith also challenge post-modernity, or at least those streams which imagined that new multiculturalism from transnational and transcultural flows would produce more widespread cosmopolitan hybridity. The old differences have not been consigned to redundancy. While it is not inevitable that classic sources of identity produce ethnic disparagement and rivalry for geo-political space, or symbolic domination and economic hierarchy, it is undeniable that the forms the classical identity formations have taken in the past decade are recognisable as a re-run of old ideas of exclusive nation, religion and political ideology. These claims for making the particular exclusive and sovereign, i.e. creating bounded national states occupied by the culturally similar, in defined territory, run dangerously against the empirical trend of increased diversification of societies everywhere. One result is race riots, ethnic conflict, segmented urban zones and the public display of exclusive identities in many parts of the world, many of which have recourse to toxic forms of absolutism, even fundamentalism. Before the present aggressive resurgence, some 25 years ago, Joseph Alpher (1986: 1) in a work devoted to nationalism and modernity in the Mediterranean, noted that there are 'four institutions which, despite the best efforts of radical revolutionaries for over a century, never seem to go away: state, nation, language and religion'.

Inventing languages to overcome identity politics

In 19th century Europe, many intellectuals, idealists and utopians visualised an imminent global age, the result of vast imperial expansion from competitive national European states, even if they could never have imagined the binary properties of bits and bytes digitisation. In remarkable acts of devotion to changing the world through grammar and vocabulary, Ludwig Zamenhof and other idealists invented languages whose very names, *Esperanto, Idiom Neutral, Interlingua, A Common Writing*, aimed to link micro-linguistic elements with extra-linguistic utopias; they wanted to make phonemes and morphemes contribute to changing human consciousness, to de-socialise humans away from the parochial, the local and the chauvinistic, and towards the ideal, the universal and the planetary. The aim of these projects was not just to make artificial languages easy to learn and use, unlike natural languages, so that every learner would be completely successful, but also to bring about personal visions of enlightenment and human progress.

Literally thousands of such projects were generated. Most were impressive in their complexity, others charming or amusing, some weird and some quirky; but all aimed to achieve ambitious socially transformative ends. Some aimed to make individuals more 'artistic' or more sensitive to beauty, others to remove male bias in speech and writing, some to eject racism from the rhetorical and semantic structures of language, others to make human thinking more logical by removing semantic ambiguity, some wanted to remove aggressive impulses, others wanted to counter Eurocentric bias in the world, some wanted to make vagueness impossible by forcing speakers to adopt direct communication styles and become more 'democratic'. Whatever the ambition being pursued, the ideologies and utopias of the language designer were rarely about language. Instead, they mostly aimed to transform human subjectivities and improve social arrangements.

Several language idealists were persecuted for their efforts. After all, the century in which many of the artificial language projects were launched was one of the most ferociously ideologically intolerant in history. Most language inventors believed that a natural language, a language of any one national community, could never serve global communication because it would entrench the advantage of some nations over others; it would privilege some thought styles over others; it would validate some histories and philosophies over others; it would legitimise some communicative practices over other, entirely legitimate, but less powerful, alternatives.

Some language inventers believed that 'native' speakers would be disadvantaged if their cherished national and natural language became the global speech form, because this would remove them from their exclusive control and make widely available, their unique 'spirit language', verbal identity form, we-code or insider speech. This would result in the loss of the personal language of sentiment and convert it instead into a mere tool in others' hands, an instrument used by cultural outsiders, foreigners and aliens, for purposes banal and ordinary, such as transacting business deals or managing traffic in sea lanes or airspace control. Romantic visions of organic speech communities would be ruptured by transactional purposes that would deplete 'spirit' languages of their deep cultural significance for their core community. Better then, to base international communication on artificial tools invented expressly for this purpose. I am referring to what we might call *a priori* artificial languages, i.e. languages invented from scratch.

However, there were also *a posteriori* language projects, aiming to change or reform existing natural languages in partial ways, like linguistic plastic surgery. Few people realise how committed many Americans were to removing English from the newly independent republic after the War of Independence. Even Benjamin Franklin apparently endorsed a plan to build a new American language, one based on German. John Adams, another early patriot, wanted to retain English but remove the vestiges of aristocracy and monarchy from it, to produce what he called 'a more democratical English'. Some patriots wanted just to change its name. Although a 1923 proposal by Washington J. McCormick to make 'American' the official language of the USA failed in Congress, later in the same year, Illinois State Senator Frank Ryan succeeded in the State House. 'American' was declared the official language of Illinois, and remained the state law until 1969 when it was changed to 'English'. There were many such attempts, including the writing of dictionaries that favoured American speech and idiom over British alternatives, and attempts to create an American language academy, such as in 1820 with William Cardell's *American Academy of Language and Belle Lettres*, whose explicit Americanising aim was as nationalist as it was short-lived. Some projects aimed for mild ways to reflect American identity in American English, others aimed to do a wholesale job of changing people's mentality. McCormick wanted a total 'mental emancipation' to accompany the political emancipation of 1776 (Lo Bianco, 2007). One dictionary writer, Noah Webster, in 1789 issued a *Declaration of Linguistic Independence*, to match the political declaration.

Identity remains and returns

Notions of identity and language are rarely separated, even within the main Anglophone centres of the world. Unsurprisingly, mass and obligatory teaching of English in China, where there are more students of English than there are Americans, provokes discussion, research, contestation and reflection on identity, all of which are the effects of large investments made by the Chinese authorities to facilitate extra-national communication in languages other than Chinese (Lo Bianco *et al.*, 2009).

Today in the USA, dilemmas of identity in relation to English remain vibrant and controversial, though the aim is neither to replace nor to reform English, but to establish it as the official language (Lo Bianco, 2007). These moves stem from the number of language rights won by minorities, political and juridical concessions to multilingualism, and especially to Spanish, which have stimulated some 25 years of a persistent and, at times, aggressive (Crawford, 2002) movement to declare English the officially sanctioned code-of-state, a movement remarkable not only for this activity in the world's greatest centre for the propagation of English as the global lingua franca, but a movement that often makes recourse to sentimental arguments about place and identity in advancing its cause. Dilemmas of identity are prominent in the UK too. At extra-national, supra-national and sub-national levels, we can see the search for a language-marked identity being taken forward by English dialect speakers, by the resisting Celtic fringe, especially Welsh, but also Scottish Gaelic, Cornish, Manx and Irish, and by speakers of new Englishes.

The connection with statehood is clear. The moves for linguistic revitalisation either anticipate and seek to hasten, or follow and so reflect political devolution. Various sub-national groups in the British Isles have gained a measure of political autonomy, and local languages have come to enjoy the attentions of earnest policy makers along with the curiosity of tourists, the devotion of folk workers and the research studies of linguists. In poetry and prose, as well as in dictionaries and political speech making, associations are made between language, place and territory. These developments underscore the claims by Giddens (1999) that the local and the traditional are asserted in the face of the alienation and impersonality of the global. All this proceeds as the assessments of the demand and status of English claim that about a third, and possibly up to half, of the population of the world will either know or be learning English by 2050 (Graddol, 2006). The efforts to recover the old Celtic languages of the UK, and interest in cultivating the old British dialects of English, with a surge in new Englishes, all gravitate around associations between identity and communities of communication, taking specific form according to the precise historical circumstances that have forged existing conditions. That these efforts are small in comparison with the global reach and power of English does not detract from the central contention that claims for identity, attempts to recover and retrieve perceived lost identity, or genres, domains and settings for the display and marking of distinctiveness, all feature in language education policy today.

It is not even particularly important whether the efforts ultimately succeed. What is relevant is the enduring nature of identity work in language. The revival efforts among the six remaining old Celtic languages, pushed to the islands, margins and edges of the British Isles, and the language maintenance efforts of immigrant language speakers, paint a picture of pervasive identity work being done in and through language in the UK today. Such developments are associated with the state, the national state, which in most European contexts is based on an established assumption of the greater efficiency of uni-lingualism. This efficiency assumption is bolstered by associating exclusive nationality with communities of communication expressed in the modernist national principle of *one people one state one language*. The narrative of the monolingual state is challenged from the supra-national level, i.e. EU and the Council of Europe COE, from the sub-national level, i.e. the political devolution process within the UK that has made Scotland, Wales, Northern Ireland and some other areas more autonomous. Uni-lingualism is also challenged from the extra-national level, from globalisation, migration and the lingering consequences of colonisation.

Teaching identity in foreign language education

Foreign language learning has often been invoked as representing a critical, and sometimes even the sole part, of the curriculum to be devoted to pluralising frameworks. Various stages have been traversed in how language teaching has incorporated the teaching of culture and the promotion of identity (Murphy, 1988; Risager, 1998). Risager's European analysis shows a clear move from assuming that languages taught in schools are spoken by distant others, in which each language represents a bordered cultural space, such as a national state, with its secure history and literature, art forms and ways of life. This *foreign-cultural* approach essentially assumes a single culture for a single country in a specific territory and isolated from the learners' culture. The aim tended to be to teach admiration for and knowledge of this culture, but it was seen to be an essentially foreign entity. According to Risager, this approach has been losing ground since the 1980s.

This practice was replaced by the *intercultural* approach, based on contrasting the target culture and the learners' culture and identity, forging hybrid interacting identities through noting similarities and dissimilarities. In some parts of Europe and in much of North America this appears to be the main approach today. A third alternative has been the *multicultural* approach, found in societies with many different cultures and languages. It seeks to impart common and shared knowledge within respect for and maintenance of different identities. Some forms of multicultural approaches in language education also see culture as a set of practices that learners can add to existing culture stocks, producing new or hybrid forms. This is claimed to be the emerging approach in multiethnic societies. According to this analysis, globalisation challenges all these ways to understand culture in language education and today what is coming to be called the *trans-cultural* approach is adopted. This tends to see cultures as interacting, not tightly bounded by national states. Since these cultures are 'available' to learners in digital and virtual form, in which learners can access selections and aspects of these cultures, rather than the authorised versions depicted by authoritative bodies or texts or individuals, unique composite or mixtures are adopted.

Identity then is alive and well in language education policies, and identity discourses have flourished through digital connections making possible multiple, hybrid and shifting forms of community and belonging, and attachments that often make use of language to do their work of constituting new identities. However, identities are insider-bonding discourses, and often rely on identification of non-belongers and their categorisation as different. When identities are made exclusive, and attached to geo-political space, they can descend into antagonism, rejection and racism, conceding to a defective variant that is exclusionary and hostile to forms of difference other than the ones it espouses. When pushed to extremes, identity discourses can combine with the search for autonomous statehood, and when practised against outsiders, have often generated communalism, sectarianism and chauvinism (Hutton, 1999). This is the dilemma of identity.

Discourses of Efficiency

In language education policies, identity talk tends towards stressing difference, but globalisation and the digital age also privilege the opposite, i.e. standardisation, portability, commonness. The most evident form this takes is the emergence of world systems in all areas of activity for the management of economic, environmental, social and political interdependency. Managing interdependency in turn relies on technical skills that privilege precision and signify a preference for controllable and systematic processes leading to predictability, and routine operations. The distribution of the symbolic and material resources of the global economy today makes these forces favour English and its instrumental use. Consider that Chile, despite speaking the third most used language on Earth, and separated from the USA by nine contiguous land borders of countries, every one of which speaks Spanish, has embarked on a massive national plan to be a fully bilingual Spanish-English country. In comparison with other languages, Spanish attracts many learners because of calculations learners make about communication efficiency, but this, and similar examples, show that for all its size and prestige, the 'efficiency' claims of Spanish struggle against those of English, the exemplar of linguistic hyper-modernity.

Efficiency, freedom and opportunity

Efficiency is such a powerful discourse in education policies that an extended word on its origins and links to language education is needed. The overarching reasoning for efficiency is often attached to ideas of freedom and opportunity. This line of reasoning draws on the thinking of the apostle of market liberalism, F.A. Hayek, and his focus on the inadequacies and limits of central planning. An Austrian economist working in the USA, Hayek argued that there are deep connections between how marketplaces are organised and issues of personal human freedoms with political consequences of state 'intrusion' into the economy, which ultimately affect all aspects of public life, including education. Hayek's many admirers among political conservatives credit his ideas as emblematic of the last part of the 20th century; 'Hayek's ascendancy' (Gruen, 2008).

The overriding aim of public policy influenced by Hayekian notions is how to achieve maximal efficiency. Hayek's view of economic liberalism ties political liberty, and individual freedoms, to the efficient functioning of markets, to the free exchange of goods and services, to the forging of independent identities for individuals and groups removed from state influence, control or definition. Though not sharing most of his conclusions, nor one of his key premises that political liberalism based on unfettered markets was a defining essence of English societies, societies the world over enact policies that contain his silent imprimatur. Efficiency as more than the simple idea of doing things in the most cost-effective way possible, but efficiency as an elevated principle of philosophy, virtue and freedom is now so widespread and assumed, that even societies that expressly reject the politics of Hayek, enact his economics.

These notions of market efficiency have a direct connection with language education and language planning. Language planning is the academic field that tries to account for the social practice of intervening to organise a society's language resources and meet its language needs. Its main aspiration in its formative decade was to achieve scientific efficiency. As Fishman (1971: 111) has stated: 'Language planning as a rational and technical process informed by actuarial data and by ongoing feedback is still a dream, but it is by no means so farfetched a dream as it seemed to be merely a decade ago'.

Efficiency and the canon

This is an image of a technically efficient mode of operating so that experts controlling discrete bodies of knowledge, untroubled by ideologies, interests or subjectivity, ending up with the 'right' choices, would make decisions about focus and priorities in language. Advocates of language rights, or of extending language education opportunities, would have to demonstrate benefits in terms of improved efficiencies, and arguments about rights would be assessed against technical criteria of measurable outcomes rather than assertions of intrinsic worth or subjective community judgments. Fishman, however, is a strong advocate of language rights, and his early vision of language planning merely reflects the domination of rationalist managerial approaches to public policy prevailing several decades ago. Efficiency reasoning leads some scholars, even as they promote the virtues of some kinds of literacy, language study and cultural education to strongly anti-pluralistic and anti-multilingual positions. This is exemplified by the apostle of 'cultural literacy', E.D. Hirsch, who has claimed that: 'Linguistic pluralism enormously increases cultural fragmentation, civil antagonism, illiteracy, and economic-technological ineffectualness' (Hirsch, 1988: 91).

Here, the cultural canon is depicted as uni-lingual, not just coincidentally, but essentially uni-lingual. High literature in standard language and normalised modes of literacy is tied to economy and technology, with the essential message that 'efficiency' is the ultimate deciding criterion. The efficiency Hirsch imagines, however, is much more profound than just effective use of resources; he imagines instead efficiency as a deep cultural value. Disturbingly, however, the world is many of the things he sees standing in the way of deep-value efficiency.

Given the reality of the linguistic and cultural diversity of the world, and the search to mark language education with identity discourses, what actions would be justified to meet Hirsch's desire or claim for cultural literacy? What actions would educators, planners and governments need to take to produce education systems, economies, technological innovation and societies untroubled by the inefficiency that he clearly sees in multilingualism?

We are all familiar with claims to make education serve economic interests more closely. Many of these conflate a series of simplifications of reality, both communicative realities in multicultural societies and realities of often irreconcilable differences of worldviews living side by side in pluralistic societies. In the past few years, public policies in many societies, influenced by the reasoning of efficiency – either market efficiencies as proposed by Hayek, or their cultural equivalents as advocated by Hirsch – advance what amount to mono-logic assumptions in literacy, mono-dialectal styles in English, mono-lingual practices in schooling. These typically naturalise English, its literacy and 'Anglosphere', i.e. native English and western parameters for governance and civic life, and make the dilemmas of identity and efficiency collide in catastrophic ways.

Literacy and script efficiency

The language form that is most closely associated with the principle of efficiency is literacy, especially standardised, predictable, stable and conventionalised alphabetic literacy in English. It should be noted that efficiency discourses, despite their specific form in recent decades, are not exclusive to either English or to modern times. China is the greatest case in the history of the world in terms of generating a national community of communication on the basis of shared writing, and it is not surprising that the distinctive feature and one of the main foci of Chinese language planning has been around orthography, the original form in the 3rd century BC, and its various modifications. Qin Shihuangdi, first emperor of a united China, pursued political unification through linguistic selection, i.e. of a single standardised writing variety (the Small Seal) and its mandated use, for greater efficiency of governance and for cultural assimilation and consolidation of his state. Since that time, China has become the site of the 'largest language engineering project in the world' (Zhou & Ross, 2004: 1) and host to language policies ever since, a large component of which have been patterned around both a simple and an elevated principle of efficiency.

Gottlieb and Chen (2001: 5) note that 'reform of script and written language is usually what first springs to the mind of language planners and the general public' in East Asia. For more than three decades, from 1954, the national official institution for language in China was called the Chinese Committee on Script Reform and was only renamed the State Language and Script Commission in 1986 (Chen, 2001); the 2001 Common Language Law is also remarkable in this respect given that issues of script are present in virtually all the articles of the law (Rohsenow, 2004: 41–43).

Script is rare if not totally absent from language policy in Europe, where alphabetisation is so entrenched that some people are barely conscious of the idea that it is possible to write in other ways. As a result, orthographic language policy in the West takes the form of debates about spelling reforms, trivial by comparison with the romanisation of Vietnamese, the adoption of Hankul in Korea, the continuing debates over the two kana scripts and kanji in the context of digitisation in Japan, and, by far the biggest issue, that arising from character simplification in China, and the repercussions for Taiwan and Singapore. Digitisation of texts is also an important issue in East Asia. Technology requires cross-national standardisation, but original and valued script forms are used to invoke distinctive identity claims and to resist efficiency rationales and their simplifying effects.

The literacies that efficiency demands are those that reduce the recognition of the local and the different. The principle of efficiency restricts the space for non-economically functional forms, just as the principle of identity resists efficiency when values and distinctiveness are challenged. Efficiency is a legitimating discourse recognised throughout public administration and governance as the least expensive, most rapidly acting and widest impacting principle for decision-making. Contesting the principle of efficiency is the most common preoccupation of pluralists who continuously come up against assumptions and criticisms whereby defending difference is construed as anti-modern and inefficient.

Worldmindedness

Thus far, I have been using two abstractions, efficiency and identity, to point out that in language education policy and practice, we often move between these two poles of thinking. Here, I want to introduce a third principle, worldmindedness, which I will propose as a (critically oriented) addition to, or softening of, this continuous oscillation between principles of efficiency and identity.

Worldmindedness, and specifically critical worldmindedness, is a construct that aims to insert a cultural critical approach to identity and culture, recognising that cultures penetrate each other, are not discrete or confined to bounded nation states. As far as foreign language education is concerned, this idea aims to impart critical generalisations beyond just the cultures of the learner and those of the society he or she is studying, beyond self and target societies. The aim is to propose a way to label openness to difference that goes beyond the representations that teachers present/do in foreign language classrooms on behalf of single target language communities, and to make a claim on all parts of language education and on other learning areas as well.

In this way, worldmindedness rejects the *foreign cultural* approach typical of much foreign language education in which learners are taught uncritical admiration of foreign cultures. Worldmindedness critiques the *intercultural approach* that is often adopted in reaction to the *foreign cultural approach*, but which is limited to contrasting target and learner cultures by looking for their similarities and differences. In such intercultural approaches, the aim is often only to note, notice and identify difference, or to treat it functionally so that differences are studied only to facilitate more effective communication. Worldmindedness also identifies and seeks to go beyond the limits of the *multicultural approach*, which is today much more common in foreign language education, and which aims for the maintenance, and, therefore, often the uncritical acceptance or non-examination of differences. As far as multiple literacies, language planning and other curriculum sites, subjects or activities are concerned, as well as policies in education in general, the aim is to search for a way to unite disparate parts of curriculum around generative principles, beyond what is available to the learner in what he or she is directly taught.

When we hear and use the word identity in language education debates, what is being advocated reflects a general tendency typical in recent decades towards favouring differentiation and localisation, validating human differences and the rights attaching to diversity. By contrast, efficiency reflects an underlying impulse in language, education and society towards standardisation and globalisation, coming originally from economic arguments linking free markets with human freedoms. The justification for proposing worldmindedness as an overarching way to talk about the goals and outcomes of language education programmes is to find common ground between various types of language learning, and to seek a way past sterile debates dominated by discourses of identity and efficiency. Worldmindedness aims to offer learners, teachers and curriculum planners a learning goal that might be incorporated into all language teaching. By cultivating attitudes about diversity beyond the narrow limits of what is directly taught, something of the vast multi-cultural diversity of contemporary school populations can at least be represented in existing programmes.

As it is imagined here, worldmindedness is neither a technical need nor an empirical necessity, since curricula for foreign language teaching are increasingly effective. Instead, worldmindedness derives from a moral commitment and a political imperative. It is justified for applied linguists from the kind of questioning of language data that critical scholars do, a kind of questioning that exposes the workings of power and interests in language and communication. It is justified in foreign language teaching because experience shows some of the limitations of the expectation that learners gain cultural insight from the study of other groups. Even when this does occur, it rarely extends beyond the specific group studied. And yet, a prevailing justification for foreign language study in curriculum documents is invariably about the culturally humanising aims of such teaching. In personal observations of class-rooms over many years, and discussions with students and teachers engaged in foreign language learning, it has often been clear to me that selecting prestige foreign languages for study often imparts no insight whatever, and occasionally no sympathetic interest, beyond the specifi-cally admired target group. In societies like Australia, post-colonial, immigrant-receiving societies with very extensive multilingualism, foreign language study is necessarily limited to a select few, and still reflects language choices made on the basis of trade, diplomacy, geography and cultural prestige. A clear example is found in the successive government policies in Australia favouring Asian languages, but which continually exclude Hindi, Vietnamese, Cambodian and other widely spoken Asian 'community' languages, overlooked in favour of the languages of larger economies of the Asian region. Worldmindedness aims to include content in language awareness and teaching programmes aimed at stimulating reflection on culture and communication, including communication problems, experienced daily either by immigrants or indigenous populations, insights that cannot be expected from the study of 'foreign' languages in schools.

Only by injecting culture-general notions, content and practices within culture-specific language education and within stand-alone language awareness training, will it be realistic to imagine some wider cultural insights, knowledge or positive predispositions. The essential aim of critical worldmindedness is for a cross-curriculum perspective on multilingualism, a focus of language awareness and a layer of common attention to culture-general ideas in foreign language teaching. The latter is necessarily limited in choice by prevailing efficiency considerations and resource limitations. Worldmindedness should, therefore, extend into literacy education and social studies, and discuss communication and cultural questions relevant to non-addressed minorities and to wider principles of language and culture in human social interaction. Specifically related to English, there is little attention paid in either ESL or mother tongue English education to world Englishes, and how 'native' English speakers ought to expand their English repertoires to include knowledge, skills and awareness of the legitimacy and inevitability of growing variety within English.

Applied linguistics, across language and literacy, should incline towards support for notions of language rights, social pluralism and valuing of diversity as a consequence of the immanence of such diversity in natural human interactions. Applied to English, the identity dilemma becomes acute, for old insiders and new users, as English grows in prominence in the world. The efficiency claims on behalf of English have seen ever larger parts of the world integrate into a common system of resource management, market economics and free enterprise. In this expanding English-mediated reality, worldmindedness should be a feature of both English and second language education projects. Multicultural education, which aimed to infuse all education practice to promote awareness and acceptance of difference (Lo Bianco, 1989, 2006), was beset with a similar dilemma of what could be transported beyond the immediate focus on learning about difference. Today, this is true for Asian studies, international education, global education, Indigenous studies and other curriculum pluralising areas, especially those that rely on language study to inculcate in learners competent and accepting awareness of human difference.

Critical worldmindedness requires substantial specification to make it an operational curriculum perspective, which could be integrated within mainstream teaching about particular cultural and communicative systems to impart more general culture and communication principles. It would have the obvious virtue of specifying cultural and communicative practices, which would include the learner, the target group of learning and generalisable principles of communication, culture and identity. Intercultural approaches to language teaching see culture residing in ordinary conversation, but this refers mostly to only two cultures, mother tongue culture and target tongue culture, imparting knowledge, or even admiration of foreign prestige lingua-cultures.

Worldmindedness aims to set in place a wider set of generalisations and curiosity about difference and interdependence, all informed by critical dimensions of language and the workings of power.

References

Alpher, J. (ed.) (1986) *Nationalism and Modernity: A Mediterranean Perspective.* New York: Praeger.

Anderson, B. (1991) *Imagined Communities: Reflections on the Origin and Spread of Nationalism.* London: Verso.

Castells, M. (1996) *The Rise of the Network Society.* Cambridge MA: Blackwell.

Castles, S. and Miller, M. (2003) *The Age of Migration* (3rd edn). Basingstoke and New York: Palgrave Macmillan.

Cha, Y-K. and Ham, S-H. (2008) The impact of English on the school curriculum. In B. Spolsky and F. Hult (eds) *The Handbook of Educational Linguistics* (pp. 313–328). London: Blackwell.

Chen, P. (2001) Development and standardization of lexicon in modern written Chinese. In N. Gottlieb and P. Chen (eds) *Language Planning and Language Policy: East Asian Perspectives* (pp. 49–75). London: Curzon.

Crawford, J. (2002) *At War with Diversity: US Language Policy in an Age of Anxiety.* Clevedon: Multilingual Matters.

Fishman, J.A. (1971) *Sociolinguistics: A Brief Introduction.* Rowley, MA: Newbury House.

Freadman, A. (2001) The culture peddlers. *Postcolonial Studies* 4 (3), 275–295.

Giddens, A. (1999) *Runaway World.* London: Profile.

Gottlieb, N. and Chen, P. (eds) (2001) *Language Planning and Language Policy: East Asian Perspectives.* London: Curzon.

Graddol, D. (2006) *English Next.* London: British Council.

Gruen, N. (2008) Much to learn from Hayek on efficiency. *The Australian*, 10 April. On WWW at http://www.theaustralian.news.com.au/story/0,25197,23513665-7583,00.html.

Hirsch, E.D. (1988) *Cultural Literacy: What Every American Needs to Know.* New York: Vintage Books.

Hutton, C.M. (1999) *Linguistics and the Third Reich.* London: Routledge.

Lo Bianco, J. (1989) A hard-nosed multiculturalism: Revitalising multicultural education? *Vox* 4, 80–95.

Lo Bianco, J. (2001) *Language and Literacy Planning in Scotland.* Stirling: Scottish Centre for Information on Language Teaching, University of Stirling.

Lo Bianco, J. (2006) Educating for citizenship in a global community: World kids, world citizens and global education. In C.N. Power, W.J. Campbell and N. Baikaloff (eds) *Towards a Global Community: Educating For Tomorrow's World* (pp. 209–255). Norwell, PA: Springer.

Lo Bianco, J. (2007) Protecting English in an Anglophone Age. In J. Cummins and C. Davison (eds) *International Handbook of English Language Teaching* (pp. 169–183). Norwell, PA: Springer.

Lo Bianco, J., Orton, J. and Gao, Y. (2009) *China and English: Globalisation and Dilemmas of Identity.* Clevedon: Multilingual Matters.

Murphy, E. (1988) The cultural dimension in foreign language. *Language, Culture and Curriculum* 1 (2), 147–163.

Risager, K. (1998) Language teaching and the process of European integration. In M. Byram and M. Fleming (eds) *Language Learning in Intercultural Perspective: Approaches Through Drama and Ethnography* (pp. 242–254). Cambridge: Cambridge University Press.

Rohsenow, J.S. (2004) Fifty years of script and written language reform in the PRC: The genesis of the language law of 2001. In M. Zhou and H. Sun (eds) *Language Policy in the People's Republic of China: Theory and Practice since 1949* (pp. 21–45). Dordecht: Kluwer.

Wright, S. (2000) *Communities of Communication*. Clevedon: Multilingual Matters.

Zhou, M. and Ross, H.A. (2004) Context of the theory and practice of China's language policy. In M. Zhou and H. Sun (eds) *Language Policy in the People's Republic of China: Theory and Practice since 1949* (pp. 21–45). Dordecht: Kluwer.

Chapter 8

Professional Ethics in Multicultural Classrooms: English, Hospitality and the Other

ALEX KOSTOGRIZ

> In order to constitute the space of a habitable house and a home, you also need an opening, a door and windows, you have to give up a passage to the outside world [l'étranger]. (Derrida, 2000: 61)

Introduction

Today, education in Australia is under enormous pressure to re-invent itself. The new Labor Government has embarked on an 'education revolution' as a way of ensuring national productivity growth through a large-scale investment in human capital. Education has been identified as a key priority in 'creating an innovative, productive workforce that can adapt to a rapidly changing world' (Rudd, 2007: 4). This agenda has triggered nation-wide reforms and debates about teaching standards and the quality of education in all types of schools (Kelly, 2008). The current government has rejected the socio-economic and cultural differences of students as an explanation of differences in educational achievement and has focused instead on teacher quality (Gillard, 2008a). As a result, improving teaching standards in the area of languages is currently identified as a key issue and, hence, has been tied to the development of a national curriculum for languages by the new National Curriculum Board. The government's emphasis on language education, particularly on Asian languages, has been considered as something that will empower the knowledge base of young people, as well as increasing their employment and career prospects. Investment in languages is also seen as a means of safeguarding national economic and geopolitical interests in the region (Gillard, 2008b). All these developments signal the government's commitment to educational reforms. However, they also signal its commitment to restructure the work of teachers by making them responsible for learning outcomes, no matter in what schools or socio-economic contexts they operate.

There is nothing particularly new or 'revolutionary' in these initiatives, given that the re-orientation of Australian politics towards the Asia-Pacific region and national curriculum debates have been on the agenda of various governments for almost two decades. What is new, however, is the increasing accountability and performativity pressures on teachers who have been identified 'as the single biggest variable effecting outcomes at school' (Gillard, 2008a). By positioning teachers in this way, the need for consensus on national professional standards has been emphasized to ensure that teachers' performance is comprehensively assessed and managed. This means getting serious about the neo-liberalization of teachers' work, thereby delineating what counts as a good teaching practice on a national scale. Consequently, excellence in teaching is to be judged, compared and rewarded on the basis of how close teachers approximate a set of performance indicators. That is to say, one becoming a high performing teacher is tantamount to one becoming a better 'managed' professional. One might ask then how teachers are going to respond and teach to difference in their multilingual and multicultural classrooms and schools, if the very idea of responsibility in teaching is reduced to some abstract performance indicators and their work is decontextualized. The problem is that the impoverished representations of 'good practice' and professional standards may contribute further to social injustice, particularly in times when the neo-liberals focus more on teachers' performance and the marketization of education rather than on reducing some profound effects of socio-economic, cultural and linguistic disadvantages on learning outcomes though democratic and culturally responsive education.

This chapter situates English language and literacy education within the context of neo-liberal reforms, particularly with regard to the development of national curriculum and its ability to respond to cultural and linguistic difference both within and beyond the nation. It identifies the blind spots and contradictions inherent in the discourse of professional standards, emphasizing the often neglected issue of professional ethics that is arguably central to teachers' work. In current conditions when cultural-semiotic boundaries between 'us' and 'them' have been constantly crossed and when the proximity of cultural-linguistic difference has challenged the normative and normalizing frameworks of teaching English to the Other, this chapter re-evaluates the contribution of Derrida, Levinas and Bakhtin to language and literacy education in multicultural conditions. It draws on their ideas of hospitality, responsibility and dialogism to transcend the monological and decontextualized views of professional ethics as caring at a distance. As an alternative, an emphasis is placed on dialogical ethics in linguistic and cultural encounters – in pedagogical zones of contact and 'face-to-face' relations with alterity – to think about the possibilities of opening up English language education to the Other and making it more hospitable to difference.

Teaching English to the Other: The Question of the 'Stranger'

English language teachers in Australia operate in what Ulrich Beck (1992) once defined as a 'risk society' – a society that is characterized by increasing uncertainties and, related to these, social and cultural anxieties. While Beck (1992) connects risks to the process of late modernization and its side effects, I would like to connect 'risks' in English language education to the processes of migration and cultural-semiotic flows that can be perceived as a 'side effect' of the globalized world and its transnational economies. Due to migration, most of the schools in metropolitan cities of Australia, to a varying degree, have become multicultural (see Gearon, this volume). In addition to students from migrant families, schools are encouraged to enroll international students. As such, teaching practices can no longer be oriented exclusively towards mainstream students and their cultural literacy. If, some three decades ago, the systems of schooling were positioned in a relatively predictable and controllable space of assimilatory education, now they find themselves located at a cultural crossroads. On the one hand, there is a need to respond productively to the increasing diversity of students, to their languages and cultural identities, as well as to the demands of the global knowledge market. Rudd's government clearly has these demands in mind while talking about the 'education revolution'. On the other hand, education remains an 'ideological state apparatus' (Althusser, 1971), whose aim is to manage 'risks' associated with cultural, religious and social differences and to ensure national cohesion and citizenship through the assimilation of differences.

This contradiction in the politics of education becomes a central concern in the current debates about national professional standards and curriculum, and embodies 'a tension between a neoliberal emphasis on "market values" on the one hand and a neoconservative attachment to "traditional values" on the other' (Apple, 2006: 21). Neo-liberal policies in Australian education have precipitated numerous efforts to delegitimize public education by highlighting, or rather constructing, deficiencies of both public schools and teachers. It is, therefore, interesting to observe how neo-liberal politics in education justifies the necessity of market competition by blaming schooling, teachers and teacher educators for the essential injustices and contradictions of hyper-capitalism. The previous education minister, Julie Bishop, explicitly stated that public schools lack values and should be protected from 'postmodern and left ideologues', who have hijacked the curriculum, 'experimenting with the education of our young people from a comfortable position of unaccountability' (Davidson, 2006: 15). The current education minister, Julia Gillard, continues this political line of reasoning, arguing that the curriculum should be nationalized to ensure both the quality of teacher training and the quality of curriculum in schools. This strategy of managing 'risks' has been widely utilized in Australia to represent teaching as a low trust profession, thereby justifying the introduction of accountability regimes to monitor both educators' performance and the curriculum.

Equally, 'moral panics' (Cohen, 1972) about cultural values and literacy have been used to create effective alliances between neo-conservative politicians, 'claim makers' and the press in establishing the 'context of influence' on education. Donnelly (2006: 8), for instance, refers to 'a long and proud history of democratic freedom based on the Westminster parliamentary system and English common law', a cultural canon and language that are Anglo-Celtic in origin and 'an industrial and economic system that guarantees a fair go for all' as a cultural-linguistic basis for a national curriculum. This heritage, as Donnelly (2006) argues, has been denied by the 'cultural Left' that infiltrated the curriculum, and students are now taught that 'Australian culture and society are characterized by inequality, social injustice, diversity and difference'. Hence, neo-conservatives suggest a return to the pre-multicultural curriculum of the 1960s and see cultural literary canon as a protective shield both from the imagined odds of the political Left and pop culture and from the 'risks' of letting strangers and their languages and multiliteracies into the cultural space of the nation-state.

Here lies the paradox. In times when classrooms become increasingly culturally diverse, teachers are urged to play down difference, see it as polluting traditional values and beliefs and, hence, as something that should be positively repressed through 'proper' education. This neo-conservative vision of teachers' work entails a typically modern design of dealing with difference through the national(ist) order-making. As Bauman (1997: 63) once put it, 'the [modern] nation state is designed primarily to deal with the problem of strangers'. It does this by using two strategies: anthropophagic (assimilation) and anthropoemic (exclusion).

Both strategies are central to the process of nation-building, described by Anderson (1991) as 'imagining' sameness by homogenizing differences and expelling strangers beyond the borders of managed and manageable territory. Needless to say, education, particularly English language and literacy education, is seen by the political Right as an ideological tool in managing differences, for if strangers are products of certain cultural or social upbringing, they are amenable to reshaping through some sort of explicitly normative national curriculum. It is for this reason that the current initiatives in educational policy making and their ethical foundations should be rigorously interrogated. If children are to benefit from 'good' teaching (Gillard, 2008a), educators need to be mindful about the limits of the national professional standards as a framework that can inform responsible teaching.

Questioning professional ethics

The current guidelines of state teacher accreditation authorities in Australia provide a very abstract and decontextualized description of standards for graduating teachers in relation to professional ethics. The Victorian Institute of Teaching (VIT), for example, requires teachers to 'be aware of the social, cultural, and religious backgrounds of the students they teach', to 'treat their students equitably', to 'develop an under-standing and respect for their students as individuals' and to be 'sensitive to their social needs' (see VIT, Professional Standards, www.vit.vic.e-du.au). These indicators of standards have been linked to the code of conduct that aims to promote 'adherence to the values teachers see as underpinning their profession', 'provide a set of principles which will guide teachers in their everyday conduct and assist them to solve ethical dilemmas', 'affirm the public accountability of the teaching profession' and 'promote public confidence in the teaching profession' (VIT, Professional Conduct, www.vit.vic.edu.au). Together, these standards and codes delineate the parameters of good professional practice and, in turn, can be used to monitor and assess teachers' work. They appeal to the moral authenticity of the profession, a sense of professional values through which individual teachers can align themselves with the community and consciously control their actions. All this was purport-edly lacking in the previous understandings of teacher professionalism. Injecting the codes of practice into professional standards can be seen, in my view, as an attempt to fill the gap in values and attitudes that has been created by managerial discourses of performativity and accountability. Clearly, teachers cannot be motivated by accountability pressures and rewards alone. That is why we increasingly hear calls to restore the moral imperative of the profession, referred to recently by Minister Gillard (2008a) as the highest 'vocational calling'.

Yet, what teacher accreditation authorities have come up with is a *deontological* view of ethics – a duty-based and objectified perspective on the righteousness of one's actions – that in their view will make up for the detrimental effects of neo-liberal politics on the profession. Due to its abstract and universal nature, deontology is not able to capture the complexity of relations in the everyday life of teachers. It is problematic to apply this type of ethics to situated professional practice because deontology tends to reduce the ethical to popular morality or even to anachronistic moralism (Kostogriz & Doecke, 2007, 2008). The righteousness of actions cannot be seen as independent of the context in which those actions occur or as a mere intention of a teacher carrying out these actions. Teaching is always already situated in relation to others insofar as teachers are obliged to respond to the call of their students and, in turn, act ethically. How one acts ethically in a particular event of everyday life and how one understands his/her responsibility 'here and now' is played out fully only relationally (Critchley, 1999; Derrida, 1999; Bakhtin, 1993; Levinas, 1986). That is why, for instance, the question of Teaching English to Speakers of Other Languages (TESOL) is the question of one's relations with the Other. This question is coming from the stranger or the foreigner, or as Pennycook (1998) would have it, from the 'SOL' of TESOL. It is perhaps necessary then, before I pose a question about the challenges of English teaching today, to clarify the question of the Other of English.

The Other as the stranger

The question of the stranger – the one who has been implicated as the Other of English curriculum and pedagogy – has played a central role in how and what kind of language should be taught to the 'English subjects' (Green & Beavis, 1996). Pennycook (1998: 22) has identified in this regard a number of connections between the (post)colonial framing of TESOL curriculum and pedagogy to 'the cultural constructions of colonialism' and the production of the non-native Other. By connecting the history of colonial discourses and the subject English within his genealogical analysis, Pennycook has explicated 'the history of the present' in English education that both contains and reproduces the binary logic in relationships between the native self and the alien Other. In this regard, one might say that the current practices of TESOL have sedimented the historical consciousness – a memory of 'the pastness of past events' (Ricoeur, 1999: 5) – that is rooted in colonialism and nationalism. These practices carry the scars and wounds of the past cultural-political projects. Few would deny that TESOL as a field has come a long way in disassociating itself from the grant-historical projects of explicit cultural-linguistic assimilation. New discourses of transnationalism, cultural-semiotic flows and human mobility have been mobilized to re-present English as the language of the borderless world. New communi-cative and student-centered approaches to language education have incorporated the liberal views of justice and human rights as their foundation. In such a context, English has been conceived as a language of empowerment that enables various 'non-natives' and 'strangers' to participate in globalized economies and cultures.

Yet, even though much has been done to transform the field in a more liberal and liberating way, English language education continues to be built around a cultural core that is exclusionary and divisive. It is this core that has enabled the cultural majority to claim the monopoly in defining what counts as a normative use of language in both curricula design and assessment. Normativity is then central to dealing with the non-normative or abnormal and, in doing so, it exacerbates cultural-linguistic stratification by excluding rather than incorporating alterity. What counts as normal is not, however, something that emerges naturally in the process of social agreement. Rather, this involves an immense amount of ideological work in the area of language and cultural politics to represent a particular as the universal and, in turn, as the national and culturally stable. The desire for a stable cultural space fuelled the engine of linguistic normalization and had a political cachet in most nation-building societies in the 19th and 20th centuries (Anderson, 1991). This ideological work also continues in current multicultural conditions as part of an ongoing nation-building project. Bauman (1997) has defined it as cultural 'order-making'. Depending on the degree of proximity to and distance from the normative center, people can either be classified as fully fledged community members or strangers. More specifically, this has to do with the idea of cultural-linguistic purity in establishing community founded on the principles of mutual understanding and unity. This project is inherently exclusive, as the idea of cultural purity (and the normative language) establishes the limits to incorporation and triggers a search for ever new strangers who do not fit within an image of community sought.

It is for this reason that modern nation-states, as Bauman (1997) argues, are in a constant process of purification. And this explains why the process of nation-building in Australia remains inherently incomplete. If, previously, the specter of Asian 'invasion' attracted much social anxiety and (b)order-protecting efforts in Australia, in current post 9/11 conditions, Muslims are the strangers in focus and at the forefront of the national security agenda. In the context of an unfinished nation-building project and globalization, educating the nation, therefore, becomes more elusive then ever before. Framing the curriculum around dominant cultural literacy and establishing communal homogeneity, while de-legitimizing the Other and announcing ever new strangers, is not feasible in these circumstances. This is because the category of the stranger will continue to stand in opposition to a national curriculum framework and professional standards that ultimately presuppose a unified 'we-horizon' (Husserl, 1970). What is needed in such circumstances is a shift towards a framework that is more response-able to 'strangers' in our classrooms. But this cannot be done only through making changes in curriculum design, teaching methods and professional standards; this is also, and importantly, an ethical issue that language educators need to face. As Butler (1993) once noted, the task of re-figuring 'outside' (e.g. the category of the stranger that constitutes the very identity of the cultural-linguistic 'inside') is a matter of re-configuring the normative and boundary-producing regime itself and, in turn, re-imagining the 'we-horizon' as a space that provides a more *responsible response* to the Other, without attempting to annul or assimilate it altogether.

Professional Ethics as Hospitality

The question of ethics has always been foregrounded in teaching practices, but often reduced to the codes of conduct in relation to students, parents and colleagues. In this way, professional ethics has been understood as a set of moral imperatives – a set of rules and principles – that regulate teachers' actions, from dress codes, to the ways of building students' trust, to the ways of enacting the core values of professional practice, such as integrity, respect and responsibility in one's practice. Even though education authorities claim that these moral imperatives can provide a recipe for actions in all situations, there are a number of issues with such an understanding of ethics, particularly if ethics is presented as something abstract and, hence, external to teachers' everyday life in schools.

Imagine yourself in a multicultural classroom – some of your students may have a similar cultural and social background to your own, but others have backgrounds that are radically different; some can operate effectively with(in) discourses of schooling and are considered to be literate, while others come from a number of war-torn countries, have disrupted schooling experiences and are identified as 'underachieving' or 'at risk' students. Ideally, an ethical teacher should respect, and respond to, all the students and their needs. He/she should welcome their cultures and religions, knowledges and texts, multiple identities and languages into the classroom. This, however, is rather difficult, if not impossible. Some knowledges, texts and languages might be welcome, but not others. Some spaces for difference might be created, but not always and not for all. There are multiple constraints on the ability of teachers to respond to differences in the classroom. And these constraints, be they curriculum, assessment, pedagogical, personal, ideological or cultural-linguistic ones, inevitably result in some sort of exclusion, domination, misrecognition or other forms of cultural, linguistic and epistemological 'violence'. Thus, given the contextual particularity of teachers' work, representing the code of conduct as an abstract set of principles and a recipe for situated action is highly problematic because this code does not resolve pedagogical dilemmas and injustices in education.

How then can we think about the ethics of situated teacher practice and responsible decision-making differently? To answer this question, we need first to address a number of more specific questions: Can English language and literacy education be ethical if it is not open to all differences? What kind of professional ethics do we have in mind, if education does not welcome the Other unconditionally? What is the relationship between ethics and hospitality in language education? And, what kind of ethics can capture the complexity of professional practice in everyday classroom events? These are all 'big' and provocative questions for the profession, which would require a book-length exploration. Here, however, I would like to limit my engagement with them to the work of Kant and Derrida on the issue of *ethics as hospitality*, in order to shed some light on the enigma of professional ethics, particularly with regard to the possibilities of opening up education to difference. Many educational researchers have productively appropriated these two philosophers in order to explore the relationships between ethics, education and justice. Thinking about justice as the relation to others, both philosophers have discussed hospitality as a cultural-political practice that counteracts violence and exclusion. Yet, their views of offering hospitality to the Other and, in turn, of opening up spaces for difference are radically different.

Immanuel Kant, in his essay on *Perpetual Peace* (1795/2005), outlined the notion of 'universal hospitality' and delineated conditions on the visitation by the Other; a visitation that would not violate peace. Kant argued that the Other (the stranger) should be given the right to visit and not the right to stay, and that during his visitation the Other should not violate peace. In this view, hospitality is limited by the conditions that restrict the freedom of the Other both before and upon his arrival to a particular state. Even though the stranger has the right to come, his visitation is regulated by law and, in this regard, hospitality, too, is circumscribed by law. Kant insisted on conditional hospitality because he believed that without these conditions hospitality could turn into violence (cf. Derrida, 1999). Yet, conditions in themselves are already a form of violence. If we apply the Kantian perspective on hospitality to a multicultural state such as Australia, we can say that the host has a monopoly in defining who can come and what one should become if one's entry is permitted. It is the host that is the final arbiter of all cultural-linguistic rights and moral values and who is the main point of reference in perceiving differences as 'nothing more than minority cultures whom it would "grant" such rights as it unilaterally determines' (Parekh, 1999: 74). A host is a host, as Caputo (1997: 111) argues, 'if he owns the place, and only if he holds on to his ownership'.

Multiculturalism, of course, has been a decisive shift away from the repressive, restrictive and xenophobic (in)hospitality of 'White Australia Policy', to a society governed by laws and principles of cultural coexistence. As such, multiculturalism is the realization of Kant's 'perpetual peace', but it is not the renouncement of one's mastery and, in turn, is not the realization of pure hospitality and justice. One can mention in this regard such events as the 'Tampa crisis',[1] or the Australian system of detention camps for asylum seekers, or current Islamophobia and, related to this, reinforcement of the security state that in itself can be seen as a retreat from the egalitarian model of multicultural society. Justice in multicultural conditions, if there is such a thing (Derrida, 1999), is yet to come and, in many ways, this depends on how we perceive and practice hospitality.

Derrida's (2000) deconstruction of Kant, in thinking about the possibilities of 'unconditional' or 'pure' hospitality, is largely informed by Levinas' approach to ethics. Levinas attempted to expel violence in relation to strangers through his formulation of a radical openness and response-ability to the Other. He argued the primacy of ethics as the first philosophy (*prima philosophia*) that comes before ontology and politics, for both politics (e.g. law-making) and ontology (i.e. the meaning of being) impose rational categories on the Other that can justify violence. Levinas focused instead on dialogical relations between self and the Other and ethical demand that the Other places on the self. It is in the relations of proximity, in their eventness, that the *I* finds itself standing before the face of the Other, which is both our accusation (for we may have oppressed or misrecognized the Other) and a source of our ethical responsibility. As Levinas (1987: 83) puts it:

> The Other as Other is not only an alter ego; the Other is what I myself am not. The Other is this, not because of the Other's character, or physiognomy, or psychology, but because of the Other's very alterity... The Other is, for example, the weak, the poor, "the widow and the orphan", whereas I am the rich or the powerful.

Levinas concentrates on the 'primordial' investigation of human relations, in which being shows itself for what it is in encounters with other beings. In these encounters, the self is not a locus of rational interpretation. The self does not discover other things or beings, but instead the self reveals its misinterpretation of its own being. The proximity of the Other – 'the weak, the poor, "the widow and the orphan"' – imposes upon me more pressing responsibilities and duties than those I have towards myself. What it means to the ethics of hospitality is that the Other can be seen as a gift that simultaneously enriches my understanding of how to act ethically and puts me under the obligation to say 'welcome' and open my doors regardless of who the Other may be.

Derrida (2000: 77) argues that the monad of home has to be hospitable in order to be considered as home – 'let us say yes *to who or what turns up*, before any determination, before any anticipation, before any *identification*' (emphasis in original). This would be an absolute hospitality rather than the one 'out of duty' that Kant alluded to. Some cultures more than others may approximate this ethic of pure hospitality. For instance, the Berbers always prepare some extra food in case they are visited by unexpected guests. They are prepared for the unexpected arrival of others. There is no culture without a principle of hospitality and some cultures can be more hospitable that others. However, cultural groups, families or individuals can also suspend this principle to protect their home and family members. In this lies the aporia of hospitality, which Derrida (1999: 70) describes as follows:

> If... there is pure hospitality, or pure gift, it should consist in [the] opening without horizon, without horizon of expectation, an opening

to the newcomer whoever that may be. It may be terrible because the newcomer may be a good person, or may be the devil; but if you exclude the possibility that the newcomer is coming to destroy your house – if you want to control this and exclude in advance this possibility – there is no hospitality....For unconditional hospitality to take place you have to accept the risk...

Derrida is concerned about the possibility of pure hospitality, arguing that when we experience the aporia (paralysis) of welcoming the stranger without conditions and, at the same time, are aware of risks associated with this, then this is the very moment of crossing the limits, of going beyond the limits of hospitality (cf. Caputo, 1997). For Derrida, responsibility starts in these aporetic moments, when we do not know what to do because, if we know what to do, we would apply a rule, or a principle, or a law. But would it be ethical? Would it be hospitable to the Other? Probably, it would not or not always, as I have argued above in my reference to teaching in the multicultural classroom. Pure hospitality in this sense acquires a messianic character, similar to justice and democracy; it has not been realized yet and is still to come. Therefore, we cannot just say that we are hospitable to any other – we are selective in our invitations, we may expect an invitation in return and, usually, we do not let people that we do not know into our houses, speaking to them on the doorstep instead. In this regard, hospitality is always demanded of us; it is a call to push our limits in welcoming the Other and be prepared to absorb a violation or forgive the unforgivable (Derrida, 2000). It is then a project for us to offer hospitality beyond our current practices, as a way of grappling with internal tensions that, in effect, keep the idea of hospitality alive (Caputo, 1997).

Such an ethics of hospitality poses a radical challenge to English language and literacy education. If education is to be hospitable to the Other, it should be open to the multiplicity of identities, knowledges, texts, languages and meanings that students bring with them into the classroom. Hospitable or welcoming education is what education is called to be in multicultural conditions. However, schooling in its current configuration – its curriculum frameworks and accountability regimes – includes all kinds of discourses and practices that marginalize and exclude, discipline and punish, homogenize and normalize. In this regard, the professional ethics of teachers, their hospitality to students and their dialogical relations with the Other, are circumscribed by the 'third' that is always on the scene. The 'third party', be it in the form of education policies and initiatives or curriculum frameworks produced by education authorities, mediates situated relations. The third injects the 'rules of engagement' into the ethical. While the neo-conservative and neo-liberal frameworks of teaching English recognize and even celebrate difference, their understanding of how to teach the Other – i.e. pedagogical responsibility for the Other – is often framed by the discourse of empowerment through the acquisition of the dominant ways of meaning-making and cultural literacy. This discourse is similar to the previous discourse of cultural-linguistic assimilation, but is very often masked behind seemingly progressive approaches to teaching.

Here lies an ethical aporia in English language education, one that Janks (2004) has defined as an 'access paradox'. As Janks (2004) argues, many English language and literacy educators see the provision of access to the dominant literacy as a way of empowering the marginalized and the disadvantaged. This social and political position drives their moral responsibility for educating the Other. Yet, the 'access paradox' contains precisely the following contradiction:

> if you provide more people with access to the dominant variety of the dominant language [and literacy], you contribute to perpetuating and increasing its dominance. If, on the other hand, you deny students access, you perpetuate their marginalisation in a society that continues to recognise this language as a mark of distinction. (Janks, 2004: 33)

No one would deny that migrant and minority students should be provided access to discourses of power and know how to use them. Still, providing access should be informed by a dialogical perspective on learning, thereby including students' life-worlds, experiences and textual practices, rather than excluding them in the name of empowerment. If English language and literacy can alienate the experiences of students, teachers should provide pedagogical spaces that are welcoming to different cultural and social experiences and, in turn, to differences in meaning-making. It is in such pedagogical spaces of hospitality that students can appropriate 'ways with words' in English rather than simply reproducing them (Bakhtin, 1981; Brandt, 2001). This approach to language and literacy pedagogy can only work if education is hospitable to, and inclusive of, students' texts and communal 'funds of knowledge' (Moll, 2000). By attending to the mediating role of culture in learning (Vygotsky, 1978; Lee & Smagorinsky, 2000), socio-cultural perspectives on language and literacy call for 'infinite hospitality' to students' cultural and textual resources. The question is how this infinite hospitality can be realized in a particular political context of education.

It is probably at this point that we need to make a distinction between pedagogical practice (i.e. teaching the Other) and ethics (i.e. response-ability to the Other). In doing so, we need then to argue the primacy of the ethical in teaching. It is only then we can say that being hospitable to and responsible for the Other is the very possibility of justice in and through pedagogical practice. In transforming cultural-linguistic mono-logism of English education, dialogical ethics as a reciprocal hospitality is particularly powerful because it addresses the very act of annihilating the Other as an ethical impossibility. Central to this is the idea that the textual and cultural practices of the Other introduce me to what was not in me, their alterity overflows my self by affecting and transforming my consciousness and understanding of the world. The value of the Other in learning is captured in Bakhtin's (1990) idea of the 'surplus of vision' that the Other provides to me. An excess of seeing through the eyes of the Other contributes to the recognition of my limitations, particularly the limits of my own worldview. We can, of course, ignore these limitations, but to do so means we may erase any chance to see, to speak about and 'read' the world differently. To welcome the Other through the dialogical engagement in learning means, therefore, expanding the horizon of meaning-making and intercultural understanding. In this regard, dialo-gical ethics springs from a recognition of the fact that the Other has a power to shape my consciousness. The Other is both my reason and my obligation (Levinas, 1969).

Returning to the question of professional ethics, hospitality injects a moral dimension into how language teachers can relate to culturally and linguistically diverse students; before these relations have become mediated by curriculum frameworks and rationalized as teaching targets and learning outcomes. The key issue here is shifting the focus away from the ideologically meditated ways of relating to migrant and minority students and to the primacy of ethics in everyday classroom events, as a responsibility for their welfare, their futures and, in turn, for the future of multicultural society in which they live. This is a question of shifting away from learning how to live side-by-side with strangers and to learning how to live with them face-to-face. Needless to say, the possibility of interrupting the cultural, linguistic or epistemological violence towards cultural-linguistic diversity will depend on the possi-bility of engaging all students in dialogical learning from and with difference and restoring a sense of the agency of those 'others' who have been excluded, marginalized or demonized in the process of inhospitable education.

This brings into view a set of issues about English language and literacy education that will be responsive to the Other's appeal. Developing this critical agenda in English language and literacy education requires laying aside the orthodoxies of the normative curriculum and normalizing teaching practices (i.e. their cultural monologism) as an impediment to a responsible education in multicultural conditions, but also recognizing that hospitable education, in a sense of pure, unconditional hospitality to difference, is currently impossible. In this respect, the idea of hospitable English education is a project that is yet to come; it is a 'messianic' project that will continue to 'haunt' schooling, if it is to be just and democratic (cf. Derrida, 1994). One of the ways towards a more hospitable and just education is transculturation (Kostogriz, 2004, 2005; Kostogriz & Tsolidis, 2008).

Concluding Remarks: Towards Transculturation

Current debates in Australia about a national curriculum have brought to the fore the issues of the cultural and the multicultural, the language and languages, cultural literacy and multiliteracies, the metanarrative and minor narratives (Luke, 2005). These debates reflect the binary logic of engagement with the national and the particular, where the national is itself one particular among many that have been mobilized in the process of educating and imagining the nation. The challenge for English educators in multicultural and multilingual Australia is how to teach ethically within the national curriculum frameworks that remain regulated by laws of conditional hospitality, whereby the difference of Other vanishes in the political space of professional obligation to the nation. It is in this space that a singular responsibility for generalized others harbors injustice to a concrete Other. In contradistinction to this culturally monological approach, dialogical ethics keeps the idea of hospitable education alive, 'haunting', as it were, teaching practices and demanding justice in relation to the Other. The ethical question in English language and literacy education thus becomes an issue of transcultural pedagogy – a practice that enables one to respond to a call from the Other by acknowledging its Otherness (Kostogriz, 2004, 2005). This pedagogical practice is centrally about the recognition of a transcendental potential of transculturation as a way of learning and meaning-making between cultures.

Transculturation is a phenomenon of the 'contact zone', which, according to Pratt (1998: 173), refers to the space 'where cultures meet, clash, and grapple with each other, often in contexts of highly asymmetrical relations of power'. Textual practices in the contact zone are not constituted in separate communities, but rather in relations of cultural differences to each other – that is, in their co-presence and dialogical interaction. Central to this pedagogical process of transculturation are the ways the Other is acknowledged. While dialogical interaction can start initially from locations that are outside the contact zone, power relations between self and the Other can intervene so that this zone becomes an are(n)a of conflict and struggle for meaning. This, according to Bakhtin (1984), represents a clash of the extreme forms of monologism because both self and the Other do not transcend their preoccupation with self-consciousness, enclosed within itself and completely finalized. However, even though there is a clash of different meanings, the self cannot negate the Other completely because alterity is the main source of self-understanding. To engage in a pedagogical dialogue is to listen and to be open to the Other; it is to be immersed in the discursive space where both teachers and students become responsive and answerable when face-to-face with alterity. The Other, therefore, is the origin of our everyday experience, and we become conscious of our answerability as educators only while revealing ourselves to another, through another and with the help of another (cf. Bakhtin, 1984).

Recognizing the transformative power of the Other is perhaps the most challenging task in teaching ethically. This would depend on how far language teachers can push back against the powerful constructs of nationalism and neo-colonialism that are sedimented in the curriculum and pedagogical practice, in order to develop tools necessary for the re-imagining of pedagogy beyond cultural borders and between self and the Other. To transcend the current policies of assimilating differences in and through education, as Luke (2004: 1438) argues, we need to re-envision a teacher in a globalized, multicultural society as 'a teacher with the capacity to shunt between the local and the global, to explicate and engage with the broad flows of knowledge and information, technologies and populations, artefacts and practices that characterise the present historical moment'. In a word, we need a vision of a new professional who can work on and between cultural borders and take responsibility for the future of difference by creating possibilities for transculturation in meaning-making – i.e. classroom events of hospitality. A pedagogical focus on such events acquires a paramount significance for teachers working in multicultural classrooms. Because members of these communities of difference are caught in a double bind between 'here and there', between dominant culture and other cultures, the paradoxical nature of transcultural literacy is that it can never be understood as a 'pure' or fixed system of meanings (Kostogriz & Tsolidis, 2008). It evolves as a distinctly new cultural-semiotic way of making sense of multi-cultural complexity in and beyond classrooms.

Transculturation is a central process of cultural transformation itself (cf. cultural hybridity in Bhabha, 1994). For this reason, it becomes important to re-think the professional ethics of English language and literacy pedagogy in times when classrooms are becoming increasingly multicultural and when the neo-liberal politics of managing difference through assimilation stifles a possibility of large-scale transformations. As an act of hospitality, transculturation would enable students to understand and negotiate differences, their connectedness and meaning dynamics in a dialogue of acknowledged differences, at a cultural crossroads. This, in turn, can inform the re-visioning of teaching and learning such as needed for a hospitable multicultural society. As Pratt (1998: 184) has emphasized, 'our job... remains to figure out how to make that crossroads the best site for learning that it can be', looking for the 'pedagogical arts of the contact zone' in order to foster a dialogue between differences in schools and beyond. This delineates the ethical horizon of English language pedagogy today. It is through its openness to the ethics of hospitality that language education can meaningfully perform its social justice agenda.

Notes

1. The 'Tampa crisis' refers to a diplomatic dispute in August 2001 between Australia, Norway and Indonesia after the Norwegian vessel *Tampa* had rescued 438 refugees from a distressed fishing boat in international waters. The refugees wanted passage to nearby Christmas Island. The Australian government sought to prevent this by refusing *Tampa* entry into Australian waters, transporting the asylum seekers to the small island country of Nauru. The Australian government was criticized both at home and internationally for evading its human rights responsibilities.

References

Althusser, L. (1971) *Lenin and Philosophy and Other Essays* (B. Brewster, trans.). New York: Monthly Review Press.

Anderson, B. (1991) *Imagined Communities* (2nd edn). London: Verso.

Apple, M. (2006) Understanding and interrupting neoliberalism and neoconservatism in education. *Pedagogies: An International Journal* 1 (1), 21–26.

Bakhtin, M. (1981) Discourse in the novel (M. Holquist and C. Emerson, trans.). In M. Holquist (ed.) *The Dialogic Imagination* (pp. 259–422). Austin, TX: University of Texas Press.

Bakhtin, M. (1984) *Problems of Dostoevsky's Poetics* (C. Emerson, ed. and trans.). Minneapolis, MN: University of Minnesota Press.

Bakhtin, M. (1990) *Art and Answerability.* Austin, TX: University of Texas Press.

Bakhtin, M. (1993) *Towards a Philosophy of the Act* (V. Lapunov ed. and trans. and M. Holquist ed.). Austin, TX: University of Texas Press.

Bauman, Z. (1997) *Postmodernity and Its Discontents.* Cambridge: Polity.

Beck, U. (1992) *Risk Society: Towards a Mew Modernity.* London: Sage.

Bhabha, H. (1994) *The Location of Culture.* London: Routledge.

Brandt, D. (2001) *Literacy in American Lives.* Cambridge: Cambridge University Press.

Butler, J. (1993) *Bodies that Matter: On the Discursive Limits of "Sex".* London: Routledge.

Caputo, J. (1997) *Deconstruction in a Nutshell. A Conversation with Jacques Derrida.* New York: Fordham University Press.

Cohen, S. (1972) *Folk Devils and Moral Panics: The Creation of the Mods and the Rockers.* London: MacGibbon & Kee.

Critchley, S. (1999) *Ethics – Politics – Subjectivity.* London: Verso.

Davidson, K. (2006) It's all about money, not children. *The Age,* 12 October, p. 15.

Derrida, J. (1994) *Spectres of Marx: The State of the Debt, the Work of Mourning, and the New International* (P. Kamuf, trans.). New York: Routledge.

Derrida, J. (1999) Hospitality, justice and responsibility. In R. Kearney and M. Dooley (eds) *Questioning Ethics* (pp. 65–83). London: Routledge.

Derrida, J. (2000) *Of Hospitality* (R. Bowlby, trans.). Stanford, CA: Stanford University Press.

Donnelly, K. (2006) Preserve a unique Australia. *The Australian,* 4 September, p. 8.

Gillard, J. (2008a) Politics and Integrity – Delivering an Education Revolution. The John Button Memorial Lecture. Melbourne, 18.7.08. On WWW at http://mediacentre.dewr.gov.au/mediacentre/gillard/releases/politicsandintegrity-deliveringaneducationrevolution.htm. Accessed August 2008.

Gillard, J. (2008b) Rudd Government commits to Asian languages in schools. Media Release, 13.6.08. On WWW at http://mediacentre.dewr.gov.au/mediacentre/gillard/releases/ruddgovernmentcommitstoasianlanguage-sinschools.htm. Accessed August 2008.

Green, B. and Beavis, C. (1996) Introduction: English teaching and curriculum history. In C. Beavies and B. Green (eds) *Teaching the English Subjects: English Curriculum History and Australian Schooling* (pp. 1–14). Geelong: Deakin University Press.

Husserl, E. (1970) *The Crisis of European Sciences and Transcendental Phenomenology* (D. Larr, trans.). Evanston, IL: Northwestern University Press.

Janks, H. (2004) The access paradox. *English in Australia* 139, 33–42.

Kant, I. (1795/2005) *Perpetual Peace* (M. Campbell Smith, trans.). New York: Cosimo Classics.

Kelly, P. (2008) Rudd's cultural revolution. *The Australian,* 1 August, p. 14.

Kostogriz, A. (2004) Rethinking the spatiality of literacy practices in multicultural conditions. Paper presented at the Annual Conference of the Australian Association for Research in Education, 28 November to 2 December, Melbourne, Australia.

Kostogriz, A. (2005) (Trans)cultural spaces of writing. In B. Doecke and G. Parr (eds) *Writing =Learning* (pp. 104–119). Adelaide: AATE/Wakefield Press.

Kostogriz, A. and Doecke, B. (2007) Encounters with 'strangers': Towards dialogical ethics in English language education. *Critical Inquiry in Language Studies* 4 (1), 1–18.

Kostogriz, A. and Doecke, B. (2008) English and its others: Towards an ethics of transculturation. *Changing English* 15 (3), 257–272.

Kostogriz, A. and Tsolidis, G. (2008) Transcultural literacy: Between the global and the local. *Pedagogy, Culture & Society* 16 (2), 125–136.

Lee, C. and Smagorinsky, P. (eds) (2000) *Vygotskian Perspective on Literacy Research.* Cambridge, MA: Cambridge University Press.

Levinas, E. (1969) *Totality and Infinity: An Essay on Exteriority* (A. Lingis, trans.). Pittsburgh, PA: Duquesne University Press.

Levinas, E. (1986) The trace of the Other. In M. Taylor (ed.) and A. Lingis (trans.) *Deconstruction in Context*, (pp. 345–359). Chicago, IL: University of Chicago Press.

Levinas, E. (1987) *Time and the Other* (R.A. Cohen, trans.). Pittsburgh, PA: Duquesne University Press.

Luke, A. (2005) Curriculum, ethics, metanarrative: Teaching and learning beyond the nation. In Y. Nozaki, R. Openshaw and A. Luke (eds) *Struggles Over Difference: Curriculum, Texts, and Pedagogy in the Asia-Pacific* (pp. 11–24). Albany, NY: State University of New York Press.

Moll, L. (2000) Inspired by Vygotsky. Ethnographic experiments in education. In C. Lee and P. Smagorinsky (eds) *Vygotskian Perspective on Literacy Research: Constructing Meaning Through Collaborative Inquiry* (pp. 256–268). Cambridge, MA: Cambridge University Press.

Parekh, B. (1999) A varied moral world. In J. Cohen, M. Howard and M. Nussbaum (eds) *Is Multiculturalism Bad for Women?* (pp. 69–75). Princeton, NJ: Princeton University Press.

Pennycook, A. (1998) *English and the Discourses of Colonialism*. London: Routledge.

Phelan, A. and Sumsion, J. (eds) (2008) *Critical Readings in Teacher Education.* Rotterdam: Sense Publishers.

Pratt, M. (1998) Arts of the contact zone. In V. Zamel and R. Spack (eds) *Negotiating Academic Literacies* (pp. 171–186). Mahwah, NJ: Lawrence Erlbaum Associates.

Ricoeur, P. (1976) *Interpretation Theory: Discourse and the Surplus of Meaning.* Fort Worth, TX: Texas Christian University Press.

Rudd, K. (2007) *The Australian economy needs an education revolution.* New Directions Paper on the critical link between long term prosperity, productivity growth and human capital investment. On WWW at www.alp.org.au/download/now/education_revolution.pdf. Accessed August 2008.

Victorian Institute of Teaching (VIT) Professional standards. Website for Victorian Institute of Teaching. Melbourne: Victorian Government. On WWW at http://www.vit.vic.edu.au/content.asp?Document_ID = 23. Accessed August 2008.

Vygotsky, L. (1978) *Mind in Society: The Development of Higher Psychological Processes* (M. Cole, V. John-Steiner, S. Scribner and E. Souberman, trans. and eds). Cambridge, MA: Harvard University Press.

Chapter 9

English as Additional Language Across the Curriculum: Policies in Practice

TRACEY COSTLEY and CONSTANT LEUNG

Within the European Union (EU) much has been made of 'old' immigration countries, such as the UK, in terms of the progress and development made in relation to integrating minority migrants into mainstream society. However, in a final report, the Commission for Racial Equality (CRE)[1] claimed that while an enormous amount of positive work had been done in regard to addressing inequality, 'an ethnic minority British baby born today is sadly still more likely to go on to receive poor quality education, be paid less, live in substandard housing, be in poorer health and be discriminated against in other ways than his or her white contemporaries' (CRE, 2007: 4). This chapter takes the view that while, in general, much has been done in terms of legal frameworks, through principles of equal opportunities and anti-racism, to integrate minority migrant groups into society in the UK, there is a need to look at how policy dispositions impact upon and shape the educational experiences of minority ethnic students within state-funded education.

Using data collected for a one-year ethnographic study, this chapter explores the construction of English as Additional Language (EAL) as a curriculum subject in a London primary school in the context where mainstreaming all students is central to national educational and social policy. We look at ways in which Government funds have been utilised in a localised context, and explore some of the key features of the provision and practice at the school level. We do not claim to provide a definitive account of how EAL is practised in England; but we would like to demonstrate how pedagogy and resources are organised in an innercity school where national policy is open to a variety of interpretations. We draw from classroom observations, recordings and interviews to examine the ways in which EAL learners are conceptualised and EAL pedagogic practices are constituted in a localised school context. Methodologically, the ethnographic approach adopted has enabled us to provide a close-up view of the interaction between policy and practice in a specific context.

Approaches to Language Provision and Funding

It is fair to suggest that while the ethnolinguistic landscape of the British Isles, specifically England, has been steadily diversifying, government policy responses to the demands of teaching and learning in multicultural classrooms have taken place in two broadly distinguishable ways since the 1960s. The first of these was built on a recognition of 'difference' and the need to mitigate against any impact that such differences may have on teaching and learning. The emphasis on 'difference' characterises policy and practice up to the early 1980s. The second embraces 'difference' within a conceptual commonality and regards all students as language learners with similar needs within an undifferentiated mainstream. This mainstream view of 'no difference' provides a backdrop against which linguistic diversity is addressed. As Leung (2001: 38) suggests, provision for EAL in England has therefore been conceived either as a 'distinct' or a 'diffused curriculum concern'. (For detailed discussion on the history and social context of EAL in England see Derrick, 1997; Edwards, 1984; Leung, 2001, 2007; Leung & Franson, 2001; Levine, 1993; Stubbs, 1985.)

Where are We Now?

Since the mid 1980s and particularly since the implementation of the National Curriculum in 1991, education policy has been in favour of mainstreaming all students. That is, 'irrespective of ethnicity, language background, culture, gender, ability, social background, sexuality, or religion' all students are to participate in an undifferentiated common curriculum (DfEE, 1999: 12). The National Curriculum is regarded as being an entitlement (both social and legal) for all students and seeks, through standardised curriculum objectives, schemes of work and assessment practices, to ensure that each individual is provided equal access to mainstream provision. In practice, this means that EAL students are expected to follow the National Curriculum irrespective of their English language competence.

The National Curriculum's position that the mainstream classroom can and should accommodate the needs of all students draws heavily from the influential Swann Report (DES, 1985). Taking into account principles of equality, anti-discrimination and multiculturalism, the report stressed the need for consistency and commonality in regard to teaching and learning for all students regardless of their backgrounds. The report emphasised successful language development as being a crucial learning outcome for all students, with the belief that the mainstream classroom afforded the best environment for this development to take place. In so doing, language teaching thus became the job of all teachers and language learning the job of all students. Crucial to the teaching of ethnolinguistic minority students is the idea that '"language development" was simply assumed to be "English development"' (Brumfit, 1995: 18). With this in place, all students are regarded as having similar learning needs and developmental trajectories.

While policy rhetoric has constructed a mainstream whole, there has been *de facto* recognition that in educational establishments in England, and indeed in society at large, inequality and discrimination are still likely to feature in the day-to-day lives of ethnolinguistic minority students and individuals. Large numbers of ethnolinguistic minority students have for some time been identified as underachieving in schools across the country (see DfES, 2004; McEachron & Bhatti, 2005). In fact, since 1966 there has been special funding for additional provision for ethnolinguistic minority students. These have a taken a number of names, such as Section 11, Ethnic Minority and Traveller Children Achievement Grant (EMTAG), Ethnic Minority Achievement Services (EMAS) and have generally been regarded as extra means by which schools and Local Education Authorities (LEAs) can seek to remove 'barriers' to education (Blair & Arnot, 1993). At present, the funding takes the form of the Ethnic Minority Achievement Grant (EMAG).[2]

What is EMAG?

EMAG is ring-fenced funding that is 'intended to narrow achievement gaps between pupils from those minority ethnic groups who are at risk of underachieving and to meet particular needs of bilingual students' (DfES, 2004: 2). The grant is further described as having two specific purposes:

(1)　To enable strategic managers in schools and LEAs to lead whole-school change to narrow achievement gaps and ensure equality of outcomes.

(2) To meet the costs of some of the additional support to meet the specific need of bilingual learners[3] and underachieving pupils (DfES, 2004).

Aiming High, a document produced by the Department for Education and Skills (DfES) to explain EMAG funding and provision, claims to establish 'a framework for a common national approach to support for bilingual pupils' (DfES, 2004: 4). At the same time, however, the document states that 'the varying nature and size of the bilingual population between and within LEAs leads to many different ways of meeting the needs of bilingual learners' (DfES, 2004: 5). The document offers examples of 'best practice' in relation to ensuring that students, from all language and community groups, achieve their maximum potential and these are presented as mini case studies that provide an overview of the types of work that schools and LEAs have engaged in as a result of EMAG funding. The document provides examples of 'best' practice under the following five headings:

(1) supporting bilingual learners;
(2) leadership and a whole school approach;
(3) using data;
(4) analysing rewards;
(5) improving teacher-pupil relationships. (DfES, 2004: 7–12)

Some of the areas of focus that the case studies highlight as being important and effective in relation to raising, and ensuring, achievement through EMAG-funded provision are:

- promoting cultural diversity, celebrating cultures and citizenship;
- small group tutoring and support classes/programmes;
- monitoring performance and target setting for students and parents;
- recognising and awarding achievement across the school population;
- raising awareness to appropriate school behaviour from both teachers and students. (DfES, 2004)

The terms 'best practice' and 'case studies' suggest that the document will provide advice at the level of pedagogy, but the document does not actually do this. The focus of the publication is not on pedagogy, but more on providing managerial direction regarding staffing. The document contains a lot of advice about the need to identify members of staff who are to take charge of EMAG provision with the implicit idea that better management leads to better provision and achievement. Where sections of the document do come close to what we might call pedagogy, the document offers little beyond a brief mention of how classes are organised in terms of timetabling. Little or no attention is paid to the variety of demands that learning curriculum content through the medium of English may pose for students as well as teachers.

While there is little in the document that constitutes or represents an available methodology that schools and teachers can take away and adopt in to their practice, a recurring theme within the document is that EMAG funds and provision play a key role in developing particular attitudes and behaviours in students, teachers and parents, attitudes that ensure success and achievement. Such a focus is highly significant in terms of the 'message' that this sends out to teachers, schools and LEAs and has implications for the ways in which EMAG students may be conceptualised.

Mainstreaming language learning means that, ultimately, it is the job of all teachers to focus on the language (English) development of their students. EAL is not currently a curriculum subject within the National Curriculum framework and a consequence of this is that there is no Initial Teacher Education (ITE) in relation to EAL in England. As a result, teachers generally do not have explicit professional knowledge about EAL teaching and learning (see Edwards, 1999; Leung, 2007; Ofsted, 2002). It is most likely to be the case that teachers with EAL specialisms are teachers who trained and previously worked outside the UK in countries such as Canada, the USA and Australia; or teachers who have undertaken degree programmes in such fields as linguistics and second language acquisition, largely of their own volition.

Data and Context

This chapter will draw from research data[4] collected between March and December 2007 at an inner-London primary school, Park Tower School.[5] The research adopted an 'ethnographic perspective' and used 'ethnographic tools' to develop an account of the ways in which EMAG funds are used to develop localised teaching and learning strategies and approaches for EAL students (Green & Bloome, 1997). Ideas and themes discussed in this chapter are informed by the following data sources compiled during the nine-month data collection period:

- Audio-recordings: approximately 40 hours of classroom audio-recordings with teachers and students in Years 4, 5 and 6.
- Field notes: detailing classes, classroom layout and activities of audio-recorded classes as well as classes and other interactions that were not recorded.

- Interviews: conducted at various stages in the research process with teachers and students.
- Lesson materials: students' work, school reports, school policy documents and other school-based artefacts.

This discussion will try to present an 'emic' or insider's perspective; by this we mean to 'describe what happens in the setting, how the people involved see their own actions and those of others, and the contexts in which the action takes place' (Hammersley & Atkinson, 1995: 6). In keeping with more established ethnographic research, this type of perspective comes from a sustained engagement with a particular group, topic or site, for example, that is of interest to the research/ers. In this case, it meant spending between 1 and 4 days a week, for approximately 36 weeks, at the school observing and participating in lessons (Duranti, 1999), and often 'hanging around' at lunch times, break times and being involved in a range of events throughout the school day in order to 'soak up' different experiences and details (Jeffrey & Troman, 2004).

The Borough of South River and Park Tower School

South River (pseudonym), the London borough in which the research was carried out, is representative of many inner-London boroughs in that it is characterised by both extremes of wealth and poverty. The particular area of South River where Park Tower School is situated has a high density of high rise, social housing with high levels of unemployment and low income jobs.[6]

In the spring of 2007, there were just over 300 full-time students on the school roll, making Park Tower an above average size primary school. A 2008 Ofsted report stated that the number of ethnic minority students at the school is 'much' higher than the national average and that 'over two thirds of the pupils require extra support in learning English as an additional language when they arrive' (Ofsted, 2008).[7] Previous reports describe the school as being 'ethnically and culturally diverse and approximately 50% of the pupils are from Black Caribbean heritage and Black African heritage and 10% of the pupils are refugees or asylum seekers' (Ofsted, 2003). This ethnically and linguistically diverse school population means that Park Tower School is eligible to receive EMAG funding.

EMAG staffing at Park Tower School

In addition to mainstream class teachers and teaching assistants, Park Tower School, at the time when research took place, had one full-time

EMAG teacher. South River's Ethnic Minority Achievement Unit funded this post, which is designed to support 30 identified students per year across all year groups in the school. As highlighted earlier in this discussion, it is not uncommon for EAL/EMAG provision to be carried out by 'non-qualified' staff. The teacher, in this case Miss B, although having a recognised teaching degree from her own country, does not have recognised teacher status in England. Miss B describes[8] herself as 'not being a class teacher' and she does not refer to herself as being a classroom assistant. She always uses the title of EMAG teacher and in the local context this distinguishes her from other mainstream qualified teachers. Although lacking 'formal' teacher status in England, Miss B is referred to in this discussion as 'teacher' to stay as close as possible to the ethnographic description. In relation to English, Miss B describes herself as never having formally learnt English and describes herself as being 'self-taught'.

EMAG provision at Park Tower School

During her first year in the post, Miss B worked with the targeted EMAG students in the mainstream classrooms, very much in line with policies of mainstreaming. Miss B described her role at this time as sitting in the class alongside 'her' targeted students and being on hand to help students. Miss B described the type of 'help' students needed as being:

- help with understanding what the classroom teacher was saying;
- help with reading;
- help with writing; and/or
- help with vocabulary and spelling.

In more general terms, Miss B described her work as being focused on trying to help the students 'get through the lessons'. Miss B felt strongly that this type of environment was not the best and most conducive way for her to support the students and to do 'her work'. She felt that in working in this way, i.e. working in a way that can be described as 'between the scenes', was somewhat restrictive and not of optimum benefit to the students.

We use 'between the scenes' deliberately here as a result of discussions with Miss B in which she was very clear that in this working pattern, 'helping' the students could only take place at certain moments, in certain places and in certain ways within the classroom. Her role was not one of lead teacher or equal status, but a secondary position of response.

For example, Miss B said that she was often aware of her students 'not understanding', 'getting lost' and 'getting behind' when the teacher was talking directly to the class and providing content input. Miss B, however, felt that it was disruptive to the class and disrespectful to the classroom teacher to interrupt and/or communicate with 'her' students when whole-class teaching was taking place. As such, Miss B's work took place at moments during the class that she felt were 'okay', or moments sanctioned or framed as 'okay' by the class teacher and herself.

At the policy level there is a recommendation that in cases where students may be in need of extra support or specialist help to achieve their full potential, provision is most effective and successful when the specialist teachers 'engage in direct teaching of targeted pupils in partnership with mainstream teachers' (DfES 2004: 5). The reality for Miss B, however, was quite different (for more in depth work on examples of partnership teaching in relation to EAL provision, see Creese, 2000; McEachron & Bhatti, 2005).

Withdrawal from the mainstream

After almost a year of working in the mainstream classroom 'supporting' students, Miss B said that she approached the head teacher in order to propose a different way of working to support EMAG students. Miss B put forward a case for working with EMAG students in individual groups separate from their mainstream classes – a withdrawal programme of sorts – arguing that her work would be more effective in targeting students' particular needs in small, individual groups rather than in the mainstream classrooms where she felt somewhat restricted in terms of what she was able to do. A key part of this argument, as described by Miss B, was that 'her' or the EMAG students needed 'different' things and to work in 'different' ways to their mainstream counterparts. This sense or feeling of 'difference', and difference in relation to provision and practice, is, we argue, crucial in understanding how EMAG at Park Tower School is framed and conceptualised. Interestingly, Miss B said she had the full support of the mainstream teachers, and the head was also open to this idea as long as it was in line with EMAG policy regulations and that any inspections of the school, carried out by Government school inspectors, supported the work being done. As noted earlier, EMAG policy is sufficiently loose to allow for this type of working pattern and, where considered appropriate, the policy recommends small group teaching (DfES, 2004).

EMAG Literacy

As highlighted above, prior to working alone with the students, Miss B provided in-class support. She worked in mainstream classes that were timetabled as literacy lessons. In these lessons teachers worked on key objectives and criteria laid out in the Primary National Framework (DfES, 2003). The framework incorporates the goals and objectives of the National Literacy Strategy, which was introduced in 1997 to raise literacy (and numeracy) levels within and across the Primary (and later Secondary) curriculum. After one year, Miss B stopped her participation in these lessons. Instead she held EMAG literacy classes in the library. An interesting aside here is that English, as a curriculum subject, does not feature in any of the timetables for any of the year groups in the school. English as a subject was never really mentioned in and around the school, instead the term 'literacy' was used (see Medway, 2005, for a discussion of uses of the term literacy).

What is literacy in EMAG classes?

In an interview in March 2007, Miss B was asked to describe what she does with her EMAG students. In *Extract 1*,[9] the explanation Miss B provides gives an overview of the ways in which EMAG Literacy is marked out, in her mind, from what we might call 'Mainstream Literacy' and how what she does with 'her' students is similar to or different from what the mainstream teachers do with 'their' students.

Extract 1

1   **MB**:   and what I do what I did this year (.) I may not follow exactly what
2   they are doing at the same time but I I cover what they need the
3   reason why I won't follow them is that they may work for example for
4   two days (.) in er the class teacher may have in their plan their weekly
5   plan two days for story opening or beginning of a story and I know
6   for a fact that with my children I need a week
7   **R**:   Yeah
8   **MB**:   on that class teachers class teachers have curriculum targets each

9   Target
10 **R:**   Yeah
11 **MB:** I follow them as well but again they might do erm do different
           things
12 **R:**   Uhuh
13 **MB:** but for example I will give a quick example they may work on
14   adjectives and connectives and adverbs and synonyms for
           example
15   and I will just work on adjectives and connectives coz I know
           my group can't
16   take much more than that.

MB = Miss B
R = Researcher

Miss B's comments suggest that the notion of pace (in relation to acquisition and cognition) has a significant impact on the types of activities, topics, work and tasks EMAG students are involved in. More significantly, this also highlights that there are very different expectations in place in terms of what the students are able to do. From this extract, EMAG Literacy then is seen to be, by necessity, slower and easier than mainstream literacy.

In the following extract (*Extract 2*), also from the March interview, Miss B introduces ideas about the students', and indeed their families', sociocultural backgrounds and highlights their importance in relation to understanding EMAG Literacy. *Extract 2* serves as something of a rationale for slower, easier and essentially different provision for these students. In the utterances by Miss B we are able to see how ethnicity appears to shape and determine students' school identities and competencies (Toohey, 2000).

Extract 2

1 **MB:** Somali Somali children erm very often come as I said before
          come
2   come from Somali with no previous school
3 **R:**   Hmmm
4 **MB:** education, parents are not literate themselves they have a
          different
5   culture and religion but may not be relevant here and they have a

6		different way of live and deal with the children and many other things
7	**R**:	Uhuh
8	**MB**:	and coz because they arrive to school (4) and they have to deal with
9		war and other things priorities erm for the parents, because I think
10		we can't talk about children in primary school without parents. For
11		the parents I think they don't know erm much about the school
12		system and um er for the children when they are arrive here I think
13		and for the parents for the families I think it's a shock
14	**R**:	yeah
15	**MB**:	They arrive here in shock for in every way (.) so they came from a
16		certain house, bigger or smaller but there was always a big open space
17		outside and they are living in a small flat and erm they have to follow
18		certain rules like in school

In these lines, we can see the framing that goes on renders EMAG students *as* different. The students and indeed their families are different from 'other' students in terms of their:

- educational experience/s;
- life experience/s;
- familial relations;
- values, attitudes and dispositions.

One of the most salient points in this extract is how the 'relevance' of the students' (and their families') experiences and practices are questioned in relation to how well they fit the context of the school.

When read in relation to ideas expressed in *Extract 1*, the notion of 'relevance', we posit, plays a significant role in the construction of EMAG Literacy. EMAG students are seen as arriving in class with a set of experiences, values and attitudes that are regarded as being qualitatively different from non-EMAG students. Their ethnic and cultural differences are highlighted in a way that places them in deficit and EMAG Literacy seems to be charged with the task of helping them to understand more than adjectives and connectives. In the interview, Miss B carried on to say that:

1 **MB:** I think they have shock with society with the way we live
         because er
2   well if you think they come from a country that is a totally
         different place

This was a sentiment that was regularly repeated by Miss B as well as other teachers in the school and indicates that in conceptualising these students' needs in relation to teaching and learning, the students are regarded as being in need of making some sort of adjustment. In other words, a key role of EMAG Literacy is to aid the students' assimilation in both the classroom and society at large. Furthermore, this places Miss B in the role of what we can call 'cultural sponsor'. Her job is more than teaching the somewhat formal and/or functional literacy of the National Strategy or indeed English language. From such a perspective, lesson content or the EMAG Literacy curriculum is concerned with developing a particular set of values, attitudes and dispositions in the students. In a sense, Miss B is charged with and takes on the task of fostering a sense of 'Englishness' in the students that they are not considered to be in possession of.

The EMAG class

There was an observable pattern to the EMAG classes. The students would arrive in class and would usually remain in this classroom for between one and three hours, depending on their timetables. Approximately the first 20 minutes of the class would be spent on reviewing students' homework. This took the form of a Reading Journal in which students were required to read one to three pages of their graded reading texts and make comments and summary statements about what they had read. When this activity was completed, attention would then be shifted to what can be described as whole class writing or whole class reading.

The shift in tasks was marked by Miss B moving to the whiteboard to write the date and lesson objectives and students being given a separate exercise book and asked to copy down what was on the board. The students would then be given a context, task or directive that would constitute the main focus of the lesson (Figure 9.1).

In the case of whole class writing, the students would be asked to do everything in draft form on a piece of scrap paper before writing it into their exercise books. At regular intervals the students would take their

Tuesday 8th of May

To write a paragraph using adjectives, connectives and different punctuation

The lost family
A family went on holiday to Brazil and they got lost in a forest.

Who was the family?
Why did they go to Brazil?
When did they go?
Where did they stay?
Why did they go to the forest?

Figure 9.1 Activity task for students by EMAG teacher

initial pieces of work to Miss B for correction and they would then be told to make changes and/or extend the text before writing it up.

In the case of whole class reading, students would each be given a copy of the class text and Miss B would instruct the class to read aloud together. At different moments, Miss B would call upon students to answer questions about the text and would provide oral summaries of the text. This type of activity would generally be followed up by the students writing a summary of what they had read or answering questions relating to the text written on the whiteboard by Miss B. Again, students would be required to write in draft form first. This pattern of lessons followed for all the groups of EMAG students across the school from Year 2 through to Year 6.

Although lessons generally followed this format, during the time spent observing and participating in these classes it was rarely the case that this cycle would be completed in one lesson. A lesson with a specified lesson objective, such as in Figure 9.1, would usually take between two to three lessons to complete regardless of the number of students or the year group. While this may echo Miss B's comments in *Extract 1* in relation to the pace at which EMAG students are considered to be able to work, we suggest that it reflects an alternative or additional EMAG curriculum coming to bear on class time. While learning objectives, linked to broader National Curriculum aims and objectives, were used to set up and frame the lessons, actual topics and foci of discussion were quite different. In regard to time, it was these 'other', non-curricular topics that were given priority in terms of class time.

EMAG Curriculum content

The following extracts (*Extracts 3, 4, 5, 6* and *7*) are taken from audio-recordings of EMAG Literacy classes that took place between March and December 2007. The extracts are taken from a range of classes with students from Years 4 and 6. These extracts have been chosen as they exemplify themes and topics of discussion that appeared to dominate EMAG classes at Park Tower School, and which we suggest reflect the EMAG curriculum in this particular context. These extracts are regarded as being illustrations of how Miss B's conceptualisations of the students presented in the interview data (*Extracts 1* and *2*) are taken up and actualised in practice.

As suggested earlier in this discussion, a key concept in relation to EMAG students at Park Tower School was the notion of difference in relation to experiences and ways of doing and being in the world. The following extract (*Extract 3*) is taken from a Year 6 group. There were five students in this class and the extract is from a lesson that took place in the week leading up to the students' SATs (externally set standardised examinations). The class was officially classified as a 'revision' class in which the students were working on extended independent writing. The students had been set a task that required them to finish a story using a prompt they had been given. The students had begun this task and Miss B was asking the class questions about their ideas for their stories (see Figure 9.1).

After listening to their initial responses, Miss B asked the students to stop what they were doing and listen to her. She seemed to be unhappy with the students' responses and frustrated by what she thought were unimaginative answers.

Extract 3

1 **MB:** at home I tell you (I am going to talk to the parents) at home so they
2   Know how to behave your mums at home should open a book and read to
3   you like a teacher does in Somali or in Arabic or in English if they know they
4   should read to you if they do not read they should tell you stories

From here, Miss B went on to make the point that the students should ask their parents to tell them stories as it helps to develop their imaginations and that a good imagination is necessary for thinking creatively. In this statement there is an implication that the students' parents are not doing what they need to be doing in order to support their children's development and progress in school. This sense of a divide between home and school practices was repeatedly highlighted throughout this particular class, as well as featuring regularly in other EMAG classes.

Extract 4 occurred in the same lesson and was similarly used to explain why students in the class were having difficulties. This time the topic was concentrating and focusing on the task, i.e. extended independent writing.

Extract 4

1 **MB:** your mums are doing wrong you know you can tell them I said it
I don't care
2   you know your mums are doing wrong by by giving you a TV in
the bedroom
3   who has got a TV in the bedroom

Again, what we find is a situation in which the practices of the home are seen to be at odds with the practices of the school. In this case, a student is unable to concentrate because they have a TV in their room. In these extracts, the overwhelming sense is that the students' parents are assumed to be doing things incorrectly and that they need to be told, by the school and if necessary their children, how to do such things correctly. The learning point of this lesson, we suggest, is not just about adjectives, connectives and punctuation, but also about actions, behaviours and practices within the students' homes need to be changed in order for them to do well at school. During these types of interaction, the students are rarely given the opportunity to respond to or refute these claims; their role is to be in silent receipt of this guidance and instruction that develops and strengthens an insider/outsider relations.

Another theme that is closely linked to the idea of bridging home/school divides and difference is that of prioritising school. Across all of the EMAG classes, Miss B regularly highlights the importance of school in relation to being and becoming a 'good' and 'successful' person. The need to prioritise school over other activities, such as playing with friends, watching TV and playing computer games, is regularly linked in class to the idea of being responsible and taking responsibility for learning. Miss B thus links being responsible both in and out of school to being a successful student. While we do not necessarily question the value of such a proposition, our interest, from an analysis of these classroom moments and interactions, are the frames of reference or the content of discussion that are used to highlight this as a specific learning need for these particular students and their families.

Extract 5 is taken from a Year 4 class of seven students. One of the students, Hasaan, had just explained to Miss B that he did not have time to do his homework as he was doing other things, such as attending an after school football club as well as going to the mosque with his elder brother. In choosing to go to the mosque instead of doing his homework, Hasaan has not only demonstrated lack of responsibility in relation to school, but both he and his mother, from Miss B's perspective, have demonstrated a lack of 'Englishness' in prioritising the mosque over homework. As such, their behaviour reflects a lack of understanding of what is and what is not appropriate and reflects a set of values that are not appropriate to studying in England.

Extract 5

1 **MB:** I don't know it's up to your mum but your mum mustn't forget homework
2 comes first because you are here to study and this is England not Morocco
3 where the the the the the the the the mosque comes first

At a later stage in this lesson, Miss B returns to Hasaan and the notion of success in school and introduces another theme that is prevalent in discussions in the EMAG classes, which is the idea of time in relation to how long students have been in the school and in the country.

Extract 6

1 **MB:** you two should do much better because you have been here longer and
2 you know the school how do we work what I want what Miss C wants for
3 homework and you making constant silly mistakes and this these two are
4 quite new in our school and they follow everything

The notion of time is interesting here in that there is a clear association between time spent in school and the familiarity with the ways things need to be done. The assumption is that the longer a child is in the school, the more successful they will be. Hasaan, however, appears to challenge or buck this trend, as Miss B suggests that as a result of the time he has spent in the school he *should* know better but doesn't. *Extract 7* quickly followed the previous interaction with Hasaan and offers, we suggest, an additional perspective to the notion of time, which is time in relation to becoming 'English'.

Extract 7

1 **MB:** this boy okay if I if I am going to write a book that boy is doing in fact much

2   better than you that is not because he is clever and you are not clever (.) or

3   he has a pencil at home and you don't or he has a table or he has a book (.)

4   you two are equally it's because that boy came from Somalia last year and he

5   had never been in school before (.) but he's like his sister Faisa he goes

6   home and he wants to work and he sits down every day Hasaan I mean it

The progress that Moses ('this boy'), also present in this conversation, is considered to be making is set against the lack of progress Hasaan is considered to be making, even though Moses has spent considerably less time in school and in England. Underpinning the positive comments to Moses is a sense that he is achieving against all odds. His sociocultural, ethnolinguistic background, family and life experiences, and time in school should place him in deficit; however, he appears to be doing very well in spite of these disadvantages. The key to Moses' success and, by implication, to Hasaan's failings is that Moses has adopted a set of behaviours, values and practices that are in line with those of the school. Taken further, Moses, his sister and his family have adopted a set of practices that, in relation to school, offset their 'Somali-ness', whereas Hasaan, in prioritising the mosque and continuing to make 'silly mistakes', has failed to adopt these similar characteristics and his 'Moroccan-ness' is holding him back in terms of school success.

Policy, Curriculum and Contradiction

Although EMAG-funded provision exists as we have seen, it is loosely formulated in relation to pedagogy and vague in identifying what the learning needs of such students might be. This looseness means that teachers are left to draw from a broad range of sources and ideologies to shape, inform and decide EMAG practice and provision. The Park Tower School example is a version of EMAG support that has been recognised by the school, external inspectors and other evaluative bodies as constituting sufficient and appropriate provision for identified EMAG students. While we do not suggest that Park Tower School is character-istic of all EMAG provision across the country, from our experience we believe it to represent commonly held perceptions of ethnic minority students within the English education system and society at large. We would suggest that the main reason why official curriculum documents continue to insist on 'no difference' (as we have discussed earlier) is that this 'focus on difference' continues to exist within the education system.

While the position held by official documents suggests that a 'no difference' view should prevail, the discussion here suggests that EMAG policy represents something of a contradiction in regard to policy and practice in relation to ethnolinguistic minority students. On the one hand, the policy of mainstreaming means that *all* students are regarded as having similar learning needs that can be accommodated through the National Curriculum. In this framework, a student's ethnic, linguistic and socioeconomic background is not considered to have an impact upon their educational success and 'difference' is thus rendered invisible. Yet, on the other hand, from the perspective of EMAG, a significantly large number of the student population of English (parti-cularly London) schools are seen as being at risk of failing to achieve and in need of extra support. EMAG policy brings the 'invisible in the mainstream' characteristics to the fore and, in effect, highlights ethnicity, language and background as being the things that place students at risk of underachievement and potential failure thus making 'difference' highly visible.

We have shown that in the case of the school in focus, EMAG provision and practice are partly framed around a perceived need to inculcate in students a set of values and dispositions that they putatively do not yet possess. That is, one of the tasks of EMAG is to aid the students' assimilation into the English school system and society through adopting a set of 'local' practices and understandings. It is not just through language per se that students are able, in the context of EMAG in this school, to demonstrate their academic abilities and achievements, but through a particular presentation of self that is regarded as being 'appropriate' and that sufficiently mediates any 'difference'.

Notes

1. The Commission for Racial Equality was set up under the 1976 Race Relations Act and worked as a non-governmental body identifying and advising on equal opportunities in the UK. In October 2007, this body became the Equality and Human Rights Commission.
2. EMAG funding replaces Section 11 funding and whereas Section 11 funding was controlled and distributed by the Home Office, EMAG funds were controlled and distributed by the Department for Education and Skills until this became the Department for Children, Schools and Families in June 2007.
3. The term 'bilingual' learner in national policy documents in England is often synonymous with EAL learners.
4. This research data is part of data collected as part of Tracey Costley's PhD studies at King's College London, which focuses on the Social Construction of English as an Additional Language.
5. Pseudonyms are used in all references to the school, teachers and students involved in this research and in the presentation of data, in order to maintain and ensure anonymity.
6. This information is taken from upmystreet.com and is a search engine powered by CACI information solutions. The user can input any UK postcode and receive an ACORN classification for this postcode along with a full neighbourhood profile.
7. In order to maintain anonymity, we have not included the full reference for Ofsted school reports on Park Tower School.
8. This comes from discussions with Miss B and from field notes taken during the research period.
9. See Appendix 1 for transcription conventions.

References

Blair, M. and Arnot, M. (1993) Black and anti-racist perspectives on the National Curriculum and Government Educational Policy. In A. King and M. Reiss (eds) *The Multicultural Dimension of the National Curriculum* (pp. 259–275). London: Falmer Press.

Brumfit, C. (ed.) (1995) *Language Education in The National Curriculum*. Oxford: Blackwell.

Commission for Racial Equality (CRE) (1986) *Teaching English as a Second Language: Report of a Formal Investigation in Calderdale Local Education Authority*. London: Commission for Racial Equality.

Commission for Racial Equality (CRE) (2007) *A Lot Done, A Lot To Do: Our Vision for an Integrated Britain*. London: Belmont Press.

Creese, A. (2000) The role of the language specialist in disciplinary teaching: In search of a subject? *Journal of Multilingual and Multicultural Development* 20 (6), 451–470.

Department of Education and Science (DES) (1985) *Education for All: The Report of the Committee of Inquiry into the Education of Children from Ethnic Minority Groups* (The Swann Report). London: HMSO.

Derrick, J. (1977) *Language Needs of Minority Children*. Windsor: NFER.

DfEE (Department for Education and Employment & Qualifications and Curriculum Authority) (1999) *English: The National Curriculum for England*. London: DfEE and QCA.

DfES (2003) *Excellence and Enjoyment: A Strategy for Primary School*. London: Department for Education and Skills.

DfES (2004) *Aiming High: Supporting Effective use of EMAG*. London: Department for Education and Skills.

Duranti, A. (1999) *Linguistic Anthropology*. Cambridge: Cambridge University Press.

Edwards, J. (1999) The language education of newly qualified teachers. In A. Tosi and C. Leung (eds) *Rethinking Language Education* (pp. 245–256). London: CILT.

Edwards, V. (1984) Language policy in multicultural Britain. In J. Edwards (ed.) *Linguistic Minorities, Policies and Pluralism* (pp. 49–80). Florida, FL: Academic Press.

Green, J. and Bloome, D. (1997) Ethnography and ethnographers of and in education: A situated perspective. In J. Flood, S. Heath and D. Lapp (eds) *A Handbook of Research on Teaching Literacy Through Communicative and Visual Arts* (pp. 181–202). New York: Simon & Shuster Macmillan.

Hammersley, M. and Atkinson, P. (1995) *Ethnography: Principles in Practice*. London: Routledge.

Jeffrey, B. and Troman, G. (2004) Time for ethnography. *British Educational Research Journal* 30 (4), 535–548.

Leung, C. (2001) English as an additional language: Distinct language focus or diffused curriculum concerns? *Language and Education* 15 (1), 33–54.

Leung, C. (2007) Integrating school-aged ESL learners into the mainstream curriculum. In J. Cummins and C. Davison (eds) *The International Handbook of English Language Teaching* (pp. 237–269). New York: Springer.

Leung, C. and Franson, C. (2001) England: ESL in the early days. In B. Mohan, C. Leung and C. Davison (eds) *English as a Second Language in the Mainstream: Teaching Learning and Identity* (pp. 153–165). Harlow: Longman.

Levine, J. (1996) Voices of the newcomers. In M. Meek (ed.) *Developing Pedagogies in the Multilingual Classroom: The Writing of Josie Levine* (pp. 11–24). Stoke on Trent: Trentham Books.

McEachron, G. and Bhatti, G. (2005) Language support for immigrant children: A study of state schools in the UK and US. *Language, Culture and Curriculum* 18 (2), 164–180.

Medway, P. (2005) Literacy and the idea of English. *Changing English* 12 (1), 19–29.

Ofsted (2002) *Support for Minority Ethnic Achievement: Continuing Professional Development*. London: Office for Standards in Education.

Stubbs, M. (1985) *The Other Languages of England: Linguistic Minorities Project*. London: Routledge & Kegan Paul.

Toohey, K. (2000) *Learning English at School: Identity, Social Relations and Classroom Practices*. Clevedon: Multilingual Matters.

Appendix 1

Transcription conventions

(.)	Indicating pause of 1–3 seconds
(4)	Indicating length of pause of more than 3 seconds
(With text)	Indicating unclear utterance
M.B.	Indicating utterances from Miss B
R	Indicating utterances from the Researcher

Chapter 10

Language Pedagogies Revisited: Alternative Approaches for Integrating Language Learning, Language Using and Intercultural Understanding

DO COYLE

Introduction

> We enter the 21st century with at least one certainty: that the world, in which the next generation will grow up, learn, work and play, will be very different from the one we know. (Nuffield Languages Inquiry, 2000)

This chapter sets out to challenge the state of language learning in our schools already one decade into the 21st century. The catalyst for this call to face up to and address future global linguistic demands lies in the growing crisis in the languages curriculum in the UK, emergent themes resonate with many other contexts. We are all involved in the rapid growth of the 'Knowledge Society' with its far-reaching implications not only in the 'here-and-now', but for our future workforce and appropriately educated citizens.

This chapter also sets out to challenge the reader by suggesting that without a significant re-conceptualisation of language learning in schools, which goes far beyond the syllabus of any national curriculum and subsequent examinations system, language learning is in the balance – to revert to being an elitist experience targeting future linguists or to be re-conceptualised as a fundamental entitlement for all learners of all abilities, focusing on developing life skills. Working towards the latter demands alternative approaches, a shift in mindset, dynamic theories and the involvement of key players. In general, such changes require re-thinking our approaches to the learning and teaching of languages, but in particular, in the case of an Anglophone country, the re-positioning of languages other than English, including world languages, heritage languages and community languages such as French, German, Spanish, Japanese, Mandarin, Gaelic, Welsh, Gujurati and so on, so that linguistic diversity is celebrated and regarded as an asset.

Building on innovative practice appropriate to the second decade of this century, I suggest how languages can once again be embedded in the regular curriculum and provide a range of relevant and motivating learning experiences that may reverse the trend of learners 'voting with their feet'.

My argument is divided into three parts: Part I raises challenging questions facing language teachers in a rapidly changing socio-economic climate; Part II suggests ways to begin to address these issues through adopting an 'integrated' approach to re-thinking classroom pedagogies; Part III explores how organic professional learning communities can trigger changes to classroom learning that are on-going, dynamic and inclusive.

Part I

Language learning in the UK is in crisis, according to recent reports in the national press, such as 'Free fall fears as pupils abandon languages':

schools are now shedding modern languages teachers and fear we have passed the point of no return for languages in secondary schools. Fewer youngsters taking languages also reduce the pool of graduates and potential teachers... schools need to find more imaginative ways of teaching languages. (Smithers & Whitford, 2006)

While the obvious effects of changing national policy from the statutory study of a modern language for students aged between 11 and 16 to optional status post-14, seem to be ignored, the language curriculum is generally perceived as reductive, irrelevant and exclusive. Moreover, while deep-seated social, cultural, political and pedagogical implications of language learning in an Anglophone country are being challenged on a rapidly changing global stage, the position and status of languages other than English in the UK is confusing, contradictory and complex. The call by the media for 'more imaginative ways' of language learning and teaching is increasingly urgent.

The UK is not monolingual. At the turn of this century, there were approximately 600,000 speakers of Welsh and 60,000 speakers of Scottish Gaelic (National Census, 2001). Wales has a successful bilingual education system and both Scotland and Ireland have high priority heritage language policies (Baker, 2002; Johnstone, 2001). Over 300 different languages are used in London alone and over 10% of primary children do not have English as their first language. From a survey of 850,000 school children (Baker & Eversley, 2000), the most common languages spoken other than English are Bengali and Sylheti (40,400), Panjabi (29,800), Gujarati (28,600) and Hindi/Urdu (26,000), followed by Turkish (15,600) and Arabic (11,000). Yet, at a macro level, these statistics are not reflected in well-documented attitudes towards learning languages prevalent in the UK. Nor is the wealth of plurilinguistic skills present in many of our schools seen as a national asset or a learning resource. Promoted through the 'island mentality' bringing with it a disincentive to learn languages – *we can speak English anyway* – there is acceptance of limited national capability in terms of a multilingual workforce. The national Nuffield Languages Report *Languages: The Next Generation* (Nuffield Language Inquiry, 2000: 38) not only recognised that: 'English alone is no longer enough and that the advantage of speaking a global language is eroded daily as more and more people not only speak it as well as we do, but speak other languages too', but also warned:

> It is also dangerous. In a world where bilingualism and plurilingualism are commonplace, monolingualism implies inflexibility, insensitivity and arrogance. Much that is essential to our society, its health and its interest, including effective choice in policy, realisation of citizenship, effective overseas links and openness to the inventions of other cultures, will not be achieved in one language alone. (Nuffield Language Inquiry, 2000: 14)

It seems then that the UK is neither capitalising on its multilingual wealth nor making use of its pluricultural potential in terms of language learning and ethos building in schools.

While there are pockets of outstanding teaching and learning of French, German and Spanish in our schools, for many young people the position of language learning is low on the priority list of success measures. It is an irrelevance despite European policy, which states that citizens are entitled to linguistic competence in MT+2 (mother tongue plus two other languages). For those who have English as a mother tongue this formula is inconsequential. With a government that pays lip service to the European drive to promote language learning as a key life skill, Graddol's (2005) warning, that being able to speak English as either a first or second language will not be sufficient, remains unheeded. One could make the point that given the dominance of English, offering alternative languages as well as native-speaker English in fact constitutes a highly desirable skill set. A 'new linguistic world order' (Maurais, 2003) resulting from a more transnational mobile workforce is often ignored rather than embraced for its linguistic potential and cultural diversity.

Moreover, at the micro level, classroom language experiences do not motivate learners (Nuffield Language Inquiry, 2000; Dearing, 2007). Coyle (2000) shows that learners and teachers believe that the current content of language learning is often irrelevant and 'boring'. Language syllabuses encourage out-moded approaches to grammatical progression, where problem solving, language using and authentic communication are mainly absent. In addition, focusing on measurable learner achievements as an evidential data source for national standards is demoralising both for learners and teachers.

During the past 30 years, formulaic interpretations of communicative approaches to language learning have led to 'nouvelles traditions' in the classroom, which focus on atomised language linked to grammar and simulated communication. Achieving national standards and targets is the tangible goal. There is no apparent urgency to review fundamental principles of language learning. More recently, the national move to introduce languages into the primary sector makes the future of languages at secondary level even more precarious if the same curriculum is offered. Issues of teacher supply and competence remain largely unaddressed and continuity between primary and secondary levels a major concern.

While this may paint a seemingly bleak picture of 'tired' language learning, there are signs that pioneers are successfully experimenting with a range of alternative approaches, and government policy is acknowledging the need for a more integrated curriculum (QCA, 2008). However, for language learning to return to a more high profile position, there needs to be some fundamental changes. A new generation of pedagogic innovation is required that takes account of and builds on current socio-economic conditions, changing learner identities and the technological evolution.

The contemporary world that we inhabit is often referred to as the 'Knowledge Society', a term that permeates discourse but where there is little consensus of its meaning – it is a shifting dynamic. Drucker (1993) interprets the basic economic resource of any society as knowledge where 'value is now created by productivity and innovation, both applications of knowledge to work'. Drucker refers to 'knowledge workers' as those belonging not necessarily to the 'ruling' class but the 'leading' class and who are involved in productivity through the 'technology of knowledge generation, information processing and symbolic communication' (Castells, 1996). We know that knowledge is flexible and ever-changing – no longer solely dependent on experts, but on individuals who create their own meanings and interpretations. One could argue that many of our young people are excellent communicators using mobile technologies and social networking sites. You Tube and Wikipedia, for example, are symbolic of knowledge sharing and construction. However, the rift between the effectiveness of methods used to promote language learning and the approaches needed to develop skills aligned with the needs of 21st century learners appears to be deepening. How is knowledge constructed and shared in language classrooms? How are our young people encouraged to use their communication skills for learning in the languages classroom and what kind of communication skills are required? But perhaps we are looking for answers in the wrong place. After all, according to Dahllof (1999), 'too much attention is directed towards finding the "best method", even though fifty years of educational research has not been able to support such generalisations'. Kumaravadivelu (1994) suggests that, in fact, in the field of modern language teaching and learning, we are now living through the 'post-method' era that emphasises the need to find an alternative way of designing effective teaching strategies. Subsequently, Kumaravadivelu (2001) proposes strategies that:

> go beyond the limitations of the transmission model... the result has been a greater awareness of issues such as teacher beliefs, teacher reasoning and teacher cognition... [and]... a long-felt dissatisfaction with the concept of *method* as the organizing principle for L2 teaching and teacher education. (Kumaravadivelu, 2001: 538)

However, the search for alternative organising principles for language learning and using becomes even more complex when one considers the demands of current societal needs and values. As the rift widens between informal and formal 'learning', the OECD (2000) *Knowledge Management in the Learning Society* raises concerns about the kind of knowledge that young people are working with in school and the kind of knowledge with which they should be engaging. Hargreaves (2003: xvii) notes that 'if teachers do not understand the knowledge society, they cannot prepare their pupils for it', and goes on to advise that 'teachers will have to reach far beyond the technical tasks of producing acceptable test results... pursuing teaching as a life-shaping, world-changing social mission again' (Hargreaves, 2003: 8).

The centrality of knowledge to social and economic prosperity, therefore, has deep-rooted implications for learning and teaching in general and the kind of contribution that languages can make in both formal and informal settings. The shift from knowledge transmission to knowledge creation (evaluation, organisation and management) requires learners to be skilled in using language – foreign or otherwise – to construct meaning. According to Hargreaves (2003: xix), if we are to realise 'life-shaping' potential, then it seems imperative that schooling goes beyond the knowledge economy into developing the values and emotions of young people's character; emphasising motional as well as cognitive learning; building commitments to group life and not just short-term teamwork; and cultivating a cosmopolitan identity that shows tolerance of race and gender differences, genuine curiosity towards and willingness to learn from other cultures, and responsibility towards excluded groups.

It is at this point that a pedagogic bifurcation is reached. One pathway leads to discipline familiarity – a sense of how the teaching and learning of languages has always sought to address, for example, identity issues, a curiosity towards other cultures and cognitive engagement through grammatical awareness. This path leads to a re-affirmation of the status quo with an acknowledgement that any curriculum evolves over time. The other path signals an alternative route alongside a belief that the demands of working effectively in the Knowledge Society and beyond, require language learning and teaching to undergo a radical review that is not based on finding the 'right method' in the traditional sense of the term. If we are to take account of 'life skills', re-conceptualising language learning other than solely through grammatical progression or scripted conversations is a requirement. Building human and social capital demands that language classrooms contribute to, for example, more transparent development of global citizenship, deeper cognitive learning and communication skills for authentic social and cognitive gain. No one method will be able to accommodate these complexities. This pathway leads towards concepts such as language *using* for knowledge construction and intercultural learning for knowledge sharing in a wide range of contexts. It must be added, too, that while both pathways share some commonalities, neither is a panacea.

By contextualising our young people's 'life worlds' within the Knowledge Society, the following questions emerge with regard to the teaching and leaning of foreign languages:

- How can we engage our learners in active involvement in their own knowledge construction?
- What are the implications for knowledge construction in a classroom where the vehicular language used is not the first language?

- How can a language be systematically and effectively learned (i.e. practised, used and created) at the same time as developing a range of other life skills such as problem solving and intercultural understanding?
- How do we set about functioning effectively in a post-method climate?

Part II

Over the past 10 years, there has been increasing interest in an approach to learning where subject matter and a foreign language are integrated. While described by Baetens-Beardsmore (1997) as 'a growth industry in educational linguistics', content and language integrated learning (CLIL) can be defined as:

> A tool in the learning of a non-language subject in which both language and the subject have a joint role.... It does not give emphasis to either language teaching or learning, or to content teaching and learning, but sees both as integral parts of the whole. (Marsh, 2002: 59)

The concept of integrating subject learning and language learning is complex. It is open to flexible interpretation to take account of contextual variables: the Geography curriculum for one year taught through the medium of German led by a Geography teacher and a languages teacher working in tandem; a module of Art through French lasting for one term led by language teachers in collaboration with the Art Department; a unit or sequence of five lessons in Citizenship taught through a mixture of foreign languages delivered by class teachers; the water cycle taught in Primary school through Spanish by the class teacher. All of these constitute approaches to integrating content and thematic studies with foreign language learning depending on teacher supply, language capability, demographics, socio-political demands, educational policy and so on.

Research carried out into motivation for language learning (Dornyei, 2005) highlights the need for relevant learner experiences to provide authentic opportunities for language learning in young people's life worlds. Changing the content of language learning from grammatical progression wrapped in poorly conceived topics and themes (e.g. house and home, transport and holidays) into the 'here-and-now' allows us to consider what these 'worlds' look like and provide a more relevant and challenging context for integrated learning.

In many countries where the CLIL vehicular language is English, subject teachers are often open to an approach that encourages the learning of their discipline through English, as it is often perceived as motivating for learners due to offering additional opportunities to enhance English competence. However, in countries where the vehicular language is not English, the impetus for introducing CLIL is more likely to lie with language teachers as a means to integrating more relevant and interesting content into the languages curriculum.

The idea of integrating subject or content learning with language learning is not new. Mohan's (1986) seminal work on the Knowledge Framework, based in the Canadian immersion setting, started to unpick the implications of integration built on the following premise:

> A language is a system which relates what is being talked about (content) and the means used to talk about it (expression). Linguistic content is inseparable from linguistic expression. In subject matter learning we overlook the role of language as a medium for learning. In language learning we overlook the fact that content is being communicated. (Mohan, 1986: 62)

Yet, integration is complex, bringing with it a new set of learning and teaching considerations. It is not about delivering the curriculum in another language, demanding the translation of materials, tasks and activities. Neither is it the re-packaging of grammatical tasks using a contextual theme, such as environmental issues, which relies on prior knowledge rather than on constructing new. Instead, integration demands an analysis of what learners need to learn, that is content knowledge (including, where appropriate, grammatical knowledge); how they will construct their learning (the language they will need to learn and use in order to socially construct that knowledge); and development of a learning ethos through the use of the target language in terms of challenging tasks, activities and classroom talk required to develop and extend cognitive understanding.

> It is obvious that teaching a subject in a foreign language is not the same as an integration of language and content, and many schools are still to make that transition. Language teachers and subject teachers need to work together... and together they should formulate the new didactics needed for real integration.... (de Bot, 2002: 32)

Constructing knowledge through a language that is likely to be more limited than the learner's first language, raises issues regarding linguistic and grammatical progression. In language learning, the usual conceptual framework employed to 'deliver' school curricula is built on grammatical progression. Typically, this assumes that, for example, the present tense in a foreign language is easier to understand and use than the past tense. However, knowledge construction does not rely on grammatical progression, but on a range of opportunities for socio-cognitive development, including spontaneous talk, reasoning and so on. It is likely, therefore, that regardless of their linguistic competence, learners will need to express themselves in the past tense from the very start and will need to use a range of expressions for 'meaning-making' and accommodating new learning. These are not in the usual repertoire of language classroom activities, especially in the early stages. Such conflicting demands uncover again the tension between semantic and syntactic processing, i.e. does or should linguistic understanding based on grammatical chronology take precedence over meaning-making? Yet, perhaps a better question would be to consider how meaning-making could best be supported by linguistic understanding in an integrated context where systematic grammatical progression (linguistic awareness) runs in parallel to spontaneous discourse for learning (language using). Mohan and van Naerssen (1997: 2) helpfully propose that a different set of assumptions is needed to form the basis of pedagogical thinking, where language is used as a *medium* of learning as opposed to those contexts where language is used as the *object* of learning. They outline some basic assumptions as follows:

- Language is a matter of meaning as well as of form.
- Discourse does not just express meaning. Discourse creates meaning....
- As we acquire new areas of knowledge, we acquire new areas of language and meaning.

These assumptions imply that for effective learning to take place through a vehicular language, the interrelationship between three basic elements needs to be carefully planned: subject matter, thinking and language. Learners will need access to discourse that supports concept construction through talk, debate, discussion, exploration and so on.

> As foreign language instructors we need to view our classrooms as the social organisation that it is and we need to participate in dialogic activity with learners so that they may achieve cognitive and linguistic self-regulation in ways that are socio-culturally appropriate. In short, our task is to enable learners to find their voice, their speaking personalities, their speaking consciousness. (Holquist & Emerson, 1981: 434)

If learners are to find their speaking 'personalities', then the way they access and use a foreign language will have to be different from current practice. This echoes Wells' (1999) belief that dialogic classroom interaction lies at the heart of learning: learners need to talk in order to learn, therefore, in integrated contexts, language learning will have to embrace language *using*. Van Lier (1996: 47) emphasises the importance of learner 'participability' and Wells (1999) also usefully suggests our concerns as teachers should be with 'knowing' and 'coming to know', that is processes and skills integral to constructing knowledge, including using language to learn as well as learning to use language. This position demands a shift for many language teachers whose practice and teaching methods have for so long been guided by second language acquisition (SLA) theories and less so by general learning theories. It seems that an integrated approach provides opportunities for capitalising on potential synergies between SLA and general learning theories. It could be argued that if, say, communicative approaches to language learning also took account of the need to use language for constructing new knowledge, then powerful contexts for learning would emerge. This argument is particularly interesting if one considers how Savignon (2004) describes fundamental elements of communicative principles for language learning, that is, a communicative approach: language is for communication; diversity is recognised and accepted as part of language development; learner competence is relative in terms of genre, style, correctness; multiple varieties of language are recognised; culture is instrumental; there is no single methodology or prescribed techniques; language using as well as language learning. In effect, all of these coincide with fundamental principles for integrated learning, yet such tenets bear little resemblance to language classroom practice reflected in the comment of a language learner: 'It's taken me five years to find out how to talk about nothing'. In other words, communicative principles have been narrowly 'translated' into practice through accepted teaching methods that bear little resemblance to their initial conceptualisation.

Moreover, Savignon (2004) also raises the role of culture in language learning as being instrumental. The 'food' and 'festivals' approach is tokenistic when we consider a broader and deeper interpretation of culture as the driving force behind the way learners think and behave and the language they use. Returning to Hargreaves' (2003) argument for the need to 'cultivate a cosmopolitan identity which shows tolerance of race and gender differences, genuine curiosity towards and willingness to learn from other cultures', Cummins (2000: 13) describes language-related programmes (including immersion, CLIL and content-based language instruction) as

> having the most potential for truly preparing citizens who can make highly significant contributions to their own and our global societies... [provided that educators]... locate their pedagogy and vision in the realm of global education.

The relationship between global education and language learning is not a given, and requires a critical look at approaches, materials and attitudes. Curricular linking, 'sister' classes, digital communication with young people in other countries is now arguably easier than ever before due to the advancement of technologies. Organisations such as Global Leap make it their business to put classes in contact with each other. It is here too that finding shared languages opens up exciting possibilities, for example, learners of German from England and Sweden work together, while learners of French from Australia and Italy collaborate on curricular projects. Another example focuses on a network of UK schools that joined forces to produce a French 'soap', each having the story line for three weeks to develop before video linking to the next school. The final episode was watched via video conferencing by a Dutch-speaking Belgian class who reviewed the story and wrote reports in French... the possibilities are endless. Yet, while collaborative work across cultures and nations is a potentially powerful means of engaging in addressing 'lived through' cultural and linguistic diversity, it often remains a peripheral activity in language teaching and learning.

In summary, I would argue that approaching language to be learned and used through an analysis of content demands (i.e. the subject, theme) and cognitive demands (i.e. the language and thinking needed to construct new knowledge and assimilate previous knowledge), raises the role of the language into a *learning tool* as well as a *communication tool*, which is both challenging and motivating for learners. The 4Cs Framework (Coyle, 2006), developed as a conceptual tool for integrated learning, provides language teachers as well as subject teachers with a means to consider their approaches to language in their teaching. While some of its founding principles will resonate with the Language Across the Curriculum movement in the 1970s (Bullock, 1975) and more recent Literacy and English as an Additional Language principles, the conclusion reached is that from a language perspective, grammatical progression alone can no longer be the sole guiding principle for organising, selecting and framing language for learning. Instead, an alternative – The 4Cs Conceptual Framework – is built on the following principles:

- Content matter (e.g. thematic studies, project, subject disciplines, cross-curricular strands) is not only about acquiring knowledge and skills, it is about the learners constructing their own knowledge and developing skills. Learners will need to use language that goes far beyond specific lexis, associated with the content.
- Content is related to learning and thinking (cognition). To enable the learners to progress, content must be analysed for its linguistic demands and decisions made about how to make it accessible to a wide range of learners of different competence levels and ages.
- Thinking processes (cognition) such as problem solving, hypothesising, discussing and justifying, need language to function appropriately. The linguistic demands of these processes, e.g. how to carry out a well-argued discussion (in terms of functions, appropriate subject discourse, appropriate depth of argument etc.) need to be accounted for in the planning process.
- Interaction in the learning context is fundamental to learning. This has implications when the vehicular language is not the mother tongue. Learners need to become skilled in how to operate in these rich contexts.
- Grammatical understanding is important for a deeper understanding of language and the generation of new language. However, in an integrated approach, grammatical progression in the traditional sense will have to lie alongside the acquisition of language *of* learning (content), language *for* learning (language needed for operating in an integrated classroom, e.g. for group learning, for discussing, for thinking, for understanding) and language that emerges *through* constructing new knowledge. These elements are not based on grammatical progression and require alternative strategies for learning.
- The relationship between cultures and languages is complex. Intercultural awareness is fundamental to learning in general and language learning in particular. If culture frames our thinking, then finding ways of 'adding value' to our language lessons demands finding ways – both explicit and implicit – of embedding intercultural perspectives into our work. In integrated learning lessons, intercultural development can provide a context for learning, material production and curricular linking (Figure 10.1).

The 4Cs Framework suggests that it is through progression in knowledge, skills and understanding of the content, engagement in associated cognitive processing, interaction in the communicative

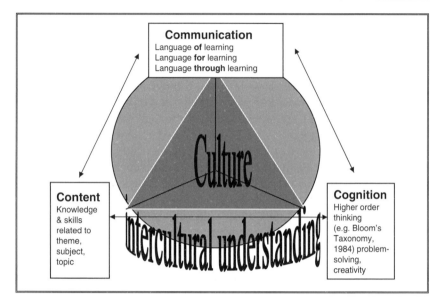

Figure 10.1 The 4Cs framework for CLIL (Coyle, 2006, with permission to reprint from APAC, Associació de Professors d'Anglès de Catalunya)

context, developing appropriate language knowledge and skills as well as acquiring a deepening intercultural awareness through the positioning of self and 'otherness', that effective integrated learning takes place. This framework is at the core of CLIL, and can support new ways of changing classroom language experiences of our young people.

The second part of the chapter intended to raise fundamental issues in the teaching and learning of foreign languages, which seek to address the growing decline in their study by young people in the UK and elsewhere. It set about considering questions emerging from Part I – and in so doing, raised many more questions in the process.

Some of the suggested changes demand a radical re-adjustment, some require adaptation of current practice; some encourage practitioners to continue to follow their beliefs and conviction; some necessitate new considerations if we are to prepare our young people for the Knowledge Society in which they will live and work; some require teachers to leave aside methods that have limited success and set about changing the tasks, activities, ethos and *modus operandi* of the class; some will not happen without 'connecting' learning with other people both inside and outside the classroom in order to give learners the widest opportunities to experiences cultural and cognitive that change the way learners and teachers work. Changes in practice are always challenging. In this case, if a more content and language integrated approach is to be developed and if the foreign language is to be used as a learning tool as well as a communication tool, then the content of language lessons will change, the language learned and used in lessons will change, the people with whom we communicate will change and so will learner motivation and engagement. As O'Connor and Seymour (1990) point out: if you always do what you've always done, you'll always get what you've always got – if what you're doing is not working, do something else.

Part III

> The greatest challenge the emerging post-method pedagogy imposes on the professional community today is to rethink and recast its choice of organizing principle for language learning, teaching and teacher education. (Kumaravadivelu, 2001: 555)

The final part of this chapter turns to a case study that shows how some of the issues and suggestions discussed in Parts I and II can be addressed and lead to changes in classroom practice. It embraces the 'post-method' era and promotes inclusive 'borderless classrooms' (Coyle, 2004), where pedagogy is not only seen as a 'mechanism for maximising learning opportunities in the classroom, but also as a means for understanding and transforming possibilities in and outside the classroom' (Kumaravadivelu, 2001: 542).

The case study is built on the idea that for change to take place, the processes must be 'owned' by the key players each having a role to play. While it has become common parlance in educational settings to talk about professional learning communities, this case study describes an inclusive concept for community building. According to Cummins (2005: 12):

> A learning community is the co-construction of learning opportunities and teachers in the "interpersonal space where minds meet and new understandings arise through collaborative interaction or inquiry".

Based on an identified need to enhance modern languages practice, organic multiple perspective learning communities have been constructed over time and place by teachers and their learners, trainee teachers and their mentors, tutors and researchers. Barth's (2001) description of 'learning-rich schools' is relevant in that schools began to link with each other to share and collaborate through trans-community networks to inform and inspire internal communities. Participants wished to engage in inquiry into how to build knowledge and capacity for radical, bottom-up changes to modern languages practice in different ways, in different contexts and with different players. Moreover, the concept of the 'borderless' classroom was explored, developed and evaluated through the use of interactive technologies that empowered schools to go beyond the confines of their classrooms. 'Borderless classrooms' are those that use interactive technologies to enable new ways of learning to take place, such as video conferencing for curricular linking through a range of vehicular languages with sister classes in other countries; lesson observations by large groups of trainee teachers to share the same lesson experience and engage in learning conversations with learners and teachers; peer observation and peer assessment by learners and trainee teachers in different contexts; sharing successful practice without spending large amounts of time in travelling to different geographical locations; simultaneous lesson data sharing through linked interactive whiteboards; empowering learners to talk to tutors, mentors and student teachers as well as their teachers about how they learn best and why and so on (Figure 10.2).

I shall endeavour to present elements of these communities to exemplify activities that respond to concerns and ideas discussed previously. However, it must be pointed out that these communities grow, are growing, develop and change according to their own contexts. A neat action plan with outcomes and targets does not exist in the traditional sense, since the transformation of pedagogies has to grow out of 'lived experiences'. On the other hand, teachers in this network of communities particularly wished to explore alternative evidence bases for effective practice using instead an articulation of Theories of Practice or 'personal theories' evolved by teachers for teachers, by learners for learners. The involvement of trainee teachers to embrace change and in some circumstances to lead it, has led to distributed leadership for learning shared between all the players including the learners. A selection of activities has been presented in tabular form (Table 10.1). They provide a range of evidence that focuses on processes and ideas for changing modern language practice. The data collected is part of ongoing research carried out by the communities (Coyle, forthcoming). Video clips, diaries, interviews, focus groups, vod-casts and pod-casts are shared through digital virtual learning platforms where the learners are considered as important as the tutors and teachers.

While possible ways of addressing the four questions have permeated the chapter, there are no solutions. Addressing the overarching need and

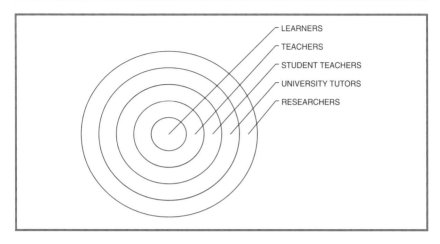

Figure 10.2 Key players in an inclusive community within a school and between schools

desire to change practices in foreign language learning also demands teachers, learners, trainees and tutors to share ideas and experiment with them. This will always be work in progress. Kumaravadivelu (2001) believes that any context-embedded change built on inclusive principles and which seeks to develop Theories of Practice involving key stakeholders has the potential to offer the 'necessary conceptualisation and contextualisation based on educational, cultural, social and political imperatives of language learning, teaching and teacher education'. I would add that working with networks of school communities who are prepared to take a risk, listen to their learners and teachers, welcome and support their trainees as contributors to the change process and work alongside tutors and researchers may also cultivate change. Schools are dynamic, unpredictable and complex social organisations. In this case, changes to foreign language practice were brought about through a preparedness to explore the implications of content and language integrated approaches, to ask why and how of learner (de)motivation and, using integrated learning as a springboard, encourage participants to construct and share their own Theories of Practice in their community and across communities. Almost 10 years ago, I urged a radical re-appraisal of the content and context for language use (Coyle, 2000). In the following years, as more and more learners have left languages behind, time is quite simply running out.

Table 10.1 Activities for learning evidence focusing on processes and ideas for changing modern language practice

Objective	Initiated by	Activity/processes	Evidence	Implications
Subject knowledge enhancement (SKE) programme for trainee teachers to develop subject knowledge and pedagogic knowledge simultaneously during a series of remotely observed lessons	University tutors and their trainees	Large groups of trainee teachers to observe the same live lessons through video conferencing, then to discuss the lesson with the teacher and learners; trainees developing their language skills especially in their second FL and at the same time improving their pedagogic language and understanding	*It deepened my own understanding of why the use of the target language for different reasons is an important part of my lessons planning* (Teacher C) *It was really interesting to observe a range of lessons at a distance but then to discuss what had happened with the kids and their teachers was brilliant* (Trainee 3) *Good use of time – I learned a lot at the same time* (Trainee 2) *It raised my expectations of what to do in and though the TL in my own teaching practice schools – but I didn't find anyone doing it there* (Trainee 8)	Teachers wanted to try exemplify effective practice for the trainees, so they had to address use of TL for real purposes because of focus on SKE (i.e. language for learning and communicating) Learners became interested in discussions between teacher and trainees and became aware of importance of communicating in TL; teacher confidence started to grow re: use of TL as they were invited to talk about what worked and what did not; this process provided CPD for the teachers (Q1, Q4)

Table 10.1 (*Continued*)

Objective	Initiated by	Activity/processes	Evidence	Implications
Global citizenship in language lessons using an integrated approach	Trainee teachers in classes with a wide age and level of learners	Trainee teachers challenged and expected to teach grammar through the theme of global citizenship while on teaching practice in their schools	*The power point was great and the learners knew that they had learned some new language but also some new information* (Class Teacher F) *Planning the lesson was really interesting because we were determined to engage them in Fair Trade issues – it was amazing that the learners were able to use difficult language and also understand easily our grammar points*	Motivating content, e.g. slave trade context, use of bartering language; great learner satisfaction; teachers keen to use trainees' materials – communal resources bank set up; lesson plans contained content objectives as well as language objectives; language objectives were organised to build on the grammar point, but also to address demands of the different tasks (Q1, Q2, Q3)

Table 10.1 (*Continued*)

Objective	Initiated by	Activity/processes	Evidence	Implications
One History lesson through French using an integrated approach	Trainee teachers and their tutors with a class of 12-year-olds in their second year of French	To trial one lesson of history (theme of Castles) in French Team teaching trainees demonstrated the lesson to teachers and to university tutors. Trainees worked in cross-discipline groups, i.e. at least one history and one FL trainee collaborating to explore issues of integration	The resources were posted on a protected website for CLIL teachers; trainees used the experience as a catalyst for their assignments; the lesson was video recorded to allow for detailed analysis after the lesson. Issues arising that are recorded as teacher commentaries: must make instructions really clear; explore further the relationship between language and talking	Lesson plans for integrated learning and resources donated to the school/teachers, i.e. exemplar materials for future use and development Trainees carried out a simple questionnaire to measure learners' reaction CPD as other teachers asked to observe the lessons; trainee confidence gains (Q2, Q3)

Table 10.1 (*Continued*)

Objective	Initiated by	Activity/processes	Evidence	Implications
Two Biology lessons through German	Teachers, learners, trainee teachers and researchers using an analytic process to identify 'learning moments', i.e. LOCIT (Coyle, 2004) (lesson observation and critical incident technique) with a class of 13-years-olds in their second year of German	FL teacher working with science teacher to create a series of Biology lessons in German; researchers to gather data to support class-based inquiry; lessons observed by researcher and trainees through VC; learners to analyse their own lesson through video editing for 'learning moments'	LOCIT process: lesson selected by teacher is video recorded; teacher, learners, trainee teachers and researchers are given a copy of the lesson; analyse to select learning moments and edit video to max 15 minutes, e.g. learners do this in ICT lessons using Movie Maker; video clips provide an evidence base, but are crucially a trigger for learning discussions	Recorded lessons used to encourage other teachers to pilot integrated methods; powerful learning capture by learners of their learning moments enables the dissemination of this practice to be used across other communities; total involvement of learners, teachers and researchers; promotes cross-disciplinary collaboration (Q1, Q2, Q3, Q4)

Table 10.1 (*Continued*)

Objective	Initiated by	Activity/processes	Evidence	Implications
A unit of Music through German	Teachers, learners and researchers with all classes of 11 years in one school and beginner learners of German	Teacher plans series of Music lessons through German ending in a small production of Peter and the Wolf; lessons planned with the regular music teacher; researcher (university tutor) acted as a critical friend; parental involvement in production	LOCIT process used (see above) for analysing practice and using the evidence as a basis for a new teacher's growing Theory of Practice; researcher involvement assist in collecting data for an evidence base, e.g. teacher interviews, learner focus groups; upload of reflective conversations into protected repository	Teacher-generated and evaluated integrated learning lessons plans and resources for others to share; learners involvement in the process; deeper understanding of classroom discourse needed when learning through a FL; deeper understanding of how language can be simple but the concepts difficult (Q1, Q2, Q4)
Sharing theories of practice	Teachers and researchers across schools	Teachers in different schools where there has been experimentation with integrated learning plan to meet together at a conference to share ideas focusing on their own theories of practice	Each teacher brings with them a series of edited video clips; these are used as a trigger for articulating theory of practice; sharing commonalities and writing agreed; theories of practice data is captured by researchers	A growing data bank of clips of learning moments and articulations of Theories of Practice for sharing across communities; increasing numbers of shared video link lessons across different cultures and countries is enriching curriculum (Q1, Q4)

Table 10.1 (*Continued*)

Objective	Initiated by	Activity/processes	Evidence	Implications
Learning Conference	Learners across schools	Learners wish to have their own learning conference where they will discuss across a range of schools through representatives, why they have chosen selected video clips from their own classroom experiences, i.e. how they articulate their own 'learning moments' to compare and contrast	Learners across different schools, ages and subject orientations meet together to discuss how they learn in integrated settings; some learners present their work in the TL, others in the MT; some learners use their experiences for coursework assignments for different courses; this is an inclusive activity, since different learners are given a voice *This is so cool:*	Learner voice; raising expectations of what learners can do in the TL; desire of learners for more sophisticated and adult approaches to their own involvement in their own learning (Q1, Q4)

Source: Coyle (2008)
Note: SKE: Subject Knowledge Enhancement
LOCIT: Lesson Observation and Critical Incident Technique

References

Baetens-Beardsmore, H. (1997) Manipulating the variables in bilingual education. In A. Buiteveld (ed.) *Report on the Conference on European Networks in Bilingual Education* (pp. 8–16). The Hague: Dutch European Platform.

Baker, C. (2002) *Foundations of Bilingual Education and Bilingualism.* Clevedon: Multilingual Matters.

Baker, P. and Eversley, J. (eds) (2000) *Multilingual Capital.* London: Battlebridge.

Barth, R.S. (2001) Teacher leader. *Phi Delta Kappan* 82 (6), 443–449.

Bloom, B. (1984) *Taxonomy of Educational Objectives.* Boston, MA: Allyn and Bacon.

de Bot, K. (2002) CLIL in the European Context. In D. Marsh (ed.) *CLIL/EMILE – The European Dimension: Actions, Trends and Foresight Potential* (pp. 29–32). European Commission, Strasbourg: Public Services Contract DG EAC.

Bullock, R. (1975) *Languages for Life: The Bullock Report.* London: Open University.

Castells, M. (1996) *The Rise of the Network Society.* Oxford: Blackwell.

Commission of the European Communities (2005) *A New Framework Strategy for Multilingualism.* On WWW at http://europa.eu.int/comm/education/policies/lang/doc/com596_en.pdf.

Coyle, D. (2000) Chapter 9: Meeting the challenge – the 3Cs curriculum. In S. Green (ed.) *New Perspectives on Teaching and Learning Modern Languages* (pp. 158–182). Clevedon: Multilingual Matters.

Coyle, D. (2006) *CLIL in Catalonia, from Theory to Practice.* APAC Monographs, 6. Gerona/Barcelona: APAC.

Coyle, D. (2010) Chapter 3 post-method pedagogies: Using a second-foreign language as a learning tool in CLIL settings. In Y.R. de Zarobe, J.M. Sierra. and G. del Puerto (eds) *Content and Foreign Language Integrated Learning: Contributions to Multilingualism in European Context.* Frankfurt am Main: Peter Lang.

Cummins, J. (2000) Immersion education for the millennium: What have we learned from 30 years of research on second language immersion. Toronto: OISE. On WWW at http://www.iteachilearn.com/cummins/immersion2000.html. Accessed 12.12.08.

Cummins, J. (2005) Using IT to create a zone of proximal development for academic language learning: A critical perspective on trends and possibilities. In C. Davison (ed.) *Information Technology and Innovation in Language Education* (pp. 105–126). Hong Kong: Hong Kong University Press.

Dahllof, U. (1991) Towards a new model for the evaluation of teaching. In U. Dahllof, J. Harris, M. Shattock, A. Staropoli and R. Veld (eds) *Discussions of Education in Higher Education* (pp. 116–152). London: Jessica Kingsley.

Dearing, R. (2007) *The Languages Review.* Nottingham: Department for Education and Skills Publications. On WWW at http://www.teachernet.gov.uk/_doc/11124/LanguageReview.pdf.

Dornyei, Z. (2005) *The Psychology of the Language Learner: Individual Differences in Second Language Acquisition.* London: Routledge.

Drucker, P. (1993) *Post-capitalist Society.* Oxford: Butterworth Heinemann.

Graddol, D. (2006) *English Next.* Plymouth: British Council.

Global Leap. Videoconferencing in the Classroom: Developing interactive videoconferencing across the curriculum in the UK and around the world. On WWW at http://www.global-leap.com/.

Hargreaves, A. (2003) *Teaching in the Knowledge Society.* Maidenhead: Open University Press.

Holquist, M. and Emerson, C. (1981) *Dialogic Imagination: Four Essays by M.M. Bakhtin* (M. Holquist ed. and C. Emerson and M. Holquist, trans.). Austin, TX: University of Texas Press.

Johnstone, R. (2001) *Immersion in a Second or Additional Language at School: Evidence from International Research.* Report for the Scottish Executive Education Department. Stirling: Scottish CILT.

Kumavardivelu, B. (1994) The post-method condition: Emerging strategies for second/foreign language teaching. *TESOL Quarterly* 28 (1), 27–48.

Kumavardivelu, B. (2001) Toward a post-method pedagogy. *TESOL Quarterly* 35 (4), 537–560.

Marsh, D. (ed.) (2002) *CLIL/EMILE – The European Dimension: Actions, Trends and Foresight Potential.* European Commission, Strasbourg: Public Services Contract DG EAC.

Maurais, J. (2003) Towards a new linguistic world order. In J. Maurais and M. Morris (eds) *Languages in a Globalizing World* (pp. 13–36). Cambridge: Cambridge University Press.

Mohan, B. (1986) *Language and Content.* Reading, MA: Addison-Wesley.

Mohan, B. and van Naerssen, M. (1997) Understanding cause-effect: Learning through language. *Forum* 35 (4), 22. On WWW at http://exchanges.state.gov/forum/vols/vol35/no4/p22.htm.

National Consensus (2001) The Office for National Statistics. On WWW at http://www.statistics.gov.uk/census/default.asp.

Nuffield Language Inquiry (2000) The Final Report of the Nuffield Languages Enquiry. *Languages: The Next Generation.* London: Nuffield Foundation.

O'Connor, J. and Seymour, J. (1990) *Introducing NLP: Psychological Skills for Understanding and Influencing People.* London: Element.

OECD (2000) *Knowledge Management in the Learning Society.* Paris: Organization for Economic Cooperation and Development.

QCA (2008) Qualifications and Curriculum Authority: An Integrated Curriculum. On WWW at http://www.qca.org.uk/qca_13472.aspx. Accessed 12.12.08.

Savignon, S. (2004) Language, identity, and curriculum design: Communicative language teaching in the 21st century. In C. Van Esch and O. Saint John (eds) *New Insights in Foreign Language Learning and Teaching* (pp. 71–88). Frankfurt Am Main: Peter Lang Verlag.

Smithers, R. and Whitford, B. (2006) 'Free fall' fears as pupils abandon languages. *Guardian Weekly* (25 August 2006). On WWW at http://education.guardian.co.uk/gcses/story/0,,1857964,00.html.

Van Lier, L. (1996) *Interaction in the Language Curriculum: Awareness, Autonomy and Authenticity.* New York: Longman Group.

Wells, G. (1999) *Dialogic Inquiry: Towards a Socio-cultural Practice and Theory of Education.* Cambridge: Cambridge University Press.

Chapter 11

Educating Languages Teachers for Multilingual and Multicultural Settings

MARGARET GEARON

I cannot imagine a future in which people of all cultures and nations are not increasingly connected by ties of travel, commerce and migration... Our future prosperity and security will depend on our ability to understand these cultures and to build bridges to the citizens of these nations and all our immediate neighbours. For that reason I am especially encouraged to learn that Japanese, Indonesian, Korean and Mandarin are the priority languages designated under the Commonwealth National Asian Languages and Studies in Australian Schools Program (NALSAS). And I am delighted that the most rapid growth in language education in the past decade has been driven by increased take up of these languages. (Major General Peter Cosgrove, Asia Education Foundation National Summit, 2003)

Introduction

This chapter is based on a project conducted in 2006–2007 by the Australian Council for Educational Research. It involved a review of languages' teacher education courses in all Australian universities as part of the then Australian government's National Statement and Plan for Languages 2005–2008. The chapter refers to part of the data collected to evaluate a small sample of the syllabuses from these courses, using the theoretical models for foreign/second language teacher education proposed by Freeman and Johnson (1998) and Vélez-Rendón (2002). It also compares the content of the syllabus of each of the university language teacher education courses to that proposed in the National Statement and Plan, and examines the extent to which such courses appear to set directions for enabling pre-service teachers to move along the continuum to accomplished teachers, as outlined in the 'Professional standards for accomplished teachers of languages and cultures' (AFMLTA, 2005).

Australia's policy on the teaching and learning of languages (Lo Bianco, 1987; DEST, 1991; Rudd, 1994) went into abeyance between 1992 and 2003. After much lobbying on the part of concerned State and Territory languages other than English advisors/departmental officers and particularly the Australian Federation of Modern Language Teachers Associations (AFMLTA), the Ministerial Council for Education, Employment, Training and Youth Affairs (MCEETYA) undertook a review of the different policies on the teaching and learning of languages across Australia in 2003. This resulted in the publication of the National Statement for Languages Education in Australian Schools, combined with the National Plan for Languages Education in Australian Schools 2005–2008. Federal Government funding accompanied the latter component, and a Languages Working Party was established to provide advice on projects of national significance to emanate from the six strands identified in the National Plan. Strand Two, Teacher Supply and Retention, included the action point: 'review the content and structure of teacher education courses with a view to improving access to, and the quality of, preparation for languages teachers' (National Plan for Languages Education in Australian Schools 2005–2008, 2005: 13). The Australian Council for Educational Research, under the project management of Dr Elizabeth Kleinhenz, successfully tendered to undertake this review (Kleinhenz *et al.*, 2007) and included in the group were representatives from languages teacher education at Monash and La Trobe Universities, and from the Research Unit in Multilingualism and Multiculturalism at the University of Melbourne.[1]

A major component of the review consisted of collecting data about the languages education courses incorporated into teacher education by those Australian universities that offered degrees or diplomas in Arts/ Education or Education alone. The data were firstly collected by accessing each university's website to determine what type of course (undergraduate, pre-service, other post-graduate), and what type of units were being taught in relation to languages education. This information was transferred to a table showing what was happening at both the National Level (e.g. Australian Catholic University) and for each State and Territory (Kleinhenz *et al.*, 2007, Appendix 1: 118–206). The second step was the preparation of a questionnaire that was emailed to identify languages education lecturers. The purpose of this was to confirm the information gleaned from the website, and to collect more up-to-date information about the numbers of languages teachers in training and the particular languages being targeted by the courses.

Part of the questionnaire sought to determine the type and range of content that the languages teacher education courses were presenting. It is this aspect that is analysed in this chapter. The analysis will be based on the propositions for languages teacher education courses of Freeman and Johnson (1998) and Vélez-Rendón (2002) to determine the extent to which such courses provide future teachers of languages other than English with the knowledge base and skills to teach in linguistically and culturally diverse contexts. In addition, the chapter analyses the selected sample of the courses to determine whether or not the content of the units appears to prepare languages teachers to implement a quality programme as envisaged by the National Statement for Languages Education (MCEETYA, 2005), in particular in relation to the following points:

> Twenty-first century education needs to engage with, and be responsive to, this changing world. It needs to develop in learners the knowledge, understanding and attributes necessary for success-ful participation and engagement within and across local, regional, and global communities, and in all spheres of activity... Education in a global community brings with it an increasing need to focus on developing inter-cultural understanding. This involves the integra-tion of language, culture and learning. (MCEETYA, 2005: 2–3)

The chapter concludes with some recommendations for further research needed to establish what knowledge base languages teachers in linguistically and culturally diverse contexts may need to implement an effective language programme in a school context, as well as a set of recommendations for modifying the existing courses to render them more relevant to linguistically and culturally diverse school settings.

Background to the Research Project

Australia is a country of vast contrasts. From the urban environments of the capital cities of the States and Territories to regional, rural and remote towns, there are many differences that influence the provision of a language other than English. Cities such as Sydney and Melbourne have a range of linguistically and culturally diverse school contexts where some reflect predominantly English-speaking communities, while others have high levels of multilingualism and multiculturalism within their school communities and in the local area. The 2006 census of the

Table 11.1 Australian capital cities showing the percentage of English-speaking and non-English-speaking families

City	English-speaking families (%)	Non-English-speaking families (%)
Sydney	64.0	36.0
Melbourne	68.1	31.9
Darwin	76.8	23.2
Perth	79.9	20.1
Canberra	81.0	19.0
Adelaide	80.4	19.6
Brisbane	83.9	16.1
Hobart	89.9	10.1

Source: Census data (2006)

Australian population produced figures in relation to acknowledged use of language other than English at home (see Table 11.1).

In general, regional and rural Australia is also predominantly English speaking, although parts of outback Australia have communities where Indigenous languages are spoken and English is the second or third language.

In addition to preparing teachers of languages to teach in Australian schools, there is also the need to be conscious that some of these teachers will work in other countries, so languages teacher education courses must address not only local contexts, but international ones as well. With increasing global movement of families, and indeed of populations of migrants and refugees, teachers of languages, and hence of cultures, must be prepared for a diversity of student populations in school communities. They need to be aware of ways in which such diversity will affect how they develop their language teaching skills within a particular context, and what this means for the belief systems and knowledge base they hold about language teaching and learning.

Vélez-Rendón (2002) believes that the literature she reviewed demonstrates that most second language teacher education courses are based on a transmission approach that focuses on providing classroom techniques and skills, knowledge about language, with little research or solid theoretical foundations to support the content, but rather a dependence on tradition and opinion, a view that is in accordance with Freeman and Johnson (1998). According to the latter, this is slowly changing with second language teacher 'candidates' developing their own theories and an awareness of the process of learning to teach. As Vélez-Rendón (2002: 457) states, '...very little attention has been paid to how second language teachers learn to teach, how they develop teaching skills, how they link theory and practice, and how their previous experiences inform their belief systems'. She believes that 'what is needed is a more theoretical and research-driven approach to preparing second language teachers' (Vélez-Rendón, 2002: 458).

In her review of the literature on what might constitute the knowledge base of languages teachers in the 21st century, Vélez-Rendón (2002: 462) cites a number of researchers who have suggested components for this core knowledge. Beginning with the work of Lafayette (1993), which I believe remains relevant to Australian language teacher education courses, Vélez-Rendón (2002: 462) notes that he proposed the following areas:

> Subject-matter knowledge consisting of language proficiency, civilization and culture, language analysis (Lafayette, 1993). The knowledge of civilization and culture component should not just constitute knowledge about these, but also the ability to develop students' cultural sensitivities, including helping students to gain awareness of themselves and others as cultural beings.

This latter point is currently being promoted as part of language teacher in-service programmes across Australia, delivered by Scarino *et al.* (2007), who have investigated and prepared a comprehensive professional learning package on intercultural competence and its development through foreign and second language programmes in primary and secondary schools. Nevertheless, as discussed later, this does not seem to have permeated pre-service languages teacher education course content.

Vélez-Rendón (2002: 463–464) proposes a model for developing the knowledge base for languages teachers. Her model has six components:

(1) The acquisition of theoretical underpinnings of the profession and the necessary analytical and reflective skills to complete the connection between theory and practice and so [that teachers] develop their own theories.

(2) The exploration of novice teachers' previous experiences as learners and the beliefs, assumptions and attitudes that they bring to their education programme.

(3) The creation of meaningful, effective field experiences that also support the integration of theory and practice, and start to develop essential teaching skills and classroom management ones. This should include classroom observation (cf: Wajnryb, 1993; Lockhart & Richards, 1994).

(4) The provision of a forum for novice teachers to share and discuss the outcomes of the field experience and classroom observations.

(5) The use of action research projects encouraging teacher-initiated inquiry, especially on topics or aspects of teaching that concern them the most.

(6) The need for language teacher educators to re-think their roles and renew their practices by also engaging in research and self-reflection through action research projects, which research classroom contexts and build meaningful relations with classroom teachers.

Language teacher educators also need to undertake needs analysis of their novice teachers and use feedback sessions to develop greater awareness of the novice teachers' stages of development so that more appropriate course content can be delivered.

Wilbur (2007), in a study of post-secondary language methods courses in the USA, makes the point that not only has teacher education failed to keep pace with socio-political changes, but second language pedagogy has changed even more rapidly, and teachers who themselves learned languages under a different paradigm need a different body of knowledge and skills. She agrees with Vélez-Rendón's comment that teacher educators and tertiary languages staff need to re-think their roles and renew their practices. This applies to the Australian context as well as to the American one. Like Vélez-Rendón, Wilbur found that there were a number of areas that were essential to the preparation of pre-service languages teachers. These included encouraging reflective practice and action research; the development of content area expertise as well as pedagogical content and knowledge; and linking theory to practice. Additional important areas included second language acquisition (SLA) theory, fluency in the second language and fieldwork experiences (Wilbur, 2007: 83). Wilbur (2007: 99) concludes her paper with a recommendation that we could certainly follow Australia; she suggests: 'A first step in a positive direction would be a national movement to identify best practices of methods instruction and to identify certain instructors and their courses as a model for others'.

Freeman and Johnson (1998) propose a re-conceptualisation of the knowledge base of language teacher education. They provide a critique of what they see as a tendency to base second language teacher education programmes on the tradition and opinion of language teacher educators rather than on theories or understandings from research (Freeman & Johnson, 1998: 398). In re-conceptualising second and foreign language teacher education programmes, they draw heavily on the work in general teacher education, which views teachers as 'individuals who enter teacher education programmes with prior experiences, personal values and beliefs that inform their knowledge about teaching and shape what they do in classrooms' (Freeman & Johnson, 1998: 401). In terms of languages education, these factors may be in conflict with current models of language learning, given the evolution from grammar-translation and cognitive approaches to an emphasis on communicative and intercultural competences. As Freeman and Johnson (1998: 401) state, 'teachers' beliefs and past experiences as (language) learners tend to create ways of thinking about teaching that often conflict with the images of teaching that we advocate in our teacher education programs' because of the power of prior knowledge and experiences in learning how to teach. They claim that 'learning to teach is a long-term, complex, developmental process that operates through participation in the social practices and contexts associated with learning and teaching' (Freeman & Johnson, 1998: 402). Their key finding is that these views of teacher learning are not reflected in current language teacher education courses in North America, and I would say the same applies in Australia. Such courses appear to promote the view that future teachers of languages need courses that:

- provide them with a body of knowledge about the language, about language learning and language teaching;
- expose them to a range of teaching practices and methodologies; and
- provide field experiences where they apply this theoretical knowledge in actual classroom settings. (Freeman & Johnson, 1998: 402)

I return to these points later, when I examine a selected sample of languages programmes in teacher education courses in Australia.

Freeman and Johnson's model of languages teacher education does not eliminate the need to understand theories of SLA, to be exposed to a range of language teaching methodologies or approaches, and to have an excellent understanding of the subject matter of the target language, but rather it sees these as necessarily being contextualised within teachers' professional lives, the settings in which they work and their circumstances in these settings. In other words, the teacher education programme must consider both personal and social contexts of language teaching as well as conceptual and perceptual knowledge required to inform and change teachers' practices. Freeman and Johnson (1998) provide a diagram of their framework for the knowledge base of language teacher education, which demonstrates the links between the nature and contexts of schools and schooling, the nature of the teacher as learner, and the activity of (language) teaching and learning.

They see schools has having a 'focus on the physical and sociocultural settings in which teaching takes place, [and] schooling [where] the focus is on the sociocultural and historical processes [...] that take place in the settings of schools' (Freeman & Johnson, 1998: 408). They justify the inclusion of schools and schooling in the knowledge base of second and foreign language teacher education by stating that 'language teaching cannot be understood apart from the socio-cultural environments in which it takes place and the processes of establishing and navigating social values in which it is embedded' (Freeman & Johnson, 1998: 409). The examination below of a small sample of language teacher education courses in Australian universities will seek to address these points.

Freeman and Johnson (1998) lament the lack of studies of language teaching as it is practiced in classrooms. In contrast, they believe that the knowledge base has been dominated by *a priori* claims, in particular in terms of the relationship between language teaching and the disciplines on which it is historically based, such as theories of SLA. Finally, they believe that language teacher educators must enable teacher learners to understand their own beliefs and knowledge about learning and teaching and to analyse and articulate what they understand is happening in their own language teaching contexts and the consequences of this through reflective practices.

Tarone and Allwright (2005: 6) have critiqued this stance by Freeman and Johnson and claim that these authors do not differentiate between teacher learning and teacher education, whereas they believe that these two should be treated separately. They do, however, agree with Freeman and Johnson that the research done on teacher learning in general should be relevant to language teacher education. They believe that there is a need for longitudinal studies on both contexts and ways in which teachers learn how to teach languages, examining novice, pre-service and experienced in-service teachers separately.

In terms of a knowledge base for second language teachers, Tarone and Allwright (2005:18) state:

> The framework for the knowledge base, in our view, should include a clear understanding of learners, who they are, why they learn, what

they need to learn, what motivates them, and how a teacher goes about negotiating the teaching/learning activities with them.

In regard to the role of SLA theories in language teacher education courses, Tarone and Allwright disagree that these theories are not of great use to teachers, but claim that 'Teacher learners should not be just consumers of SLA research but partners in on-going research to identify the knowledge and needs of second language learners in classrooms' (Tarone & Allwright, 2005: 21).

It appears that both pairs of writers, Freeman and Johnson, and Tarone and Allwright, agree about the need for a knowledge base for second language teacher learners, but disagree about what the fundamentals should be, and the degree to which the role of the language learners should be considered as critical to this knowledge base. Ultimately, they both consider that SLA has some part to play, but that more classroom-based research is needed to clarify what it is that constitutes a knowledge base for pre-service and in-service teachers. This is supported by McKay (2008) who, when asked to comment on the best ways of training languages teachers for multilingual classrooms, stated that 'research to inform language teaching and language teacher education should be classroom-based in actual contexts and include both learners and learners' views' (McKay, 2008).

In light of the above recommendations for a knowledge base for prospective languages teachers, I turn now to examining a selected sample of courses offered in Australian universities. I have chosen five from the seventeen from where data were collected over a nine-month period between 2006 and 2007.

Analysis of the Languages Method Courses

An examination of the course descriptions and some of the unit outlines for these languages teacher education programmes shows that, overall, most really do not prepare future teachers for linguistically and culturally diverse school contexts. Indeed, they appear to justify what Vélez-Rendón (2002) refers to as courses based on tradition and personal opinion of the languages teacher educators. Most of the courses indicate that they provide prospective languages teachers with knowledge about language teaching, and introduce them to a range of teaching methods and practices, two of the features mentioned by Freeman and Johnson (1998). Many refer to the importance of knowledge about SLA theories and principles as part of the required knowledge base, the key component specified by Tarone and Allwright (2005).

Few of the course descriptions for the languages component of the teacher education programmes refer to the development of intercultural understanding, and the relationship between language and culture as stipulated in the National Statement for Languages Education in Australian Schools (2005: 3). On their 2006 websites, Universities Q and T do include the following statements, which could be interpreted as addressing this aspect of languages education. University Q, Primary LOTE Curriculum Studies 2 course description states: 'The unit emphasises the importance of developing learning environments in which students can become intercultural communicators and develop strategic language learning skills' (University Q). University T, Bachelor of Education course description states: 'All third year students do... a curriculum unit that includes intercultural aspects of language.... Fourth year students may specialise in languages, including cumulative models of language teaching and learning and intercultural language learning' (University T).

Most of the course descriptions for the languages component of the teacher education programmes mention the socio-cultural environment of schools and schooling, one of Freeman and Johnson's features. For example, University U has a unit entitled, 'The socio-cultural contexts of secondary education', which includes a 'critical-reflective approach to educational practices and beliefs and which enables a critique of educational philosophy and how it influences professional practice' (University U).

Although specific mention of languages education is not made, this is one of the key components of the Graduate Diploma in Language Teaching and must be taken by prospective languages teachers. University R also seems to have a commitment to linking languages education to the nature of schools and schooling. In the description of the LOTE Education 2 unit, 'students... examine the relationship between LOTE and the school curriculum' and in the unit entitled Current Issues in LOTE, 'attention is given to the educational, sociological, psychological, and political aspects of the development of LOTE programmes and understanding of LOTE importance and role within the Australian educational context' (University S). Slightly weaker statements regarding this component are made by University T, which refers to the culture of schools and contexts of teaching as part of the general Bachelor of Education degree, and University V, which mentions that the Graduate Diploma in Education covers the social context of teaching and learning. In linguistically and culturally diverse school classrooms, this component proposed by Freeman and Johnson is clearly an essential one for languages teacher educators to incorporate in their courses to prepare future teachers of languages for a range of socio-cultural environments in schools and schooling, and is clearly a missing element that needs to be addressed if these teachers are going to be prepared adequately for 21st century classrooms.

Another key component of language teacher education programmes is that of reflective practice, referred to by Freeman and Johnson (1998) and Vélez-Rendón (2002). For one aspect of reflection, both sets of authors suggest that prospective languages teachers be provided with opportunities to 'understand their own beliefs and knowledge about teaching and learning' (Freeman & Johnson, 1998: 412) and to reflect on 'the development of personal theories of teaching, self-awareness and change' and to undertake a 'critical evaluation of their prior experiences as language learners, and their beliefs, assumptions and attitudes' (Vélez-Rendón, 2002: 463–464). In regard to these ideas, University T mentions reflection and renewal as part of the Bachelor of Education course.

Freeman and Johnson (1998: 412) add a further component to reflective practice and that is the provision of opportunities to analyse and articulate what they [teacher trainees] understand as it is happening and the consequences. University W appears to include this in its LOTE Curriculum II unit, where students are provided with 'opportunities for reflection on teaching experience through analysis of lesson segments' (Kleinhenz *et al.*, 2007: 205). This feature of a languages teacher education course is important to researching the links between theories and classroom practices, a step that is being promoted as necessary to understanding how teachers of languages learn how to teach, to develop their teaching skills (Vélez-Rendón, 2002) and to make links between theory and practice (Freeman & Johnson, 1998; Vélez-Rendón, 2002; McKay, 2008).

Examining the selected universities websites to access the languages teacher education units being offered as part of pre-service teacher education courses significantly raised awareness of how an overview of a proposed knowledge base can produce a substantially impressionistic view of what the language teacher education courses are doing in response to the characteristics of such a base as proposed by Freeman and Johnson (1998, 2005), Vélez-Rendón (2002) and Tarone and Allwright (2005). A more in-depth analysis shows that none of the courses actually meets what might be considered as the basic requirements for a language teacher education course for the 21st century. Indeed, the courses reviewed illustrate very nicely the comment by Freeman and Johnson (1998: 402) that many language teacher education courses continue to operate under the assumption that they must provide teachers with a codified body of knowledge about language, language learning, and language teaching; expose them to a range of teaching practices or methodologies; and provide a field experience in which they are expected to apply their theoretical knowledge in actual classroom settings.

It must be admitted, however, that these units are not attached to a teacher education programme that focuses solely on the preparation of teachers of languages, but rather are units within a broader, general teacher education course, which may contain units that address the characteristics shown to be absent. This raises the point made by Vélez-Rendón (2002: 465) about 'the uniqueness of second and foreign languages as subject matter'. If the latter is the case, it may be necessary for language teacher education to become a sub-programme within the general teacher education one. This assumes, of course, that those who undertake such a course wish to be solely teachers of a language or languages.

Indeed, until recently, this was the case at University U, where a Graduate Diploma in Language Teaching was offered to local and international students wishing to teach languages in secondary schools. This course appears to incorporate most of the components proposed by both Freeman and Johnson (1998) and Vélez-Rendón (2002) in the description of its overall aims together with the list of units making up the course components.

> This course aims to: enable students to achieve or consolidate specialist, professional competence as practitioners in teaching and programming for spoken and written languages; provide students with the relevant theoretical underpinning for this professional competence in a variety of contexts and the ability to reflect critically on it; and develop students understanding of the linguistic demands if teaching and learning, and of issues in language development. (Kleinhenz *et al.*, 2007: 145)

These aims include the following components from Freeman and Johnson (1998): provision of a body of knowledge about language learning; provision of a body of knowledge about language teaching; and reflective practice with the provision of opportunities to analyse and articulate what beginning teachers of languages understand as it is happening and the consequences. These aims also include Vélez-Rendón's point of how they develop their teaching skills. The titles of the units would also lead to the expectation that this course covered other factors mentioned by these authors. Units such as Socio-political contexts of Language, Literacy and Numeracy Education, Language Development, and Language Teaching Methodology cover provision of a body of knowledge about the language and exposure to a range of teaching practices and methodologies.

Currently, this course in languages education 'is now offered as the Languages major in the graduate entry degree Bachelor of Teaching in Secondary Education' (University U) and has a number of new units, many of which reflect the views of Freeman and Johnson, Tarone and Allwright, and Vélez-Rendón about preparation of languages teachers. An examination of the units offered in terms of the factors proposed by Freeman and Johnson (1998: 406–412) shows that the units entitled Language Teaching Methods 1, 2 and 3 at University U address the need to provide a body of knowledge about language learning and teaching, and exposure to a range of teaching practices and methodologies. For example, Language Teaching Methods 1 states: 'The subject combines theory with practice to provide a student with the skills and understanding required to begin to teach languages in a secondary school' (University U).

Units such as Professional Experience 1 and The Socio-cultural Contexts of Secondary Education cover the socio-cultural environments of schooling, both theoretical and practical. According to the description of the latter unit, it 'investigates the socio-cultural contexts of secondary education and social theories which seek to explain the social, economic and political forces shaping schools and classrooms. It explores the ways in which these forces interact in the Australian context to influence educational outcomes' (University U).

The course also includes the unit, Language Development, which 'provides a framework for studying first and second language development, with particular emphasis on social and function perspectives on language learning. The subject offers a survey of the principal topics currently addressed in the study of second language acquisition, and of the major research methods and paradigms used in such studies' (University U). This corresponds to one of the key aspects recommended by Tarone and Allwright (2005).

In terms of Vélez-Rendón's model for second language teacher education courses, University U's Language Teaching Methods 3, Language Education 4 and Professional Experience 1 address how teachers learn to teach, develop their teaching skills and link theory with practice. For example, Language Teaching Methods 3 states that students develop a range of approaches and strategies to use in the classroom which reflect research findings in education. They develop a philosophy of teaching languages taking account of current syllabuses and policies, and demonstrate an understanding of the professional insights and demands of the practising language teacher. (University U)

The only aspect of Vélez-Rendón's model that appears not to be covered in the course is how previous experiences inform second language teachers' belief systems.

The analysis of the Bachelor of Education at University U also shows only minimal gaps in terms of the National Statement for Languages in Australian Schools, as it does not incorporate a focus on the development of intercultural understanding or competence, or really address what knowledge, attributes and understandings languages teachers will need to engage with students in schools locally, regionally and on a global basis. This said, other university teacher education courses that offer preparation for languages teachers address only small elements of the models presented by Freeman and Johnson (1998, 2005), Tarone and Allwright (2005) and Vélez-Rendón (2002, 2006).

It is worth noting here the recent work of Kramsch (2008) alerting us to the importance of language ecology as a field that needs to be considered in the preparation of language teachers who will be working in multilingual (and therefore multicultural) classrooms, teaching either the dominant language of the nation as a second language for students, or teaching a compulsory language as part of the school curriculum (Zarate *et al.*, 2008). Her research and suggestions are based on the notions of 'trans-lingual' and 'trans-cultural' competence as the goals of language courses at university. In other words, as the notion of intercultural competence in Australian languages other than English curriculum documents proposes, language learners, and in particular, teachers of languages, will develop the ability to operate between languages, and will be able to extend this to their own primary and secondary school students. This means that teacher educators 'will need to operate in a globalized space where verbal exchanges will be increasingly plurilingual and pluricultural' (Zarate *et al.*, 2008 in Kramsch, 2008: 390). For languages teacher education, this means that a purely 'textbook' approach to the teaching and learning of another language will not suffice and so teacher education courses will need to deal with how to present, analyse and use as pedagogical tools texts which exist in the real world and which learners may or may not encounter. Kramsch uses the example of bi- and multilinguals and their dealings with each other, in the presence of a second/foreign language learner of one of the languages. She skilfully demonstrates how language is used by interlocutors who would not be considered 'native-like' in their non-first language, but who are able to manipulate and so construct 'social and cultural reality in interaction with others' (Kramsch, 2008: 407). Through these examples, she demonstrates the importance of language ecology theory/theories for learners who wish to engage and interact in real/authentic communities of the language/s that they are learning in a classroom context.

Issues of illocutionary and perlocutionary force (intended effect of speech acts and their actual effect) are particularly relevant where language learners are wishing to enter into transactions in the second/ foreign language community. Teachers who have a 'monolingual' mindset may not be able to recognise the need to address the different linguistic and cultural knowledge and skills that learners in linguistically and culturally diverse classes bring to this compulsory school language programme. Kramsch (2008: 402) states: 'Multilingual environments can elicit complex relationships between speech acts and their perlocutionary effects'. If teacher educators are not aware of this possibility and do not include it in language teacher education courses, students may reject the course content and revert to traditional stereotypes and clichéd views of interactions with speakers of the language being learned.

Conclusion

The preparation of languages teachers can no longer include just linguistic knowledge, theories of SLA and pedagogical practices that assume a homogeneous grouping of students in terms of the latter's interest in and motivation for learning the second (or further) language. The linguistically and culturally diverse classrooms that many languages teachers encounter contain students with a range of abilities and varying degrees of familiarity with the school context in which they find themselves. It is imperative, then, to develop a knowledge base for languages teachers, one which will enable them to understand the various factors impacting on their teaching and learning context, and which will enable them to select and implement classroom practices that enhance language and intercultural learning. Equally important is the recognition that teachers in school-based languages programmes can no longer rely on the types of texts proposed in textbooks that still appear to promote the view of a 'standard' language in use. Such textbooks do not take into consideration the linguistic and cultural diversity and competence of students and non-native-speaking teachers alike.

Research into ways in which languages teachers can accommodate learners who are already bi- or multilingual and are required to study yet another language as part of their schooling is essential for providing information for languages teacher education courses for the diversity of 21st century classrooms, learners, and their needs and interests, both immediate and future.

Note

1. This project was funded by the then Department of Education, Science & Training (DEST) in 2006.

References

Asia Education Foundation (2003) Report of the National Summit – Studies of Asia in Australian Schools at a Crossroad: Strategic Directions 2004–2006. On WWW at www.asialink.unimelb.edu.au/aef/pdt. Accessed 22.7.08.

Australian Bureau of Statistics (2006) Census data. On WWW at www.censusdata.abs.gov.au. Accessed 21.7.08.

Australian Federation of Modern Language Teachers Association (2005) *Professional Standards for Accomplished Teachers of Languages*. Canberra: Department of Education, Science and Training.

Cosgrove, P. (2003) Understanding Asia Culture: Helping the ADF achieve in the region. Address to the Asia Education Foundation National Summit. In Report of the National Summit – *Studies of Asia in Australian Schools at a Crossroad: Strategic Directions 2004–2006* (p. 20). Melbourne: Asia Education Foundation and Zbar Consulting Pty Ltd.

Department of Employment, Education and Training (DEST) (1991) *Australia's Language: The Australian Language and Literacy Policy*. Canberra: AGPS.

Freeman, D. and Johnson, K. (1998) Reconceptualising the knowledge-base of language teacher education. *TESOL Quarterly* 32 (3), 397–417.

Freeman, D. and Johnson, K. (2005) Response to Tarone and Allwright. In D. Tedick (ed.) *Second Language Teacher Education: International Perspectives* (pp. 25–33). Mahwah, NJ: Lawrence Erlbaum.

Guntermann, G. (ed.) *Developing Language Teachers for a Changing World*. ACTFL Foreign Language Education Series No. 22. Lincolnwood, IL: National Textbook.

Kleinhenz, E., Wilkinson, J., Gearon, M., Fernandez, S. and Ingvarson, L. (2007) *The Review of Teacher Education for Languages Teachers: Final Report*. Melbourne: ACER and Canberra: Department of Education, Employment and Workplace Relations.

Kramsch, C. (1996) *The Cultural Component of Language Teaching*. On WWW at www.spz.tu-darmstadt.de/projekt_ejournal/jg-01-2/beitreg/kramsch2.htm. Accessed September 2006.

Kramsch, C. (2008) Ecological perspectives on foreign language education. *Language Teaching* 41 (3), 389–408.

Lafayette, R. (1993) Subject matter content: What every language teacher should know. In G. Guntermann (ed.) *Developing Language Teachers for a Changing*

World (pp. 124–158). ACTFL Foreign Language Education Series No. 22. Lincolnwood, IL: National Textbook.

Lockhart, C. and Richards, J.C. (1994) *Reflective Teaching in Second Language Classrooms.* Cambridge: Cambridge University Press.

Lo Bianco, J. (1987) *National Policy on Languages.* Canberra: Commonwealth Department of Education.

McKay, S.L. (2008) There are more opportunities than challenges for the language teacher in the multilingual world. Panel Discussion at Language Teaching in a Multilingual World. The 43rd RELC International Seminar. RELC, Singapore.

MCEETYA [Ministerial Council on Education, Employment, Training and Youth Affairs] (2005) *National Statement and Plan for Languages 2005–2008.* Adelaide: State of South Australia Department of Education and Children's Services Publishing.

Rudd, K. (Chair) (1994) *Asian Languages and Australia's Economic Future, A Report Prepared for the Council of Australian Governments on a Proposed National Asian Languages/Studies Strategy for Australian Schools.* Brisbane: Queensland Government Printer.

Scarino, A., Liddicoat, A., Carr, J., Crozet, C., Kohler, M., Loechel, K., Mecurio, N., Morgan, A., Papademetre. L. and Scrimgeour, A. (2007) *Intercultural Language Teaching and Learning in Practice Project: Professional Learning Program.* Adelaide: University of South Australia Research Centre for Languages and Cultures; Canberra: Department of Education, Employment and Workplace Relations.

Scarino, A., Liddicoat, A., Carr, J., Curnow, T., Kohler, M., Loechel, K., Mecurio, N., Morgan, A., Papademetre, L. and Scrimgeour, A. (2008) *Professional Standards Project: Professional Learning Program.* Canberra: Department of Education, Employment and Workplace Relations.

Tarone, E. and Allwright, R. (2005) Second language teacher learning and student second language learning: Shaping the knowledge base. In D. Tedick (ed.) *Second Language Teacher Education: International Perspectives* (pp. 5–24). Mahwah, NJ: Lawrence Erlbaum.

Vélez-Rendón, G. (2002) Second language teacher education: A review of the literature. *Foreign Language Annals* 35 (4), 457–467.

Vélez-Rendón, G. (2006) From student to teacher: A successful transition. *Foreign Language Annals* 39 (2), 320–334.

Wajnryb, R. (1993) *Classroom Observation Tasks: A Resource Book for Language Teachers and Trainers.* Cambridge: Cambridge University Press.

Wilbur, M. (2007) How foreign language teachers get taught: Methods of teaching the methods course. *Foreign Language Annals* 40 (1), 79–102.

Zarate, G., Levy, D. and Kramsch, C. (eds) (2008) *Précis du plurilinguisme et du pluriculturalisme.* [*Handbook of Multilingualism and Multiculturalism.*] Paris: Editions des Archives Contemporaines.

University websites

University Q. On WWW at http://clbed.qut.ed.au. Accessed September 2008.

University S. On WWW at http://www.unisanet.unisa.edu.au. Accessed September 2008.

University T. On WWW at http://fcms.its.utas.edu.au. Accessed September 2008.

University U. On WWW at http://www.utsydney.cn/education/courses/gd_languages.html. Accessed 16/19.7.08.

University V. On WWW at http://www.vu.edu.au. Accessed July 2008.

Part 3

Research Directions in Diverse Contexts

Chapter 12

Multilingual Researcher Identities: Interpreting Linguistically and Culturally Diverse Classrooms

ANGELA CREESE, ARVIND BHATT and PETER MARTIN[†]

Introduction

This chapter addresses one of five research aims of an Economic Social Research Council[1] (ESRC)-funded project that looked at multilingualism in complementary schools[2] in four communities. The research aim was to 'develop innovative ethnographic team methodologies using interlocking case studies across diverse social, cultural, religious and linguistic contexts'. In this chapter, our aim is to give an account of working in a multilingual team. We focus, in particular, on the Gujarati case study and the two researchers most involved in this. The larger project consisted of four case studies and nine researchers in total. Each case study was made up of a pairing of researchers who also worked in the larger team of nine. Here, we focus on the Gujarati case study for a number of reasons. First, the two researchers have worked closely together over several research projects on complementary schools (Martin *et al.*, 2004), offering reflections that go back to 2002. The two researchers' vignettes describe their close collaboration over six years. Second, although each of the four case study pairings offers interesting insights and could be used in a chapter such as this, chapter length necessitated a choice of only one. A fuller account of all nine vignettes can be found in Blackledge and Creese (in press).

We believe it is worth studying the methodological processes of team ethnography to demystify the research process and make it more accessible and understandable to those who work, study and research in multilingual educational contexts. We hope this will further our understandings of linguistically and culturally diverse classrooms.

[†] It is with great sadness that we report on the sudden and untimely death of Peter Martin during the publication of this chapter.

Within education and ethnography, there is a substantial literature on the importance of collaborative research models between teachers and researchers (Beaumont & O'Brien, 2000; Hawkins, 2005; Conteh *et al.*, 2008; Denos *et al.*, 2009). Beaumont and O'Brien's (2000) collection stresses the importance of co-writing between practitioners and researchers in their reports of collaboration in the area of language education. Hawkins (2004) speaks of a shared agenda between teachers and researchers in untangling learning in classrooms and stresses the importance of equality. Denos *et al.* (2009) give an interesting account of professionals collaborating, discussing and understanding across their different contexts of schools and universities. They describe how teachers and academics all experience varying roles as knowers and learners and also differ in expertise and knowledge. They discuss the processes of collaboration between teachers and academics in their Teacher Action Research Group (TARG). Through TARG meetings, members attempt to transform their own practices, understandings and workplaces. They describe the processes of team meetings as building solidarity, confidence and strength through their discussions. Using teacher vignettes of classroom lives, the study illustrates how, through collaboration, teachers and academics challenge powerful structures. They describe as particularly inappropriate a narrowly conceptualised education system that constructs students into problematic and narrow identities. Conteh *et al.* (2008) describe a process of collaborative classroom-based action research in linguistically diverse classrooms between teacher-researchers and a professional researcher. They argue for a better understanding and implementation of the theory/practice interface in the lives of teachers and academics, and highlight the need to bring in the researchers' different perspectives, revealing in the process, the dialogic and transformative quality of collaborative research. An important feature of the research was the 'equal collaboration between the three participants', because 'There was no funding for "principal investigators", "research assistants" or "other hierarchical roles"' (Conteh *et al.*, 2008: 3), more equal relationships could be established and maintained.

Such work as the studies described here typically stresses the importance of collaboration, shifting and fluid constructions of knowledge and expertise, the sharing and negotiation of new understandings and the flattening of hierarchical structures. It rarely deals with contestation and disagreements in the negotiation processes. However, this literature has a strong and important foothold in teacher education and offers a theoretical and methodological framework for teachers and academics to jointly research educational contexts. Much less has been written about team collaboration processes in the various stages of ethnographic educational research. However, this is an important research area because the make-up of research teams shapes what is noticed in the field and what is reported on in final research articles regarding classroom practice. The interface between research and classroom practice also has a potential impact on teacher development and training. We believe that team diversity is a way forward for understanding and articulating classroom realities in contemporary education.

The research team we describe in this chapter was made up of individuals with different ethnic, race, gender, nationality, linguistic and class backgrounds, who worked in four interlocking case studies. Angela Creese was responsible for overall coordination and was not attached to any one case study. The case study pairings are shown below.

Gujarati case study	Arvind Bhatt (AB) and Peter Martin (PM)
Chinese case study	Li Wei and Chao-Jung Wu
Bengali case study	Adrian Blackledge and Shahela Hamid
Turkish case study	Vally Lytra and Dilek Yağcıoğlu-Ali

In this chapter, we focus on the Gujarati case study and the research pair, Arvind Bhatt (AB) and Peter Martin (PM). As mentioned above, there is no particular rationale for choosing this pair over any of the other three. Each is of interest. However, an in-depth analysis of each pairing and its work in the full team is beyond the word limits of this chapter (see Blackledge & Creese (in press) for accounts of all nine vignettes). Each of the four individual case studies was central in producing detailed and nuanced accounts of two schools in each case study. They allowed, and indeed required, each two-researcher team to bring their particular linguistic and social knowledge to their interpretation of social action in each community. In each of the case studies, at least one of the researchers was bilingual in the community language and English, and in some cases both researchers spoke the community language, but may have had different levels of proficiency. In the Gujarati case study, Arvind is bilingual in Gujarati and English. He jis both a teacher and researcher in the complementary schools involved in this research project. He was, therefore, very much involved in participant observation. Peter on the other hand, does not speak Gujarati, but is multilingual in Malay and Kelabit, both languages of Malaysia. Like Arvind, he has lived for many years in Leicester and knows the town well. Both researchers, along with Angela Creese, have been involved in researching complementary schools in Leicester over several years: for Peter and Angela since 2002 (Martin *et al.*, 2004); Arvind has at least 15 years experience as a researcher in a variety of Gujarati community and educational projects.

Our main findings from the overall research project can be found in Creese *et al.* (2007a, 2007b, 2007c, 2007d, 2008a) and cannot be reported fully here. We found that multilingual young people and their teachers used linguistic resources in sophisticated, sometimes contradictory, but creative ways to negotiate identity positions and that the teaching and the learning of community languages were enacted in sites in which values could be transmitted, accepted, contested, subverted, appropriated and otherwise negotiated (Hornberger, 2005).

Working in Linguistically Diverse Contexts: What Teachers and Researchers Share

We believe that a chapter on team research is important in a volume such as this, which seeks to consider pedagogical issues arising from diversity. We hope to show that the 'many voices, many languages and many cultures' that are represented in our school classrooms can be best described through research approaches that explicitly address how diversity shapes data collection, analysis and final written accounts. In many ways, the 'new dilemmas' facing teachers in linguistically and culturally diverse classrooms are the same facing researchers. As Eisenhart (2001a) suggests, we are all seeking new ways of adjusting our conceptual orientations to take account of changing human experiences, priorities and features of contemporary life. She argues:

> If postmodernism has taught anthropologists anything definitive, it is that we can no longer conceive of social groups of people with a culture that is clearly bounded and determined, internally coherent, and uniformly meaningful. (Eisenhart, 2001a: 117)

Researchers, then, like teachers, are grappling with finding new languages of description to understand diverse classrooms and their social practices and interactions. Old categories, marked boundaries and fixed views of identity and culture are now unhelpful. Researchers, like teachers, are looking for new approaches and methods to describe and work with the diversity of contemporary life. Indeed, 'old' research methodologies, along with established pedagogies are also being criticised and called into question. In terms of research, Eisenhart (2001a: 218) notes:

> Although feminist, ethnic and postmodern critics have influenced the way ethnographers think about their relationships with study participants and the styles ethnographers use to write their accounts, methods of site selection, data collection and analysis remain virtually unchanged.

Eisenhart's argument is that ethnographic methodology has not kept pace with its core theoretical literature. She describes the advances in conceptualising key constructs in post-modernity, such as 'culture', 'community' and 'identity', but suggests a lack of simultaneous methodological advances in ethnography to research these features of contemporary life. Eisenhart (2001a: 19) advocates various reflexive practices as one way to respond methodologically to new theorisings of social life and suggests that teams of ethnographers can be used both to introduce and represent a variety of different voices and perspectives into written research accounts. She also suggests that researchers should engage in their own critical introspection when representing those they are researching. Thus, in terms of ethnographic approaches, the research literature reports on strategies for countering narrow realist ethnographies that hinder understandings of differently situated others. As we have suggested, one strategy advocated is the use of research teams.

Research Teams: Representing Diversity

Research teams are held to offer more divergent voices in ethnographic accounts and this is seen as positive. Eisenhart (2001a: 19) notes, 'Increasingly, collaborative teams are being used to broaden the scope of work to, for example, include more settings and provide different perspectives'. According to Eisenhart (2001b: 219), collaborative approaches involve 'more different kinds of people' in designing the research process and creating the final product, which requires researchers to disclose more about their own views, commitments and social positions. Such approaches make clearer 'the social position, cultural perspective and political stance' (Eisenhart, 2001b: 219) of the researcher and how these influence subsequent actions.

Erickson and Stull (1998: 23) describe the importance of team processes in representing the researched and speak of 'plural gazes' in jointly constructing narratives. A feature of team ethnography is the presence of competing and divergent 'cultural selves' and ways in which identity politics may shape 'noticings' in the field. McCorkel and Myers (2003) believe it is important not just to acknowledge the influence of identity-play in positionings in the field, but also to show how and to what extent these structure the research processes. They argue:

> The problem is that in the act of "discovering" scientific truths, the skeletons we dig up are often our own. What passes as a scientific discovery about "the Other" is often the very assumptions and narratives we used to construct our subjects and their "difference" prior to entering the field. (McCorkel & Myers, 2003: 220)

Similarly, Ramazanoglu (1992) argues:

> Working as a research team cannot then be a process which can be taken for granted, nor can it be a set of relationships which is external to the conduct of the research. ...Their own class, gender and ethnicity, their social relationships, sexuality and personal values, that is the way the researchers are situated in social life, are conventionally deemed to be external to the processes of producing and interpreting data. [T]he ways in which the functioning of research teams can affect the production of social science knowledge has received relatively little attention. (Ramazanoglu, 1992: 1–2)

Mullings (1999) reports on a long line of feminist scholars who have argued the need to incorporate methodologies that recognise the existence of multiple viewpoints and the partiality of their own assessments. Her point is that researchers' knowledge is always partial and shaped by their 'maps of consciousness' (Haraway, 1991 in Mullings, 1999). In other words, their positionality in the social world is influenced by their unique mix of race, class, gender, nationality, sexuality and other identifiers (Mullings, 1999: 348). Maps of consciousness shape what is noticed and not noticed in the field and are always unfinished. As Rosaldo (1993: 9) argues:

> All interpretations are provisional; they are made by positioned subjects who are prepared to know certain things and not others. Even when knowledgeable, sensitive, fluent in the language, and able

to move easily in an alien cultural world, good ethnographers still have their limits, and their analyses are always incomplete.

Because researchers occupy and perform different sets of social identities, they form different relationships with research participants and this influences their noticings. The processes of self-representation in the research process are crucial to the ongoing data collection and the perpetuation of trust and confidence. They involve the researcher in a dynamic interplay of individual identities as they skilfully position themselves in relation to the researched. As Rampton *et al.* (2004: 3) argue, it takes time and close involvement to make sense of the 'complex intricacies of situated everyday activity among the people being studied', and the researcher's own social experiences and 'interpretive capacities' are crucial in this process.

Mullings (1999) describes how her own particular combination of gender, race, class and age characteristics had significant effects on the type of information collected in her study of companies in Jamaica. However, in her paper, she shows how she was able to position herself away from being constructed as a representative of a given community and the over-simplifying 'racial and gender matching' that came with it (Mullings, 1999: 12). She speaks of finding spaces in the research process that 'evoked the least threat or suspicion from the elites' whose opinions she sought (Mullings, 1999: 10). According to Mullings, there is a convergence of possibilities in the relationships with participants and researchers; some of these may stultify dialogue while other relationship open dialogue up.

Pratt and Hanson (1995: 25) agree when they note:

> Positions are not static: this is a point that needs to be underlined carefully in the contemporary context, in which "marking" by sexual orientation, class, race etc. is sometimes used not only to open up new conceptual spaces but also to discipline and silence others.

McCorkel and Myers (2003: 200) also take up researcher 'positition-ality'. They show how master narratives (Romero & Stewart, 1999) shape what is noticed and how researchers represent participants.

Insiders or Outsiders, Both and Neither

This sub-heading comes from Mullings (1999), who critiques the binary nature of insider/outsiders debates because it seeks to freeze the way researchers are able to position themselves in time and space with interactants. Insiders are typically said to be at an advantage because they are able to use their intimate knowledge of the context to gain access and make insightful observations. By contrast, outsiders are said to be at an advantage because they are likely to be perceived as 'neutral' and can stand apart from the politics of the local. Martin *et al.* (1997: 110) describe insiders as people sharing the culture and language of the researched and who are likely to 'pass' as native; and outsiders as those who do not share the language and culture and who are not included or recognised as members of the community. In their work, Martin *et al.* (1997) explicitly mention the sharing of a language as a marker of insiderness. We explore this further below.

More recently, however, it has been acknowledged that the insider/outsider dichotomy does not capture the dynamism of social life, and such boundaries are difficult to use, maintain and defend. Mullings (1999) shows how insiderness is not performed in any simple way around visible attributes such as race, gender, ethnicity or class. Instead, she described how she used her social self in a complicated positioning performance in relation to those she interviewed, attempting both insider and outsider positions with the overall aim of developing a level of trust with those she was interviewing. This also involved being mildly deceptive at times in order to manage relationships (Shaffir & Stebbins, 1991). McCorkel and Myers (2003: 204) also challenge the notion of a static insider/outsider dichotomy, particularly those 'brokered by racial and gender identities'. They show how these are constantly developing and shifting during the processes of fieldwork. However, they also acknowledge that 'difference does make a difference in research' (McCorkel & Myers, 2003: 226). In a reflexive account of their own research journeys, they show how 'position and privilege influence the production and performance of research' (McCorkel & Myers, 2003: 226). They argue that it is futile to renounce their 'privileged status as knowers' (McCorkel & Myers, 2003: 227). Rather, it is necessary to engage in strong reflexivity and turn the gaze towards themselves as researchers.

Below, we consider some of these challenges in the light of team ethnography in our work on complementary schools. In particular, we explore two different researcher perspectives. We reveal consistencies and tensions in their relationships with the researched and also with the rest of the team. We consider whether representing the voices and perspectives of individual researchers in a team of researchers can add complexity and richness to ethnography.

Researcher Identities

The chapter draws on two researcher reflections from a larger pool of nine individual researcher vignettes by each member of the team. The vignettes were written to meet the research project's fourth aim, which was explicitly methodological. This was 'to develop innovative ethnographic team methodologies using interlocking case studies across diverse social, cultural, religious and linguistic contexts' (Creese *et al.*, 2008a). One way we attempted to meet this objective was an agreement among researchers to write a one-page vignette at the time of data collection on two themes settled on by the team as of interest to them.

- Relationship to research participants.
- Negotiating a researcher identity within the team.

No further structure was given to the arrangement and the production of these vignettes. However, many of the first drafts produced accounts over two or three pages long. These were circulated around the full team. Researchers agreed that second and final draft outputs would be no longer than one page of single spaced A4 sheet. Two of these vignettes are included in this chapter. They exemplify the range of different perspectives brought to team research by a multilingual team with different linguistic, cultural and research backgrounds. They also reveal some of the complex issues about reflexivity discussed earlier in this chapter. They show the 'both and neither' aspect of the insider/outsider dichotomy and how researchers navigate this. We discuss two sites for negotiating the insider/outsiders dichotomy: the field and the university. We will see that these two contexts are sites where researchers experience different levels of insider- and outsiderness. The vignettes also explore the importance of language in identity politics in complementary school. This is an important factor that is often ignored in the sociological literature that tends to prioritise race, gender, ethnicity and nationality as most important in the positioning work that researchers engage in. We will look at how researchers describe language choice as a way to build rapport and create space for trust. We will also show that this is not done in any simple structural and mechanistic way, with language automatically linked to ethnicity. Rather, we show how researchers use their linguistic repertoires to negotiate ways in and out of the research process.

The remaining sections of this chapter are structured in the following way. First, Arvind and Peter's vignettes are given in full. Following each is a brief summary of some of the main points covered. We then turn to discussing the two themes we feel are most salient in the researchers' accounts: (1) insider/outsider positionality and (2) language and cultural background in the team.

Arvind Bhatt, researcher Gujarati case study

Relationships to participants: Now that I have completed observations at one participant school, I am asking myself: Why am I doing this research? and, Why am I doing this research?

The first question implies my professional motivation (other than being employed) – to promote an understanding of multilingualism and complementary schools and to investigate the complexity of social aspects of multilingual interactions in complementary schools. The second question involves reflexivity and subjectivity on a more emotional level. The tension between being objective, scientific and 'naïve' and being a committed advocate for multilingualism and for complementary schools perturbs my relationships with the participants. Ethnography, as an ideological practice, presents a sort of reality over a fixed period of time. Ethnographers impose, wittingly or unwittingly, a coherence which may or may not be *the truth*. As a recognised member of the community we are searching and as a member of the research (or academic) community, I have to tread a cautious path. Also significant is the fact that my relationships with the participants are more enduring than those with my academic colleagues due to the fixed period of my contract with my employer(s); I cannot take the 'research and go' stance.

Because of my connection with a University, I am ascribed a high status by the participants. This is shown by special linguistic markers and by being invited to special occasions. I am also expected to give the benefit of my 'wisdom' to the school and to individual teachers. Thus the deputy at the school expects me to suggest improvement in curriculum, teaching methodology and recruitment of students. And, of course, after observations I am often approached for an 'appraisal' of the lesson. I play down both the status and expectations by asserting that I am 'only a researcher'. I use my 'insider' persona to build trust and my 'outsider' persona to keep my distance.

Negotiating a researcher identity: The boundaries between 'researcher' and 'community member' are not so much permeable as punctured and I decide where they overlap (or get punctured). This luxury is not, however, available vis-à- vis my academic colleagues. Here I have to establish and maintain my 'researcher' credentials through use of appropriate language and formality (though these, too, get blurred due to friendships built up during our last collaboration, particularly in the 'pair' situation). In the larger team setting, new but temporary (and pleasant!) friendships are being created but are constrained by the demands of the research routines. Also, I am seen as an 'expert' in some aspects of the research where my skills and expertise in a particular language are valued. In many ways, negotiating a research identity in the team and the pair is much easier because of the commonly agreed roles, parameters and well defined objectives of the project.

Overall, I feel that I am not only researching a community but also, to some extent, representing it.

At the beginning of Arvind's vignette, he poses two reflexive questions about his motivation for doing this research. Arvind has been involved, with others, for more than 20 years in trying to establish Asian and other minority languages in the (British) education system. For most of the time, Arvind sees this as a struggle against the prevailing winds of monolingualism and of power imbalances between European and Asian (or community) languages. So, the research allows him to do two things: to highlight the potential of community languages and of complementary schools and to take a relatively detached look at the dynamics of bi- and multilingualism in complementary schools. There is thus a tension, for Arvind, between commitment and detachment. Additionally, as a team member, he contributes his linguistic and cultural expertise and is aware of being seen as an 'expert' within the team. At team meetings and discussions, Arvind sometimes found himself cautioning his research colleagues against over-interpreting the data. For example, working as a teacher in both mainstream and complementary school contexts allowed Arvind to see consistencies in student behaviour across the two contexts. He is guarded against ascribing behaviour as exotic in complementary schools. Though complementary schools offer a unique blend of language and culture that is so different from the mainstream, Arvind notes that there are no differences in the two settings with having to deal with learners who are forging new identities for themselves. In the vignette, Arvind speaks of consciously using his fluid insider-outsider identities to 'protect' complementary schools from 'exoticism' or the stigma of being 'old fashioned'. But as a researcher, he also notes the fascination of the research process that he sees as a creative tension in his discussion with research team colleagues.

The engagement in the research raised by Arvind's account is on the political and personal level. There is a commitment to the politics of multilingualism as well as commitment to enduring relationships for those he studies and works with. He is aware of positioning himself as both an insider and outsider and he views this as an important skill in building trust and maintaining distance. His role as a university researcher accords him high status, but with his insiderness comes the responsibilities of giving back to those he researches. For Arvind, the university offers less freedom than the field. This is because in the university, roles are fixed and structures are in place, which allow little opportunity for negotiation. Time limited contracts militate against enduring relationships, for example. He is aware of how his cultural and linguistic knowledge is used by the team and sees the project as a way of representing a community as well as researching it.

Peter Martin, researcher Gujarati case study

Relationships to participants: In both sites in the Leicester/Gujarati project there was some link with previous research.[3] In School A (IES), the link was through the head teacher who was a teacher in a school in the previous ESRC complementary schools project. School B (JBV) was one of the schools from the previous project. Strangely enough, at the beginning of the current/recent fieldwork, I felt more comfortable in the 'new' school (IES) than in the one I had previously studied. This was a new endeavour, and the Head (KB) welcomed us with open arms. That is not to say that School B did not welcome us back, too. They did. And, in fact, the Senior Administrator (GB) of this School was particularly welcoming (more about this later), as was the Head Teacher and the other teachers with whom I have come in contact. But the bottom line for me is that I still can't get away from the feeling of being 'manipulative' (cf. Fraser, 1992) and feeling that my presence disrupts the flow of the school/classes which I observe. (For example, I feel uncomfortable when teachers, during the lesson, stop to explain something to me.) In School B particularly, where I had previously carried out fieldwork, I felt I was invading their space again. For this reason, in re-establishing contacts, I took pains to point out how the outcomes of the previous project had, in some small way, raised the profile of complementary schools in Leicester and beyond. Nevertheless, I did wonder whether some members of the school community wondered 'why have they come back'. To some extent, the actions of GB have allayed these fears in that, in an announcement to the school, he made quite a play of the fact that 'researchers from the University of East London have chosen our school' to do their research. The fact that it was a non-local university – that the researchers had come from afar to see their school – seemed to increase the status factor of the research. Also, and this has come to light subsequently, GB has plans – which he first aired to me in an interview 3 years ago, for his school to purchase a building and set up an Education Trust, which would network with academic and funding institutions (including research).

There are issues to do with use of languages which I would like to explore – though no space here. In any fieldwork I have been involved with I have tried to learn at least to greet people (and perhaps more) in the language of the community. However, there are issues due to the particular sociolinguistic context here, and the subtle use of mixtures of languages that have made me reassess this situation.

Negotiating a researcher identity: In my observations and thoughts about what is occurring in the sites (and I have noted this in the fieldnotes in this project and the previous one), I often make reference to 'wondering' whether the more linguistically and culturally sophisticated other (AB) agrees with my interpretation of what's going on. I also often feel frustrated at not being able to understand what is going on, and also the subtle nuances in the switches between languages. Some of the best quality interpretation came in the previous project in meetings between the researchers, debating what exactly was going on in the sites, with each researcher offering different viewpoints. These remain quite vivid discussions even three years later.

The intrusive role of ethnographic research is described in Peter's account. He refers to feeling manipulative in that, in returning to one school to carry out a new project, he is invading their space once again, and thus feels he is exploiting a trusted relationship. On the other hand, the overwhelmingly friendly welcome to both schools suggests that the feelings of being exploited were not felt by the participants in the schools. The need not to interfere, disrupt or take without paying back is apparent in the vignette. Peter makes reference to the success of the previous research and the way that the profile of complementary schools had been raised in Leicester. The report from the previous project (Martin *et al.*, 2004) had been widely disseminated and it was clear that both schools seemed proud to have been 'chosen' for further research. Peter's vignette shows an incremental commitment to those he has researched, with relationships developed in the first research project extended and developed in the second one. In many ways, there is a development of trust. There is an awareness too of how University status is used for negotiating access to the school research sites. Although both Peter and Arvind lived locally, the fact that they worked for a university some distance away seemed to increase the status of the project.

Peter's awareness of language and its cultural subtleties and his reliance on Arvind are also mentioned as significant in the vignette. Peter was frustrated by his lack of facility in Gujarati all the more so as in previous work in multilingual sites, he has had access to the languages of the communities he has worked with. Finally, his confidence in the interpretations of the full research team at the university is also significant. Discussions between the research team members allowed for different voices to be heard and different interpretations to emerge.

Discussion

Reading across these vignettes, there are two themes around positionality we would like to develop further below. They include: insider/outsider and language/culture.

Insiders and outsiders: Relations in the field

The researcher accounts show an interest in the subtleties of the insider/outsiders debate and acknowledge how feelings, attitudes and stances towards insider and outsider categories vary in the two different sites of research: the complementary school and the university, and even between schools. The vignettes show the fluidity of the insider/outsider categories as researchers engage with different participants and negotiate themselves and the project in relation to both research participants and the fuller team. Arvind, for example, speaks of needing to move in and out of insider and outsiders positions with research participants in order to bring closeness and maintain distance. He is aware of needing to perform particular identities in order to gain access. We hear of the importance of emotion, connection and long-term commitment to a community and a group of people. In contrast, Peter speaks of imposition, manipulation and feelings of discomfort and invasion. There is an expression of the need to 'payback' to those whose classrooms he is disrupting.

Insiders and outsiders: Relations in the team

A similar range of belonging and distance was expressed in terms of the other arena of practice, that of the university where the team came together to met around every five weeks. The purpose of full project meetings were generally two fold. Mornings were generally spent on business, while afternoons were spent on cross case study analysis and discussion of data. In their vignettes, we see Peter speak of his ease and interest in full research team meetings, while Arvind comments on transitory relationships and the structures and demands of the institution. We see two versions of full team meetings as a learning, open discursive space, but also as more fixed and hierarchical. Peter mentions the importance of the university meetings as a place to be critically reflective, listen to others and hear new interpretations. Arvind mentions the ongoing identity work of researcher performance. He recognises that this requires careful negotiation and caution, not only with the rest of the team, but also in representing the research participants. His caution is also with ethnography, which can still carry a tinge of 'us' and 'them'. His comments on 'fixed realitities in ethnography' point to the danger of over-interpreting data so that what is 'normal' for the community is represented as 'exotic'. Although there were points of disagreement on interpretation, discussions were frank and researchers were sufficiently trusting and confident with one another to treat differences with equanimity.

Language and Culture

A second theme that is salient in the two vignettes is the relevance of 'language and culture'. Arvind mentions how he is constructed by the team as expert in particular areas of language and culture. Peter speaks of Arvind as cultural expert and broker, who helps him understand elements of the research process. The vignettes show the complex role that language(s) played in the project, with researchers describing how both English and community languages are important in developing trust with research participants. The vignettes show the importance of language choice in shaping relations with those in the field.

Conclusion

Eisenhart (2001b) makes particular mention of collaborative research teams in meeting the challenges of conventional ethnography. She discusses the possibilities they offer for portraying internal tensions and inconsistencies as well as producing accurate, balanced, insightful and respectful ethnographic accounts. We do not suggest that team ethnography is the panacea for overcoming all the issues facing ethnography in the postmodern era. In fact, in many ways, this chapter raises more issues than it solves. Despite a broadly positive experience of doing team ethnography, we see that voices compete and contrast in describing the processes of constructing an ethnography. Where does this get us? In revealing the different perspectives of this team and how they compete and complement, engage and retreat, we believe we are able to represent different voices in our final accounts.

Eisenhart (2001b) has argued that conventional ethnography is not known for its attention to divisions, struggles or inconsistencies or for its scope or its mobility. She suggests that ethnographers will need to respond in two ways to new theoretical developments in the field of education and culture. According to Eisenhart (2001b: 22), ethnographers need to be 'pushed by theoretical and social currents to trace cultural forms "upward" and "outward" so as to consider how they are manifested and produced in networks of larger social systems'. In other words, in order to understand 'community' in contemporary life, we will need to trace relationships across time and space to understand how they are performed locally, but also shaped or controlled elsewhere. She goes on to argue that ethnographers are also likely to be 'pushed "downward" and "inward" to see how cultural forms become part of individual subjectivities or imaginations' (Eisenhart, 2001b: 22).

We believe that team ethnography and its attention to the different social, cultural and linguistic perspectives of team members offers possibilities to be pushed upward and inwards. A team of researchers offers different instantiations of micro experiences resulting in the production of divergent and overlapping views of the social order. A multilingual team, in particular, offers rich descriptions of how language and culture play a part in the construction of meanings and knowledge in the everyday practices of the field, and the university. The different multilingual perspectives also offer different voices through the individual reflexive accounts as well as different noticings and representations of research participants in the field.

In this chapter, we have shown that language is an important social marker, along with race, gender and social class, in the positionality of the researcher in the field. However, we agree with research that shows it is not a static marker that guarantees either insiderness or outsiderness. Rather, it is used agentively by the researcher to build trust and confidence with research participants. However, language is also social capital and social structure, which is used by all participants to include and exclude. We have shown the researcher aware of the value of language and how it positions players differently in the research process.

We have argued that in making the processes of meaning-making and representation explicit, we can demystify the processes of team ethnography. The multilingual and socially produced knowledges and skills of different team members increase the number of voices brought into the frame. Understanding how a multilingual research team builds relations with those they are researching in multilingual settings also opens up opportunities for dialogue and understanding between teacher, learner, parent and researcher.

The new dilemmas facing teachers in linguistically diverse classrooms are similar to those facing researchers. Both are grappling with better understandings and responses to the possibilities and complexities of difference and diversity. In this chapter, we have argued that bringing different voices and perspectives to understanding the processes of our multilingual schools and classrooms will produce more nuanced and richer accounts of classroom practices and their participants. This is necessary in what should be a symbiotic and productive relationship between educational research and educational practice.

Notes

1. The Economic Social Research Council is the UK's research funding council for the social sciences.
2. Complementary schools are voluntary schools and are outside the state's mandatory educational structures. They are also known as supplementary schools, heritage language schools, community language schools and ethnic schools. We use the term 'complementary schools' rather than the term 'supplementary schools' to stress the educational value these schools bring to their communities. We have argued that the latter term has connotations of deficit and educational failure.
3. See Martin *et al.* (2004).

References

Beaumont, M. and O'Brien, T. (eds) (2000) *Collaborative Research in Second Language Education.* Stoke on Trent: Trentham Books.

Blackledge, A. and Creese, A. (in press) *Multilingualism: A Critical Perspective.* London: Continuum.

Conteh, J., Kumar, R. and Beddow, D. (2008) Lining theory and practice in improving learning: Collaborative action research in multilingual primary classrooms. *Naldic Occasional Paper 21.* Luton: Naldic Publications.

Creese, A., Bhatt, A. and Martin, P. (2007a) *Investigating Multilingualism in Gujarati Complementary Schools in Leicester.* University of Birmingham. On WWW at http://www.esrcsocietytoday.ac.uk/esrcinfocentre/viewawardpage.aspx?awardnumber=RES-000-23-1180.

Creese, A., Blackledge, A. and Hamid, S. (2007b) *Investigating Multilingualism in Bengali Complementary Schools in Birmingham.* University of Birmingham. On WWW at http://www.esrcsocietytoday.ac.uk/esrcinfocentre/viewawardpage. aspx?awardnumber=RES-000-23-1180.

Creese, A., Lytra, V., Baraç, T. and Yağcıoğlu-Ali, D. (2007c) *Investigating Multilingualism in Turkish Complementary Schools in London.* University of Birmingham. On WWW at http://www.esrcsocietytoday.ac.uk/esrcinfocen tre/viewawardpage.aspx?awardnumber=RES-000-23-1180.

Creese, A., Wu, C-J. and Wei, L. (2007d) *Investigating Multilingualism in Chinese Complementary Schools in Manchester.* University of Birmingham. On WWW at http://www.esrcsocietytoday.ac.uk/esrcinfocentre/viewawardpage.aspx? awardnumber=RES-000-23-1180.

Creese, A., Baraç, T., Bhatt, A., Blackledge, A., Hamid, S., Li Wei, Lytra, V., Martin, P., Wu, C.J. and Yağcıoğlu-Ali, D. (2008a) *Investigating Multilingualism in Complementary Schools in Four Communities.* University of Birmingham. On WWW at http://www.esrcsocietytoday.ac.uk/esrcinfocentre/viewawardpage.aspx? award number=RES-000-23-1180.

Creese, A., Bhatt, A., Bhojani, N. and Martin, P. (2008b) Fieldnotes in team ethnography: Research complementary schools. *Qualitative Research* 8 (2), 223–242.

Denos, C., Toohey, K., Neilson, K. and Waterstone, B. (2009) *Collaborative Research in Multilingual Classrooms.* Bristol: Multilingual Matters.

Eisenhart, M. (2001a) Educational ethnography past, present and future: Ideas to think with. *Educational Researcher* 30 (8), 16–27.

Eisenhart, M. (2001b) Changing conceptions of culture and ethnographic methodology: Recent thematic shifts and their implications for research on teaching. In V. Richardson (ed.) *Handbook of Research on Teaching* (4th edn; pp. 209–225). Washington, DC: American Educational Research Association.

Erickson, K. and Stull, D. (1998) *Doing Team Ethnography: Warnings and Advice.* London: Sage.

Fraser, E. (1992) Talking about gender, race and class. In D. Cameron, E. Frazer, P. Harvet, M.B.H. Rampton and K. Richardson (eds) *Researching Language: Issues of Language and Power and Method* (pp. 90–112). London: Routledge.

Haraway, D. (1991) *Simians, Cyborgs and Women: The Reinvention of Nature.* New York: Routledge.

Hawkins, M. (2004) Becoming a student: Identity work and academic literacies in early schooling. *TESOL Quarterly* 39 (1), 60–82.

Hornberger, N.H. (2005) Introduction: Heritage/community language education: US and Australian perspectives. *International Journal of Bilingual Education and Bilingualism* 8, 101–108.

Martin, D., Stuart-Smith, J. and Dhesi, K.K. (1997) Insiders and Outsiders: Translating a Bilingual Research Project. Paper presented at the British Association of Applied Linguistics Annual Conference, September.

Martin, P., Creese, A., Bhatt, A. and Bhojani, N. (2004) Final report on complementary schools and their communities in Leicester. University of Leicester/University of Birmingham. Unpublished document. (ESRC R000223949.) On WWW at http://www.uel.ac.uk/education/staff/docu ments/complementery_schools.pdf.

McCorkel, J.A. and Myers, K. (2004) What difference does difference make? Position and privilege in the field. *Qualitative Sociology* 26 (2), 199–230.

Mullings, B. (1999) Insider or outsider, both or neither: Some dilemmas of interviewing in a cross-cultural setting. *Geoforum* 30 (4), 337–350.

Pratt, G. and Hanson, S. (1995) *Gender Work and Space*. London: Routledge.

Ramazanoglu, C. (1992) Methods of working as a research team: Women risk aids project: *Wrap Paper 3*. London: Tufnell Press.

Rampton, B., Tusting, K., Maybin, J., Barwell, R., Creese, A. and Lytra, V. (2004) UK linguistic ethnography: A discussion paper. Unpublished. On WWW at www.ling-ethnog.org.uk.

Romero, M. and Stewart, A. (eds) (1999) *Women's Untold Stories*. New York: Routledge.

Rosaldo, R. (1993) *Culture and Truth: The Remaking of Social Analysis*. Boston, MA: Beacon.

Shaffir, W.B. and Stebbins, R.A. (1991) *Experiencing Fieldwork*. Newbury Park: Sage.

Chapter 13

Negotiating Teacher-Researcher Collaboration in Immersion Education

DIANE DAGENAIS, DANIÈLE MOORE and CÉCILE SABATIER

Background

Immersion education and diverse classrooms

Although immersion programs have been lauded for developing bilingualism among students in Canada, recently there have been calls for such programs to expand beyond a focus on only two languages of instruction, namely French and English. Our research in French Immersion classrooms in Vancouver, Canada, revealed that languages other than French and English received only scant attention and that while multilingual immersion students engaged in a rich and varied repertoire of language practices at home, it was rarely used as a resource at school (Dagenais, 2008; Dagenais & Moore, 2008). Swain and Lapkin (2005) observed similarly that population shifts in Canada and elsewhere beg for a change in immersion pedagogy to more overtly recognize a range of home languages. They argued that principles of multilingual education must be applied to immersion programs in contexts of diversity, and that it is vital to introduce multiple languages in learning activities in order to support the development of bilingualism/multilingualism.

The Language Awareness Project

In response to this situation, we established an action-research project over three years with teams of researchers and teachers in Montreal and Vancouver, to explore whether language awareness activities might provide a forum for discussing language diversity.[1] The aim of the project was to enable elementary school students to examine a variety of languages (German, Arabic, First Nations languages, Chinese, Korean, Spanish, Greek, Italian, Japanese, Malay, Dutch, Portuguese, among others) in these activities and document how they co-constructed representations of languages, language speakers and language learning during their grades five and six academic years.

Since our work is focused on innovations in French language education, we turned to studies of language awareness activities designed for instruction in French. They are known collectively as *Éveil aux langues* through large-scale projects such as Eole (Perregaux *et al.*, 2003) and Evlang (Candelier, 2003; Sabatier, 2005). Several recent applications also draw on advances in research on multilingualism (Cenoz & Genesee, 1998; Coste, 2002; Martin-Jones & Jones, 2000) and developments in critical pedagogies (Fairclough, 1992; Norton & Toohey, 2004).

The school we worked with in Montreal provided instruction in French and the school in Vancouver provided instruction in both French and English in the context of a French Immersion program. This three-year action-research project expanded on a prior case study of language awareness in the same schools (Dagenais *et al.*, 2008). That study documented how such activities enabled students to recognize that they had a larger collective multilingual repertoire as a classroom community than merely school languages. As well, they learned how to draw on this repertoire as a basis for approaching new languages and develop metalinguistic awareness.

In Vancouver, the teachers whose classes formed our research sites and the research assistants, who were practicing teachers as well as graduate students, collaborated with university researchers and a university videoethnographer on developing, implementing and documenting language awareness activities and disseminating results in conferences and publication outlets. The Vancouver school is part of a large suburban school district in which 40% of the student population speaks a language other than English at home. However, in this particular school, only 7.5% of students are designated as learners of English as a second language. While most students speak English at home, some speak a language other than French or English.

The project built on cultures of collaboration already established at two levels; one between the schools and universities and the other between peer groups of researchers, teachers and students. Students attended to language diversity by examining the role of language in society and comparing the patterns of their own languages and other languages. They gathered information on monolingual, bilingual and multilingual signage in their communities, examined the visibility, use and status of different languages and considered stereotypes related to language contact (Dagenais *et al.*, 2008).

In this chapter, we draw on final interviews, conducted in French and translated into English here, with the two participating teachers, who have been given pseudonyms, to examine how the tensions between participant agendas were navigated during collaboration in the Vancouver site. We wished also to understand more about barriers and opportunities for innovation in language teaching in action-research projects based on school-university partnerships.

Theoretical Framework

Teacher-researcher collaboration

Over the last two decades, teacher research has emerged as a powerful approach to documenting the daily reality of teaching. In a North American context, Cochran-Smith and Lytle (1999) adopted a retrospective stance to examine the evolution of this type of research in the 1990s. They identified contexts in which teacher research was adopted and described different conceptual frameworks that underpinned it, such as teacher education programs, professional development activities and school change initiatives. Collaborations in these contexts gave rise to a new understanding of teachers' multilayered roles in research and educational change as decision makers, consultants, curriculum developers, analysts, activists and school leaders. Three frameworks that oriented teacher research included social inquiry, ways of knowing in communities and practical inquiry. The social inquiry framework is based on critical theory and focuses on transformation through action-research aimed at equity and democracy. The ways of knowing framework centers on research as a form of agency for change and the generation of local knowledge from grassroots perspectives. It emphasizes collaborations that blur the boundaries between research and practice activities and alter the relations of power between researchers, teachers and students. The practical inquiry framework concentrates on reflective practice and draws, in particular, on Clandinin and Connolly's (1995) notion of 'professional knowledge landscapes' to situate the contexts of teachers' stories and interpretations of practice.

In addition, Cochran-Smith and Lytle (1999: 22) took a prospective stance to suggest that in the first decade of the 21st century, teacher research would emphasize the idea of 'teacher as knower and agent for change that... affirms a commitment deeply felt by many who are involved in the educational enterprise'. They highlighted challenges that face those involved in this kind of work in light of recent neo-liberal agendas focused on standards and accountability, wondering, how to reconcile the idea of co-construction of knowledge by teachers and their students with the current move toward increasingly specified curriculum frameworks, how to hold on to the larger goals of democratic education in the face of intense pressure to evaluate success based on students' performance on high-stakes tests, and how to support communities of teachers working together on the questions that matter to them in light of mandates at many levels to collaborate on the implementation of system policies. (Cochran-Smith & Lytle, 1999: 22)

We have taken on this challenge in our teacher-researcher collaboration on new initiatives in immersion pedagogy, to engage students with a broader range of languages beyond Canada's two official languages. While pushing back against the narrow focus of the curriculum, we examined its language carefully to see where it might allow teachers to justify their innovative practices in terms of program and policy objectives related to education about diversity, multiculturalism and anti-racism in a democratic society.

In this sense, our work is in keeping with other teacher-researcher collaborations that sustain extended dialogue and close partnerships across professional groups to develop equitable classroom practices (Cochran-Smith & Lytle, 1999; Connelly & Clandinin, 1995; Dagenais *et al.*, 2008; Day, 2004; Norton & Toohey, 2004; Rogers *et al.*, 2006). We assumed that each participant and group of professionals would bring to our teacher-researcher collaboration diverse perspectives that emerged from different institutional cultures, professional traditions, personal ancestries and experiences with diversity. We also expected to move beyond traditional boundaries between schools and universities and disrupt established comfort zones as we negotiated our relationships.

We understand educational collaboration to be a 'a process in which two or more individuals work together to integrate information in order to enhance student learning' (Jenni & Mauriel, 2004, cited in Montiel-Overall, 2005, np) and more broadly, the collaborative partnership as a

> shared creation [in which] two or more individuals with complementary skills interact to create a shared understanding that none had previously possessed or could have come to on their own. Collaboration creates a shared meaning about a process, a product, or an event. (Schrage, 1990: 40–41)

Moreover, whereas Wells and Chang-Wells (1992: 14) define 'collaborative research as a mode for professional development for teachers', we argue that it is a form of professional development for researchers as well. For example, our analysis of interviews that were conducted in the second and third year of the project with our teacher partners led us to reconsider and reconceptualize our own roles in such partnerships. New insights we gained from the first round of fieldwork and interviews enabled us to acknowledge that our prior understanding of how language awareness was implemented elsewhere was based on assumptions that did not necessarily apply to this particular context and that we needed to be ever more sensitive to our school partners' priorities and frames of reference.

Agents of social change

Central to our project is the notion of teachers and researchers as agents of social change who examine classrooms from their variously informed perspectives. For Freeman (1998), engaging teachers in researching their own practice is a political activity, since it positions them as insiders and empowers them as experts about their workplace, while also serving a functional purpose to generate new understandings and knowledge from the inside out. While Freeman focused on teachers examining their own work, our research on classroom practice involved close collaboration across institutions and professional affiliations. In this way, we sought to bridge the gap between school and university by drawing on our relative distance and proximity to practice and theory, and on the emic and etic perspectives that we applied to our analysis of classroom life at different stages in the process of collaboration.

Referring to recent advances in theories of organizations, in particular the concept of the butterfly effect that has emerged in chaos theory and research on educational change (Fullan, 2003; Morgan, 1999), we conceptualize innovation in education as a shift in the smaller spaces of daily work through grassroots partnerships. We understand this can lead to a broader restructuring of relationships across institutions, as social actors mobilize to militate for changes in pedagogy, curriculum documents and policy discourse. This perspective on change is similar to the one adopted in Casey's (1993) study of women teachers who committed to political activity by engaging in social change on a daily basis in their classrooms and communities. Casey signaled how this commitment involved them in terrains of political struggle related to issues of language and personal identity. Similarly, participation in our project brought to the fore tensions around differences in the ways we understood language education and our roles as actors engaged in educational research and change.

Integrating diverse perspectives on change

Drawing on the sociology of organizations, Sainsaulieu (1987) proposed a theory of institutional change that understands professional affiliations in the workplace to be heterogeneous. He suggests that research on change closely examines the cultural dynamics in place when diverse groups are confronted by their differences as they interact during the change process. Moreover, he emphasizes how professional identities and group affiliations are constructed and shaped according to the way people perceive their reality and their own position in the social structure.

During change processes, groups tend to affirm the original boundaries of their affiliations, relying on them to make their positions known and to defend their interests. In the context of inter-institutional collaboration and multiple professional identities, differences are made evident, leading to the confrontation of organizational cultures and individual perspectives (Dagenais, 2000).

According to Sainsaulieu (1987), the confrontation of differences is resolved in two ways: either the perspectives of diverse groups become a source of conflict and differences are reaffirmed as participants withdraw from interaction; or their differences become the object of negotiation and are transformed through collaboration and extended discussion. In the first case, the status quo is reproduced, and in the second case, change becomes possible.

Negotiating Change

Participant stances

The researchers thus brought to the project a political agenda for change based on their knowledge of theoretical developments in the field of language education, an understanding of action-research as a form of educational transformation, and experience with other innovations in language awareness pedagogy. Our initial project also drew on Norton and Toohey (2004), who suggested that critical pedagogies focus on language education as a means of pursuing equity. It also referenced Pennycook (1999), who proposed that a critical educational stance means connecting language to broader political contexts and ethical concerns with issues of inequality, oppression and compassion. Thus, in every phase of the project, some of our discussions involved clarifying what was meant by redistributing power relationships between researchers, teachers and children as we sought to understand the links between critical pedagogies and language awareness activities that would enable students: (1) to become aware of the unequal values attributed to diverse languages and their speakers; (2) to modify their linguistic representations; (3) to take ownership of their learning; in order to (4) question and act upon social inequalities (Fairclough, 1992, as cited in our initial project proposal submitted to the funding agency, September, 2004, translated from French).

France, the grade six teacher, had as her political agenda to change the status quo of immersion practice by integrating a study of family and community languages in classroom activities. Her aim was to allow for more small-group interaction among students, based on her prior experience as a research assistant in the earlier case study of language awareness, which was the focus of her master's thesis research.

> **France:** Yes that's it. [One of the researchers] taught me a few master's level courses... we had looked at language awareness approaches... it would be a good theme for my master's thesis and since I already found it interesting and read a lot on that and it became central to my research project... and we implemented language awareness activities in my class for a year... so that I lived with language awareness for two and half years and diving into that again interested me even after finishing my master's project... (Interview excerpt, 27 February 2008)

The agenda of Paule, the grade five teacher, was to expand her own practice by adopting language awareness activities after observing her colleagues' classroom innovations in the earlier project. At that time, her son had been a student in her colleague's class and she had noticed that he was interested in the language awareness activities, which further stimulated her curiosity and led her to participate in this project.

> **Paule:** Actually, at the beginning... I had an opportunity to follow an in-service program in French education and [one of the researchers] came for an hour, an hour and a half to talk precisely about the concept of language awareness... and it drew my attention, but not in a way where I could see that... it could necessarily be used in my classroom, but simply because it is a new concept used in Canada. Knowing France, who is my colleague... who used it, in fact who implemented, with her master's, in her classroom... I was more and more curious to see the impact it could have. And how mostly we could apply it throughout the curriculum we already teach. And I had the opportunity to have my son, who was in France's class, who would

talk about the activities that sometimes took place in the classroom. I found it very interesting. (Interview excerpt, 26 June 2007)

Whereas France's discourse indicates that she had a long-term commitment to engaging in language awareness activities and research in this area, Paule's discourse evokes how the opportunity to participate in language awareness was serendipitous in the sense that she had heard about this approach through various sources: a workshop, her colleague and her son. Paule's interest in language awareness was also that it could potentially be integrated in the established curriculum. Thus, each teacher embarked on the project with different background knowledge, interests and expertise in language awareness. This had an impact on their engagement with the team. Whereas France chose to work on developing activities with the research assistants over the summer, Paule positioned herself such that she asked to have activities developed by the research assistants and then found that she was left to make sense of them as she read over them before lessons.

France: It is interesting to work on a research project... in the beginning I didn't think about working on the preparation of the project itself I thought only about teaching the lesson in my class, but finally since I had the opportunity to work in the summer on the development of lessons, that I really liked because I felt like the lessons belonged to me, that I knew them, that I was teaching something I felt like teaching rather than taking something that was given by someone else. So that is why I became involved... (Interview excerpt, 27 February 2008)

Paule: I had to get into it... when you are not the one who constructs an activity... you try to read the activity that someone else constructed... you try to read an activity... you try to respond to expectations... I tried sometimes to understand the message. In general, it was very, very, very well explained, but I had to read over two or three times. And... the girls [the research assistants] were extraordinary also regarding their help. The material was already all well prepared, so it was very good for me. But on the other hand... on students' responses were always different than what I expected. That was really interesting. (Interview excerpt, 26 June 2007)

On the one hand, France emphasizes her partnership with project members to develop activities, which led her to feel like an equal member of the research team with ownership over the projects' orientation. This enabled her to establish greater agency in the collaboration. On the other hand, Paule highlights the difficult, more passive position she found herself in when her decision to have activities developed by others disempowered her somewhat since she could not shape the direction of lessons or gain more agency in classroom innovations. This is reminiscent of a more traditional and vertical model of curricular change that conceptualizes innovation as developed by external agents, such as university researchers, and implemented by local teachers who are required to reproduce change as conceived by others.

While the point of departure in an action-research project in classroom innovations in language awareness may at the outset appear clear in a proposal, the enacted curriculum is determined rather by the constraints and the reality of classroom life. This has been documented in Candelier (2003) as follows:

> The path that has led us successively from a projected, hypothetical curriculum, to one that is enacted in classrooms... enables us first to define the multiple constraints that weigh on all reflections about elaborating a sort of ideal language awareness curriculum. (Candelier, 2003: 298–299, our translation)

Confronting differences

The confrontation of differences, though difficult at times, was rewarding in many respects. It forced us to continually renegotiate our respective understandings of the process and content of change (Fullan, 2003), communicate what were the constraints of our own professional contexts, clarify what were our respective criteria of credibility, readjust our mutual expectations and co-construct a shared path for challenging the status quo. As we indicate below, our different frameworks and work orientations emerged in discussions about our concerns related to the micro-level of social interactions, such as exchanges between students and teachers, as well as those between teachers and researchers. They also emerged in discussions related to the macro-level of policy frameworks.

For example, when discussing the micro-level of classroom interactions, the researchers took the stance in writing the initial project proposal that multilingualism enriches society and that children's multilingual repertoires must be included in immersion activities as valuable tools for knowledge construction. The researchers' perspective on teaching was informed largely by literature and research in the area as well as their experiences working with pre-service and in-service teachers. They referred to Cummins (1996), who has argued that the way in which teachers define their professional roles directly impacts their relationships with children of diverse language origins, which can affect students' academic progress in school. The researchers also assumed that the relationships that teachers establish with multilingual students and their pedagogical approaches are closely linked to their views of language as a problem, a right or a resource (Riuz, cited in Baker, 1993).

However, French Immersion teachers generally tend to describe their mandate in terms of creating a Francophone space in their classrooms and resisting the overwhelming presence of English in the larger community. For the teachers, becoming involved in this project meant repositioning themselves in their stance on classroom interactions as supporters of using multiple languages in student-teacher exchanges, including English, to negotiate meanings and make comparisons across languages. This went against the grain of the traditional exclusion of family languages and teacher-imposed sanctions for using English in some immersion classrooms. For example, in an activity that required students to take photographs of bilingual/multilingual signage in their communities, students took pictures in groups (Dagenais *et al.*, 2008). In front of an automatic teller that presents texts in English, French and Chinese, they negotiated in English what to capture in their picture and then switched back to French to continue the activity. This type of code-switching, though often not tolerated in immersion classrooms, was accepted by the teachers participating in this project. In examining the macro-context of education, teachers and researchers discussed how language awareness activities related to Canadian policy discourse. The researchers were concerned about implicit contradictions in policy discourse that established a hierarchy of languages through official language policy, which enables the state and schools to privilege French and English over other languages as a legitimate means of communication at school. However, policies of multiculturalism and intercultural education that orient educational practice in the country are based on the notion of the equality of all citizens, regardless of cultural, religious or linguistic origins. The teachers were concerned that the activities and curriculum materials developed in the project should reflect provincial curriculum orientations related both to policies of official languages and multiculturalism.

Negotiating change

At one level, the team members negotiated the content of change (activities developed) and at another level, we had to negotiate the process of change (how activities were implemented), as well as what counted as knowledge (expected learning outcomes). For instance, Paule's primary pre-occupation at the beginning of the project was to ensure that it did not disrupt her from her regular curriculum agenda, that is, what and how she planned to teach that year. She also wanted to ensure that what the students learned could be justified in terms of the mandated curriculum.

> **Paule:** Well, it was mainly for me, it was how could we integrate this concept [language awareness] throughout the curriculum that we already had in the classroom. And I could say, in all honesty, that I was very skeptical... to be able to try to create activities that would fit and not cause a surplus of work... in addition to all the subjects that we teach. (Interview excerpt, 26 June 2007)

Participation in an innovative project of this nature necessarily involves extra work for those involved and participants must come to an agreement as to what are the mutual expectations, commitments and workloads. As indicated in this excerpt, tensions arose particularly at the beginning of this project as members tried to make sense of what they were doing. Whereas the researchers were guided by a philosophical and ethical change agenda based on research and theory, Paule was guided by her professional responsibility to ensure that she respected the mandated curriculum. These asymmetries were, to some degree, resolved through extended dialogue, as well as shared moments of planning and debriefing where our perspectives shifted back and forth. They were also addressed inadvertently as we moved the location of our meetings, alternating between the university, the school and the homes of one of the teachers who had young children, the researchers' homes and cafes near the school to debrief and eat together. These conversations and shifting locations recognized our multiples roles and identities as women and professionals, facilitating movements across boundaries in the positions team members took up at different times in the project. As the following excerpt illustrates, one of the teachers assumed the role of a researcher as she interviewed her colleague at the end of the school year.

> **Interviewer (France):** That's it! How did you experience the presence of researchers in your classroom? The fact that you were tape-recorded, that you were filmed, that they were IN your class/
>
> **Paule:** In the beginning it intimidated me a lot... a lot... but they were so nice... they put me at ease. Often, in fact, the camera was not turned on me. When I gave instructions, I was so... I wanted so much to do well at the level of my instructions [laughs] that the

camera didn't bother me at all. I didn't see it. And when the children worked together, I didn't exist anymore, it was really the children, the camera was turned on them. And for the person who was taking fieldnotes, I never had visual contact with the person, very discreet, she took notes. Even, I had a right to the notes afterwards, so I found that it was very open. (Interview excerpt, 26 June 2007)

In this excerpt, Paule reveals that at first, she positioned herself as someone who was being evaluated by outsiders and that she later began to understand that she was an equal partner in action-research who had valuable expertise to contribute to the orientation of the project and the implementation of activities. When she realized that the focus was not only on her, but that it was on the students and the social interactions as well, she began to relax and engage more as a co-investigator to examine reflexively what happened in the classroom as she read field notes and watched the videotapes.

> **Paule:** And usually that was all. Yes, yes. It happened at the very beginning when the team was larger... there was a moment where I felt that they needed to talk to me... to... and what was interesting, because they showed me some videos, some moments. And then we paused and there we said: "well, there should I have intervened? Or what should I do? Should I let them talk"... So, it was good for me to see myself... It was good and not so good. But... it made me readjust. (Interview excerpt, 26 June 2007)

In the end, the camera lens was not only a research tool, but it also became a useful professional development tool for Paule. As she reviewed video excerpts, she began to question her practice and seek new ways of interacting with her students during language awareness lessons.

France and Paule were not the only ones to shift positions at different moments in the research. The videoethnographer participated in team meetings as a full project member as well. Despite the fact that she did not speak French, throughout the project, she shared not only her technical expertise, but also her understanding of classroom processes based on her extended participation in several ongoing research projects over many years. In addition, she contributed her knowledge as a parent of French Immersion students. The researchers' stances also shifted as the project progressed and the collaboration developed. Unfortunately, we did not systematically audiotape all our meetings in which we sometimes engaged in heated debates about what to do and what roles to adopt, so the interviews with teachers are the only data we have available to analyze here. We recognize now how useful it would be to audiotape all meetings throughout the life of a project in order to document how engaging in collaboration changes peoples' relationships with one another and their positions in the group.

Tensions also arose over our understanding that language awareness activities are integrated throughout the curriculum and not limited to one particular lesson. As well, the budget of the project limited us to having the videoethnographer film the classroom interactions only once a week at a pre-determined time: 'Linda came to film once a week but you know I was doing other [language awareness] activities aside from that' (Interview with France, 27 February 2008). Eventually, in the last year of the project, we countered this difficulty by leaving a video camera and audio recorders with the teacher and children so they could film themselves whenever they engaged in activities related to language awareness. However, tensions between our ideals about what we hoped to accomplish and the limits of time constraints were never completely resolved, as France reveals:

> **France:** Well for sure I wasn't able to do everything I wanted to do there were activities that I had to drop because I had no more time. We planned activities for Wednesdays when the team came in other words when Linda was there and the members of the team came to observe... we lacked time I needed to teach science, social studies, mathematics there were interruptions at school with assemblies and special presentations and all that. (Interview excerpt, 27 February 2008)

In this project, teachers felt keenly the pressure of time in a very demanding curriculum framework and a busy school schedule, so that they tried constantly to grapple with how to link language awareness activities with what was already expected of them.

At another level, the students accepted the presence of the research team in their classroom space and began to engage as co-investigators in the project by taking photographs of the local multilingual signage in the community as part of the language awareness activities. The data they gathered determined the content of subsequent activities (Dagenais *et al.*, 2008). As well, they took responsibility for documenting the date and the name of the participants who were recorded in audiotapes; they checked the functioning of audio and video equipment and they audiotaped and filmed themselves. As their role in the project was negotiated, they were empowered to take responsibility as agents of transformation in the classroom and in their communities in their own right.

> **Paule:** And I think that, that had an impact on the students... after having done the project... I think that they are now more observant about what surrounds them in the community. (Interview excerpt, 26 June 2007)

Participation in this innovation led students to observe their communities differently according to teachers and it also led them to view their students differently:

> **France:** Yes well especially a few years ago when I did this with my students the first time it really changed my way of seeing learning and really the notion of co-construction and of collaboration was really strong. I told myself it was really something that I needed to develop elsewhere than just in language awareness. I need to give children a chance to collaborate between themselves, to help each other. And also what is interesting is to see sometimes, I let the children place themselves in pairs and there were two who were not strong who placed themselves together. Even though they were both weak, they were able do something so much better than when they are both in isolation. Added together, that enabled me to see them, to discover this with them. (Interview excerpt, 27 February 2008)

In this excerpt, France reveals that collaborative practices she established with students in language awareness activities allowed her to see the powerful impact they have on improving students' capacity to learn. As well, it enabled her to envision how collaboration between learners might be supported in other areas of the curriculum.

> **Paule:** Well, actually, it brought me back to the beginning of my teaching career. Because I saw again, actually, that children still need to work cooperatively. And I think that with the years of experience that I have and with the number of subjects that we need to teach, the teacher-led lesson always remains the easiest and I think we forget still too often that children among themselves it's incredible how much they can help each other and... I think that that... reminded me that I needed to make a change myself that I turn to the past a little to as I was in my first years of teaching. And to have patience and to give children the time to work together more. (Interview excerpt, 26 June 2007)

As Paule indicates, participation in this innovative project reminded her of practices she had adopted at the beginning of her career, but later dropped. She now saw the value of returning to practices that allowed students to collaborate and empowered them in co-constructing knowledge together.

Finally, participation in the project and engagement in a collaborative and reflexive process led to another interrogation about the lasting impact of pedagogical change and raised a question as to whether participants are ready to continue with the innovation afterward, given the constraints of the situation that do not necessarily change. For example, as both teachers noted, the required curriculum and school-wide activities present considerable challenges for teachers who wish to innovate and change the status quo.

> **Paule:** It would require a change. Am I ready for a change after so many years of teaching? Probably if I left some things behind, yes. But I couldn't add more right now, that I know. But if some activities such as these ones arrive already made? It's perfect. But for me to have to construct activities to be able to respond to certain objectives? I don't think I would have the time. (Interview excerpt, 26 June 2007)

Conclusion: Co-constructing a Shared Understanding

Though we embarked on this collaborative classroom innovation based on prior research and an articulated vision in an initial research proposal, our pre-conceptions were reshaped as we made sense of the content and process of educational change and stasis in relation to our interactions, extended conversations and ongoing feedback to one another throughout the project.

The feedback reflected each member's own issues, concerns and urgencies that differed according to the centrality of the research in her own professional universe. Having agreed on the principle of working with a plurality of languages, our team needed to learn to work with a plurality of professional and individual perspectives and priorities.

This led us to renegotiate our boundaries in our relationship with one another as teachers and researchers. As we shifted the spaces of our work and moved out of established comfort zones, as teachers and researchers, we engaged in a back and forth movement at two levels: (1) in the exploration of possibilities between official policy, curriculum documents and innovative practices; (2) in disrupting the traditional role boundaries of teacher and researcher work. Our professional identities were reshaped while each member of the team shifted her gaze between research and practice concerns, etic and emic perspectives, at different degrees at varying times in the process of collaboration. As our discussion of final teacher interviews indicates, thinking about our respective roles in the project led us to engage in a heuristic analysis of our collective action and co-constructed a pedagogy of diversity (Allemann-Ghionda *et al.*, 1999).

These shifting spaces of negotiation in collaborative efforts open opportunities not only to reconfigure the enacted curriculum, but also to concretely demonstrate to policy makers how immersion pedagogy, official curriculum and educational policy might expand beyond bilingualism to include societal multilingualism and multilingual repertoires in classrooms.

Note

1. This longitudinal study, Éveil aux langues et à la diversité linguistique chez des élèves du primaire dans deux métropoles canadiennes, was supported by a standard grant from the Social Sciences and Humanities Research Council of Canada awarded to Dagenais, Armand, Lamarre, Moore and Sabatier, 2005–2008. We are grateful to students and teachers who welcomed us in their classrooms and collaborated closely on this project. We recognize as well the invaluable work of our research assistants Mary-Lou McCarthy, Brooke Douglas, Kelly Evans and Emmanuelle Gauthier.

References

Allemann-Ghionda, C., de Goumoëns, C. and Perregaux, C. (1999) *Pluralité Linguistique et Culturelle dans la Formation des Enseignants*. Fribourg, Switzerland: Editions Universitaires Fribourg Suisse.

Baker, C. (1993) *Foundations of Bilingual Education and Bilingualism*. Clevedon: Multilingual Matters.

Candelier, M. (ed.) (2003) *L'éveil aux Langues à l'École primaire. Evlang: Bilan d'une innovation européenne*. Brussels: De Boek.

Casey, K. (1993) *I Answer with My Life: Life Histories of Women Teachers Working for Social Change*. New York: Routledge.

Cenoz, J. and Genesee, F. (1998) (eds) *Beyond Bilingualism: Multilingualism and Multilingual Education*. Clevedon: Multilingual Matters.

Clandinin, D. and Connolly, F. (1995) Teachers' professional knowledge landscapes: Secret, sacred, and cover stories. In F. Connolly and D. Clandinin (eds) *Teachers' Professional Knowledge Landscapes* (pp. 1–15). New York: Teachers College Press.

Cochran-Smith, M. and Lytle, S. (1999) The teacher research movement: A decade later. *Educational Researcher* 28, 15–25.

Coste, D. (2002) Compétence à communiquer et compétence plurilingue. *Notions en Questions* 6, 115–123.

Cummins, J. (1996) *Negotiating Identities: Education for Empowerment in a Diverse Society.* Ontario: California Association for Bilingual Education.

Dagenais, D. (2000) La représentation des rôles dans un projet de collaboration inter-institutionnelle. *La Revue des Sciences de l'Éducation* 26 (2), 415–438.

Dagenais, D. (2008) Developing a critical awareness of language diversity in immersion. In T. Fortune and D. Tedick (eds) *Pathways to Bilingualism and Multilingualism: Evolving Perspectives on Immersion Education* (pp. 201–220). Clevedon: Multilingual Matters.

Dagenais, D., Armand, F., Maraillet, E. and Walsh, N. (2008) Collaboration and co-construction of knowledge during language awareness activities in Canadian elementary school. *Language Awareness.* On WWW at http://www.multilingual-matters.net/la/AoP/default.htm.

Dagenais, D., Beynon, J. and Mathis, N. (2008) Intersections of social cohesion, education and identity. *Pedagogies: An International Journal* 3, 1–24.

Dagenais, D. and Moore, D. (2008) Représentations des littératies plurilingues, de l'immersion en français et des dynamiques identitaires chez des parents chinois. *Canadian Modern Language Review* 65 (1), 11–32.

Dagenais, D., Moore, D., Sabatier, C., Lamarre, L. and Armand, F. (2008) Linguistic landscape and language awareness. In E. Shohamy and D. Gorter (eds) *Linguistic Landscape: Expanding the Scenery* (pp. 253–269). New York: Routledge/Taylor and Francis Group.

Day, C. (2004) Change agendas: The roles of teacher educators. *Teaching Education* 15 (2), 145–158.

Fairclough, N. (1992) *Critical Language Awareness.* New York: Longman.

Freeman, D. (1998) How to see: The challenges of integrating teaching and research in your own classroom. *The English Connection* 2 (5), 1–8.

Fullan, F. (2003) *Change Forces with a Vengeance.* New York: Routledge.

Jenni, R.W. and Mauriel, J. (2004) Cooperation and collaboration: Reality or rhetoric? *International Journal of Leadership in Education Theory and Practice* 7 (2), 181–195.

Martin-Jones, M. and Jones, K. (2000) *Multilingual Literacies.* Philadelphia, PA: John Benjamins.

Montiel Overall, P. (2005) Toward a theory of collaboration for teachers and librarians. *School Library Media Research*, 8. On WWW at http://www.ala.org/ala/aasl/aaslpubsandjournals/slmrb/slmrcontents/volume82005/theory.cfm. Accessed 12.6.08.

Morgan, G. (1999) *Images de l'Organisation.* Québec: Les Presses de l'Université Laval.

Norton, B. and Toohey, K. (2004) *Critical Pedagogies and Language Learning.* Cambridge: Cambridge University Press.

Pennycook, A. (1999) Introduction: Critical approaches to TESOL. *TESOL Quarterly* 33 (3), 329–348.

Perregaux, C., de Goumoëns, C., Jeannot, D. and de Pietro, J-F. (eds) (2003) *Éducation et Ouverture aux Langues à l'École.* Neuchâtel, Switzerland: CIIP.

Rogers, T., Marshall, E. and Tyson, C. (2006) Dialogic narratives of literacy, teaching, and schooling: Preparing literacy teachers for diverse settings. *Reading Research Quarterly* 41 (2), 202–224.

Sabatier, C. (2005) *Rôle de l'Ecole dans la Construction et le Développement du Plurilinguisme Chez des Enfants Issus de la Migration Maghrébine en France*. Lille: ANTR.

Sainsaulieu, R. (1987) *Sociologie de l'Organisation et de l'Entreprise*. Paris: Presses FNSP.

Schrage, M. (1990) *Shared Minds: The New Technologies of Collaboration*. New York: Random House.

Swain, M. and Lapkin, S. (2005) The evolving sociopolitical context of immersion education in Canada: Some implications for program development. *International Journal of Applied Linguistics* 15 (2), 169–186.

Wells, G. and Chang-Wells, J. (1992) *Constructing Knowledge Together: Classrooms as Centers of Inquiry and Literacy*. Portsmouth, NH: Heinemann.

Chapter 14

Languages in the Classroom: Institutional Discourses and Users' Experiences

HANNELE DUFVA and OLLI-PEKKA SALO

Introduction: Languages as Objects of Learning and Teaching

In this chapter, we will discuss language education, drawing theoretically on the work of the Bakhtin Circle and contemporary authors who have discussed dialogism in relation to language learning and teaching research (see Hall *et al.*, 2005; Ball & Freedman, 2004). We focus on the language learners' and teachers' conceptualizations of language and suggest that different, open-ended ways of studying the experienced aspects of the language learning process (see also Breen, 2001; Benson & Nunan, 2004) are important research tools. Furthermore, we argue that tasks and activities that elicit learners' beliefs are also important as pedagogical tools. We briefly survey research on beliefs about languages, which has been carried out in the context of Finland in different projects by our colleagues and ourselves. We are currently involved in a research project, studying language learning and language teaching while drawing on the dialogical philosophy of language.[1] In addition to this project, we also draw in this chapter on findings from a study of foreign language teachers' life stories (Kalaja *et al.*, 1998), a project in which Finnish children's metalinguistic awareness and its relation with foreign language learning was explored (Dufva & Alanen, 2005; Aro, 2004), and an on-going study of how university students of foreign languages develop as language professionals (Kalaja *et al.*, 2008). The terms 'conceptualization' and 'belief' are used here as near-synonyms – shorthand expressions for all kinds of personal knowledge the language users have about language – ranging from 'myths' and 'attitudes' to 'academic knowledge' and 'scientific theories'.

First, we argue that the theory of language that is present in the works of Bakhtin and Voloshinov (for a discussion of the Bakhtin Circle, see Brandist, 2002) is particularly relevant to the field of language education because it provides a meta-theoretical framework that is directly concerned with real-life language use and suggests certain pedagogical solutions (see, particularly, Bakhtin, 2004). The theoretical commitments and arguments that seem most appropriate for the theory and practice of language education include:

(1) Bakhtin's view of language as heteroglossic (rather than invariable and static);
(2) a functionalist stand (rather than a formalist one);
(3) the insistence that it is concrete language use that should be analyzed by linguists (rather than the alleged invariance at the underlying level);
(4) a view of language as dynamic eventing (rather than as a set of static objects) (see e.g. Lähteenmäki, 1998, 2001, 2003).

These arguments have also been brought forward in the theory of language education to illustrate the fact that language learning is a process of socialization, influenced in a situated fashion by various social and cultural factors that on the one hand, provide affordances and resources, but on the other hand, also set constraints (see e.g. Kramsch, 2002; van Lier, 2004; Lantolf & Thorne, 2006).

The linguistic argumentation of the dialogists points also to a view where languages are regarded as culturally and historically situated *social and political entities* that consist of on-going and constantly varying situated practices and actions. In that, dialogism offers an alternative to the asocial and, therefore, abstract and decontextualized representations of language that have been typical of, for example, the mainstream tradition in linguistics and, also, in second language acquisition (SLA) research. Within SLA, languages have often been named anonymously as L1, L2 or L3, a conceptualization that seems to suggest that languages are autonomous, abstract and neutral codes that can be internalized in succession, in a process where social and cultural factors are not important. While not rejecting the view that there are features in the process of language learning that are not language-specific and that may even be universal, we wish to point out that it is important to pay more attention to what particular languages ('Finnish', 'German', 'French') are involved as mother tongues and additional languages, and in what kind of social milieu the language learning occurs. Equally, it is relevant to examine how the languages are subjectively experienced by learners and teachers, i.e. what kind of conceptualizations are involved.

In recent years, the studies of first, second and foreign language development have experienced an increase in socially oriented research. This research has shown how important such questions as interaction, social participation, identity issues and social networking are for language learners (for a review of 'social turn', see Block, 2003). Acknowledging the importance – and also the primacy – of social considerations, we nevertheless wish to point out that the experienced, phenomenal aspects of language learning and teaching need to be accounted for. Indeed, they seem to be highly important for the learning process – as they obviously can have an effect on, for example, learners' motivation – and, therefore, are also pedagogically relevant.

The dialogical approach to language learning not only focuses on the social plane of interaction, but also includes a socio-cognitive plane of individuals involved. As Voloshinov (1973, 1976) suggests, the social uses of language are turned into individual ways of speaking (and thinking) in a reciprocally determined process of semiosis. Thus, from the point of view of learning and teaching, it is important to consider how the languages in question are positioned in the social field of legislation and policy making, how they are represented in various institutional documents, such as language curricula, and how they are conceived by people in their everyday life. It is almost self-evident that all these official representations set constraints in a very direct fashion on how languages are practiced, talked about and perceived by people. However, in addition, the discourses of a more informal kind – those expressed as 'opinions' in the media, on websites and in everyday talk – mediate views and perspectives that may be equally powerful though less institutional.

Our own focus foregrounds the analysis of unofficial beliefs about language. In this analysis, we wish to underline the *multi-voiced* nature of beliefs. As knowing emerges in the processes where a person participates in the socially available discourses that appear in various contexts of talk and written texts, and as language use at the social level is always heteroglossic (Bakhtin, 1986), it follows that beliefs are multi-voiced, both inter-individually and intra-individually (for a more detailed argument, see Dufva, 2003). Thus, any actual classroom situation where languages are taught and learned is an ensemble of different voices, echoing a variety of conceptualizations where professional and academic knowledge of language exist along the multiplicity of mundane views. Sometimes these views co-exist in seeming harmony, sometimes they clash with each other. Moreover, each learner – and also teacher – nurses multiple beliefs about languages, depending on the perspective taken. It is this diversity – the multi-voiced mindscape of the classroom – and its possible relevance to research and teacher education, which we wish to discuss below. We will start our discussion from the domain of language and education policies in Finland.

Language Education in Finland: The Social Context

Finland is often represented as a homogeneous country, one reason being that most citizens (91.2% in 2007) speak Finnish as their mother tongue. Public voices frequently stress the importance of national unity, and education is often regarded as a primary means to socialize citizens – including immigrants – into a 'Finnish way of life'. These centripetal discourses of national unity and identity are widely used to project the image of a successful nation and its future. The mission of basic education is articulated as follows: 'to furnish society with a tool for developing educational capital and enhancing equality and a sense of community' (NCCBE, 2004: 12). One way of analyzing language education from a socio-cognitive perspective is to apply a chain-of-effect analysis (Salo, 2008), which aims at mapping the influential societal factors and institutional discourses at the same time regarding their potential manifestation at the individual level of language users' experiences.

Figure 14.1 gives a simplified picture of the chain-of-effect in the context of Finnish language education. First, all basic education is strictly governed by legislation and the national core curriculum. These documents define which subjects are to be studied, their core content and the number of weekly lessons. Further, as the teaching profession is strictly regulated by acts, all teacher trainees basically undergo similar education, regardless of their university and department. In addition, because of its fairly small size, the national community of teacher educators is able to work in close cooperation. In Figure 14.1, an important position is given to the producers of study materials because, as many Finnish educationalists (see Heinonen, 2005) have pointed out, the materials seem to guide teaching practices more than curricula. Regarding the study materials as implementations of the curricula objectives, teachers largely base their teaching on textbooks.

The description of foreign language objectives in the national core curriculum (NCCBE, 2004) draws heavily on the ideas put forward in the Common European Frame of Reference for Languages (CEFR, 2001),

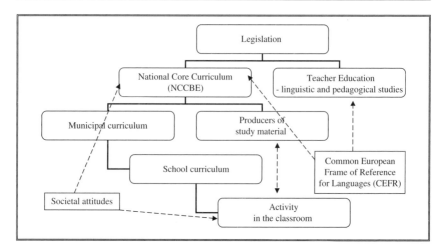

Figure 14.1 A simplified diagram of the chain-of-effect of language education in Finland

which provides a singular rationale for language education in various European Union (EU) countries (see Salo, 2007). For instance, in line with the functional view of language promoted by CEFR, the Finnish NCCBE (2004) states that foreign language instruction is to give the pupils functional skills for coping in communicative situations. However, it is the grassroots-level activity in the classroom that eventually determines whether the objectives set in official documents are met. Even if acts and curricula, designed at the level of societal macro-structures, do influence language education, it is the individual voices – based on individual experiences and beliefs – that create the multi-voiced language classrooms.

Does this language education policy work and how do people perceive it? In general, the Finnish education system is considered to be a successful one, and it has been evaluated highly by the Programme for International Student Assessment (PISA) (see OECD, 2007). Although major international studies of language skills have not been made, the students' command of foreign languages can be judged to be relatively high. In 1995, when the language proficiency of the general Finnish population was studied in an Adult Education Survey, the results showed that almost three in four (72%) adult Finns could speak at least one other language than their mother tongue. Women were more proficient in foreign languages than men, and younger Finns more proficient than older ones (Taavitsainen & Pahta, 2003: 6). In addition,

Table 14.1 Language studies in the national core curricula in Finland

Language	Grade 1	Grade 2	Grade 3	Grade 4	Grade 5	Grade 6	Grade 7	Grade 8	Grade 9	Upper secondary school
A1	--------------------------Compulsory--------------------------									
A2				-----------Optional-----------						
B1							Compulsory			
B2							-----------Optional-----------			
B3										Optional

more than three in four Finns (77%) believe that people in Finland are proficient in other languages as compared to the EU average of 44%.

When one compares the position of particular languages, the situation in Finland is similar to the overall picture presented in the 2005 Eurobarometer survey. The survey indicated that English was the foreign language that most Europeans knew. According to the same survey, more than half (60%) of the Finnish population knew at least some English, about 38% of them knew Swedish and 17% German (Special Eurobarometer, 243). These three languages were also those that Finns considered most important for their children to study. The vast majority of Finns (90%) believed that speaking foreign languages either is, or could be, useful for them personally. It may not be surprising that Finns perceived English to be by far the most useful language to know (88%), followed by Swedish (38%), German (19%) and Russian (10%). Moreover, Finns saw formal education as the most common way of learning languages, as two-thirds (66%) of them mentioned language lessons at school as a preferred way of learning languages. Moreover, 54% of those who had studied languages at school considered that the lessons had been the most effective way to learn languages.

The official bilingualism in Finland sets certain constraints on language education. Finland has two official languages: Finnish with 91.2% of the population as mother tongue speakers (in 2007) and Swedish with the corresponding number of 5.5%.[2] The official bilingualism is also pinpointed in the national core curriculum, where it is established that in addition to their mother tongue (i.e. Finnish or Swedish), each Finn is to study the other official language for a minimum of three years during the nine-year basic education that is compulsory for all. As Finland is also strongly dedicated to reaching the target of 'mother tongue plus two' – set by the EU – the national core curriculum for basic education (see NCCBE, 2004) puts much weight on foreign language teaching (Table 14.1). This results in the fact that all Finnish students are supposed to learn at least two additional languages during their basic education, one of them being either Swedish or Finnish, and the other most usually learned language is English (99.2% in 2007). Despite the generally favorable attitudes towards learning foreign languages, the public opinion of the majority – according to the 2005 Eurobarometer survey – is that the 1 + 2 target is too high and that only one foreign language (read: English) would be sufficient. Table 14.1 shows schematically what options are involved in studying languages at Finnish schools.

Finnish children usually begin studying a foreign language in the third grade (at the age of 8–9). For the first foreign language (called A1), mostly either English or one of the national languages (Swedish or Finnish) is chosen. However, certain schools offer other options, such as German, French or Russian. It is to be noted that the number of pupils with an A1 language other than English or the second national language is trivial (2.5% in 2007).

Studying of the second foreign language (B1) usually begins in the seventh grade as a compulsory subject. Before that, the students are offered a possibility to start studying their second foreign language in the fourth or fifth grade (as a so-called A2 language) as an optional choice. The compulsory B1 language is usually Swedish (99.3% in 2007); most Swedish-speaking pupils study Finnish as their A1 or A2 language. Finally, the children can also choose a third foreign language (B2) as an optional language in grade 8 (in some schools in grade 7). This optional language (B2) is usually German or French, but some schools provide instruction in Spanish, Italian, Russian or Latin. More optional languages (from B3) can be taken at the stage of upper secondary school – at the age of 16–20.

According to Statistics Finland (2008), nearly all students who completed their studies at the upper secondary school in 2007 had studied English and either Finnish or Swedish as part of their syllabus. German had been studied by 33%, French by 19%, Spanish by 11% and Russian by 6%. Other foreign languages were studied by around 4% only. There are gender-related differences: about twice as many female students study an additional language as compared to male students. Also, even if foreign languages *are* studied, it has to be noted that many students end up taking only a few courses of the languages and do not necessarily complete their studies. In addition, despite national efforts to *increase* the number of pupils studying foreign languages other than English, the number of students studying German or French, for example, has declined dramatically in recent years, especially in basic education. In 2001, almost every fifth Finnish student (19.3%) had studied German during basic education, whereas six years later only one in eight (12.5%) had done so.

Thus, on the one hand, foreign language teaching is highly valued. On the other hand, there are many societal controversies and also problems at the level of municipal and school-level policy making – all of which seems to result in unfortunate consequences that diminish options in foreign language studies. To map future needs, a major national project on surveying and developing Finnish language education policies was carried out between 2005 and 2007 (Luukka & Pöyhönen, 2007). The results of the project, along with the above statistics coming from different sources, show that despite the good intentions of the policy makers, the social capital of knowing foreign languages seems to be actually diminishing or, at least narrowing into knowing fewer languages, possibly English only. All things considered, in recent years the position of English has strengthened while the command of Swedish has deteriorated. The number of people studying German, French or Russian, and non-European languages, is on the decrease.

The reasons for the declining skills in Swedish are partly due to the fact that instruction in the B1 language was cut by one third in the 1994 national curriculum. Latomaa and Nuolijärvi (2002) observe that this development may eventually pose a problem for the national policy of bilingualism, as it has become increasingly difficult to hire Swedish-speaking people for jobs that require fluency in both national languages, such as in nursing or in tax offices (see McRae, 2007). The Language Act (423/2003), introduced by the government, emphasized that the purpose of the law is 'to ensure the constitutional right of every person to use his or her own language, either Finnish or Swedish, before courts and other authorities' (section 2). By contrast, proficiency in English is now estimated as being at a much higher level than some decades ago. The main reason for this is not usually seen in the improved quality of instruction, but rather in the cultural circumstances that favor the wide use of English in the country, both in the (popular) media and in working life (for the use of English in Finland, see e.g. Leppänen & Nikula, 2007).

In the following section, we will discuss whether and how the social situation has an influence on people's beliefs about languages.

Conceptualizing Languages: Exploring Teachers' and Learners' Beliefs

It can be argued that both language learners and teachers hold conceptualizations that are, at the same time, socially informed and subjectively and privately constructed. Thus, personal knowledge is, to some extent, shared, as it partly consists of conceptualizations that are 'around' in each particular context, but it is also unique in the sense that it is based on a series of events in which learners as individuals have participated (for a similar argument, see Pietikäinen and Dufva, 2005). Personal knowledge about languages is also often mediated by 'significant others' – particularly teachers, but also parents, family members, friends, acquaintances, writers and celebrities who have influenced the individuals' thinking about languages (Aro, 2009).

In the everyday characterizations of language users, languages are not value-free and neutral constructs, but rather entities that are judged in terms of 'the good, the bad, and the ugly'; a view that also happens to correspond with the dialogical argument about the non-neutrality and ideologically laden character of language. Dufva *et al.* (1989) found that university students evaluated languages in terms of their social prestige ('cultured' versus 'primitive'), aesthetics ('beautiful' versus 'ugly') or their utilitarian value ('useful' versus 'not useful'). Furthermore, they also commented on the 'learnability' ('difficult' versus 'easy'), 'complexity' ('complex' versus 'simple') and mentioned the perceived distance between their mother tongue and the language in question ('different' – 'similar'). Similar responses to languages appear in written narratives, such as life stories or stories about language learning, which have been collected for research analysis (Kalaja *et al.*, 1998; Dufva *et al.*, 2003; Dufva, 2006a).

Considering the two important languages in the Finnish language education – English and Swedish – they are spoken about and experienced in very different terms. It is commonplace to call Swedish *pakkoruotsi* ('forced Swedish'), a well-known formulation in the community that connects the image of the language with something compulsory, obligatory and non-optional, primarily in terms of education. The formulation, connected to the past history and language situation of our country, still regularly appears in Finnish newspapers and webchats. By contrast, many surveys show that the attitude of the Finnish-speaking population towards Swedish is mostly positive, and most people (70%) see Swedish as an essential part of Finnish society (Allardt, 1997). There is also a widespread interest in Swedish-language immersion both in day-care centers and at school (see Buss & Mård, 2001). The ways of speaking about Swedish are divided.

Clearly, personal opinions about Swedish are polarized, and this has an effect on how the language is considered as an object of study at school. Salo (2008), in a study of teachers of Swedish, found that about half of them had faced motivational problems at school, mainly because their pupils tend to consider Swedish as an 'unnecessary' subject. Still at the university level, the number of students who would prefer not to study Swedish is relatively high, although the students are aware of the usefulness of these language studies for their future working life (Jauhojärvi-Koskelo & Nordqvist-Palviainen, 2007). What all these facts seem to suggest is that the conceptualizations of Swedish as an object of study may be strongly polarized (between 'love' and 'hate' or between seeing it as 'useful' or 'futile'). This certainly presents a challenge for the teachers, but at the same time, makes it an important issue to address, both in teacher education and in classroom practices.

If the case of Swedish is sometimes felt problematic – by learners who oppose learning and teachers who encounter less motivated students – the perception of the English language is very different. Widely used in Finland in the contexts of, for example, the media and working life, it has sometimes been named a 'third domestic' language (Leppänen *et al.*, 2008). In everyday talk and/or in the media, it is frequently spoken of as 'useful' or, using other epithets, as 'international' or 'global'. Dufva (2006b) discovered that university students saw English in terms of an important social capital because of its 'utility around the world' and its 'importance for one's future working life'. English was also seen as 'nice', but it was seldom experienced 'passionately' as an object of study as, for example, French. Neither was it seen as a 'difficult' language, in contrast to German (and interestingly, also Swedish). Thus, typically, the omnipresence of English was recognized, but it was not seen as a source of any deep emotion. On the other hand, although the students did not mention this at all, in the media, English is also spoken of as a 'danger'. Hence, the language is seen as 'harmful' and the many borrowings from English as a 'corruption' of the Finnish language. Sometimes the widespread use of English in the country is seen to threaten the position of the Finnish language. English is then spoken of as a 'killer language' that might endanger 'smaller' languages and lead to their extinction (for a discussion, see Dufva, 1992).

Consequently, conceptualizations of English seem to be divided, although in a rather different manner to those of Swedish. English is seen either as a 'social capital' of the global world or as a 'danger'. However, there is another interesting aspect that often appears in the conceptualizations of English, this time particularly in the context of school and young children's beliefs. This is how the children seem to distinguish between the 'institutional English' and the 'everyday English'. The results of a longitudinal study (grades 1–6, age 7–12) of Finnish children's metalinguistic knowledge and their foreign language learning show that pupils in interviews often spoke about English (their first foreign language) in terms of formal 'language objects', their 'internalization' and 'memorization'. This occurred when they spoke of English as an object of study – or when they thought this was what the interviewer was asking (see e.g. Dufva *et al.*, 2003; Dufva & Alanen, 2005; Aro, 2009). However, it seemed evident that there was also another

English: the English that the children frequently used in such everyday activities as playing computer games. Whenever we asked about *learning* English, they usually never mentioned these activities. Thus, there seemed to be two Englishes: the classroom English, which was a literacy-based school subject, regarded in terms of studying, memorizing and evaluation, and the everyday English, which 'was there' just to be used.

To sum up, we argue that languages, as objects of study, are subjectively felt and experienced, often emotionally and evaluatively. There are widespread conceptualizations – highly evaluative ones – that exist for English and Swedish, although different. The emotional involvement in the case of Swedish may be higher and more polarized, while the perception of English seems to be more neutral and perhaps less divided. Between these two languages, there is also an interesting difference in how 'close' or 'foreign' they are generally perceived. In the Finnish context, Swedish is what is called a domestic language – a national language and an official language of the country. Nevertheless, it is experienced by many learners as a truly 'foreign' language. By contrast, English, traditionally a 'foreign' language, is often named as 'close' and 'almost like a mother tongue' (Dufva, 2006a).

Languages in Classroom: The Pedagogical Context

We argue above that beliefs about languages are multi-voiced. It is only natural that there are differences between individuals. For example, it can be assumed that some people feel strongly pro-Swedish, while others are as vehemently against studying it. However, it is argued that there is polyphony, multi-voicedness, also at the individual level. The beliefs the individuals nurse may vary quite a lot and arise in a situated fashion to the level of talk or writing whenever they are evoked by certain topics or called forth by certain other participants (Dufva, 2003). Hence, it can be argued that individuals do not have one conceptualization about, say, Swedish or English, but many. At the same time, this fact opens up possibilities for developing language awareness by means of different tasks and activities that elicit beliefs and make it possible for learners to reflect upon them, articulating and possibly re-articulating them.

Different tasks that have been used for research purposes are suitable for pedagogical purposes as well. One example is a written narrative in which participants are asked to write their life story – as a foreign language learner (Leppänen & Kalaja, 2002) or, as a foreign language teacher (Kalaja *et al.*, 1998) – with the aim of collecting data for research purposes. However, similar tasks can be used as course activities (Kalaja & Dufva, 2005), making learners reflect on their own learning process. Different types of meaning potential and different means for expression are provided by visual modality. Visual means have been used in studies where foreign language learners were asked to draw their self-portraits (Kalaja *et al.*, 2008), projects in which multilingual Sami-Finnish children were engaged in representing the 'language sites' important to them by photographs (Pietikäinen, 2008) and in a study where the use of English in Finland was examined by asking teenagers to record their daily language activities by taking photographs (Nikula & Pitkänen-Huhta, 2008). These learner-oriented activities let 'subjects speak for themselves' (Roebuck, 2000) in multiple and multi-modal ways. Such activities may not only be helpful for the learners in assisting them to analyze aspects and shades of their learning experiences, but also for the teachers who may thus gain insights in how their students conceptualize the language themselves as learners or reflect on their learning process.

Thus, we feel that the talk about how each and every learner conceptualizes languages – or the kinds of beliefs she/he has about them – should be foregrounded in foreign language classrooms, and therefore, in foreign language teacher education as well. In other words, we see it as an important tool to enhance language learners' *awareness of language(s)*. By this, we do not mean the formal and structural aspects of the language only or its semantic, pragmatic and communicative aspects, but also such socially and culturally loaded aspects that make languages 'the good, the bad and the ugly' and that relate to the experienced relationships between the learner and the language. It is important to evoke beliefs about languages and talk about them in the classroom. Nevertheless, they should not be dismissed lightly as 'lay knowledge' or 'false beliefs' only. Although certainly not being theories of language in any strict sense of the word, everyday conceptualizations may still offer perspectives that have often been neglected. As we have pointed out, in some respects, views that have sometimes been called 'naïve' resonate quite well with the dialogical arguments. This brings us to our final point, to the teachers' beliefs.

Teachers' views are also multi-voiced. When writing *outside* classroom and institutional contexts, teachers often use similar characterizations as learners and 'naïve' speakers: they similarly 'love' or 'hate' languages and speak of them in terms that are most intimate and personal (see Kalaja *et al.*, 1998). When in a classroom, however, the decontextualized discourse seems to be much stronger: language is often spoken of in terms of rules of grammar and items of vocabulary and it is seen as a set of language objects to be internalized. This atomistic view seems to reject the idea of languages as socially, culturally and emotionally experienced phenomena. Furthermore, even in professional discourse, each teacher seems to have a niche of his/her own – his/her specific conceptualization of language and hence a teaching focus or approach. As Salo (2008) shows, teachers of Swedish have different kinds of Swedishes. Some teachers emphasize the communicative nature of the language in general. Others point out that the important thing about Swedish is to know it sufficiently enough to pass the national language test for qualifying as a public servant. Some teachers see Swedish as a formal system to be acquired and, thus, put emphasis on rules and structures in their instruction.

In classroom interactions, different voices are heard. As we have pointed out, the powerful representations and discourses that have been typical of formal linguistics certainly appear in the classroom. The powerful discourse of decontextualization tends to represent language in terms of an abstract code. In fact, this view, which owes much to de Saussure's notion of language, was criticized by Voloshinov (1973), who saw it as an attempt to reduce language to a set of formal objects (such as sentences, words, syllables, phonemes). This, according to Voloshinov, detached language from its life-world to be studied and dissected in linguistic laboratories. Further, as Voloshinov argued, the tradition was closely related with the tendency of regarding language through its written forms (for a closer discussion on written language bias, see e.g. Linell, 2005). At the beginning of the 21st century, many teaching materials (Salo, 2006), resources and classroom practices still recycle this tradition and mediate a formalist and literacy-based conceptualization of language (Dufva *et al.*, 2003; Dufva & Alanen, 2005). We cannot help feeling that this tendency often prevents language learners from understanding languages as semiotic resources and, thus, conceptually alienates language from its learners/users, presenting it as a collection of formal objects and/or operations that seem to be devoid of any personal signification and authenticity (see also van Lier, 1996).

Conclusion

The research we have briefly surveyed above seems to indicate the multiplicity of ways in which languages are spoken about and represented in various institutional texts, media and everyday talk. As language learners and teachers – and also as researchers – individuals draw on this variety of views that affect how they think about languages and what kind of beliefs they have. We have argued that the heteroglossia of the socially available discourses leads to the multiplicity of individual beliefs and that even seemingly monolingual and monocultural classrooms are places where a variety of different conceptualizations can emerge. As the linguistic and cultural background of the participants increases, so do the potentially available discourses and ways of thinking.

We see the study of the phenomenal and personally experienced aspects of language learning as a highly relevant topic of research. This kind of research not only allows us to explore the learners' views, but also highlights the chain-of-effects that are involved in language education and that influence teachers' beliefs. Finally, the approach may bring new theoretical insights for researchers – as we attempted to show in arguing for the relevance of dialogical perspective in the analysis of learners' and teachers' beliefs about language.

We have discussed the diversity of the classroom from the point of view of how languages are conceptualized, pointing out that every classroom is a multi-voiced ensemble where different notions of language exist – both consciously discussed, but also unconsciously held and nursed. We have argued that it is highly probable that persons – whether learners or teachers – do not have one single conceptualization, but several. Making these conceptualizations audible – or visible by such means as drawings or photographs – is an opportunity for increasing the learners' language awareness, thereby making language learning personally meaningful and significant.

Notes

1. This paper is part of a research project called *Dialogues of appropriation: perspectives on language learning and teaching*, funded by the Academy of Finland.
2. In addition, Sami languages, Finnish Sign Language and the Romani language all have certain rights recognized in, for example, the Constitution and the Language Act. The number of residents who have neither Finnish nor Swedish as their mother tongue is 3.3% of the population (Statistics Finland, 2008).

References

Allardt, E. (1997) *Vårt land, vårt språk. Tvåspråkigheten, finnarnas attityder samt svenskans och finlandssvenskarnas framtid i Finland/Kahden kielen kansa. Kaksikielisyys, suomalaisten asenteet sekä ruotsin kielen asema ja tulevaisuus Suomessa.* Finlandssvensk rapport nr 35. Helsingfors. [*Our Country, Our Language: Bilingualism, the attitudes of Finns, and the status and future of Swedish in Finland.*]

Aro, M. (2009) Speakers and doers. Polyphony and agency in children's belief about language learning. *Jyväskylä Studies in Humanities*, 116. http://urn.fi/URN:ISBN:978-951-39-3532-0.

Bakhtin, M.M. (1986) *Speech Genres and Other Late Essays.* Austin, TX: University of Texas Press.

Bakhtin, M.M. (2004) Dialogic origin and dialogic pedagogy of grammar: Stylistics as part of Russian language instruction in secondary school. *Journal of Russian and East European Psychology* 42 (6), 12–49.

Ball, A. and Freedman, S.W. (eds) (2004) *Bakhtinian Perspectives on Language, Literacy and Learning.* Cambridge: Cambridge University Press.

Benson, P. and Nunan, D. (eds) (2004) *Learners' Stories: Difference and Diversity in Language Learning.* Cambridge: Cambridge University Press.

Block, D. (2003) *The Social Turn in Second Language Acquisition.* Edinburgh: Edinburgh University Press.

Brandist, C. (2002) *The Bakhtin Circle: Philosophy, Culture, and Politics.* London: Pluto Press.

Breen, M.P. (ed.) (2001) *Learner Contributions to Language Learning. New Directions in Research.* London: Longman.

Buss, M. and Mård, K. (2001) Swedish immersion in Finland: Facts and figures. In S. Björklund (ed.) *Language as a Tool: Immersion Research and Practices* (pp. 157–175). Proceedings of the University of Vaasa. Reports 83. Vaasa: University of Vaasa.

CEFR (2001) *Common European Framework of Reference for Languages: Learning, Teaching, Assessment.* 2001. Council of Europe, Modern Languages Division, Strasbourg. Cambridge: Cambridge University Press.

Dufva, H. (1992) "Happily ever äfterkö?": Suomen ja englannin yhteinen tulevaisuus. [Happy ever after?: The common future of Finnish and English.] In H. Nyyssönen and L. Kuure (eds) *Acquisition of Language: Acquisition of Culture.* AFinLA Yearbook 1992 (pp. 79–96). Jyväskylä: AFinLA.

Dufva, H. (2003) Beliefs in dialogue: A Bakhtinian view. In A.M.F. Barcelos and P. Kalaja (eds) *Beliefs about SLA: New Research Approaches* (pp. 131–151). Dordrecht: Kluwer.

Dufva, H. (2006a) Logical German and easy English: How language students perceive different languages. A paper presented at the Annual BAAL/IRAAL Conference, 7–9 September 2006, Cork, Ireland.

Dufva, H. (2006b) How people speak of languages: Rethinking the role of languages in intercultural communication. In F. Dervin and E. Suomela-Salmi (eds) *Intercultural Communication and Education/Communication et education interculturelles: Finnish Perspectives/perspectives finlandaises* (pp. 33–54). Bern: Peter Lang.

Dufva, H. and Alanen, R. (2005) Metalinguistic awareness in dialogue: Bakhtinian considerations. In J.K. Hall, G. Vitanova and L. Marchenkova (eds) *Dialogue with Bakhtin on Second and Foreign Language Learning: New Perspectives* (pp. 99–118). New York: Lawrence Erlbaum.

Dufva, H., Alanen, R. and Aro, M. (2003) Kieli objektina: Miten lapset mieltävät kielen? [Language objectified?: How children see language.] In M. Koskela and N. Pilke (eds) *Kieli ja asiantuntijuus.* AFinLA Yearbook 61 (pp. 295–316). Jyväskylä: AFinLA.

Dufva, H., Hurme, P. and O'Dell, M. (1989) The good, the bad and the ugly: Cross-cultural aesthetics and ethics of spoken language. In J. Niemi (ed.) *Papers from the Eleventh Scandinavian Conference of Linguistics* (Vol. 2; pp. 530–544). Joensuu: University of Joensuu.

Hall, J.K., Vitanova, G. and Marchenkova, L. (eds) (2005) *Dialogue with Bakhtin on Second and Foreign Language Learning: New Perspectives.* New York: Lawrence Erlbaum.

Heinonen, J-P. (2005) *Opetussuunnitelmat vai oppimateriaalit: Peruskoulun opettajien käsityksiä opetussuunnitelmien ja oppimateriaalien merkityksestä opetuksessa.* [Curricula or teaching material? Teacher conceptions on the importance of curricula and teaching material in teaching.] Helsingin yliopisto. Soveltavan kasvatustieteen laitoksen tutkimuksia 257.

Jauhojärvi-Koskelo, C. and Nordqvist-Palviainen, Å. (2007) Jag behöver inte svenska i jobbet! Inställning till svenska hos unga finskspråkiga studenter. [I won't need Swedish at work! Young Finnish-speaking university students' attitudes towards Swedish.] A paper presented at the NORDAND Conference, 10–12 May 2007, University of Helsinki, Finland.

Kalaja, P., Alanen, R. and Dufva, H. (2008) Self-portraits of EFL learners: Finnish students draw and tell. In P. Kalaja, V. Menezes and A.M.F. Barcelos (eds) *Narratives of Learning and Teaching EFL* (pp. 186–198). Basingstoke: Palgrave Macmillan.

Kalaja, P. and Dufva, H. (2005) *Kielten matkassa: Opi oppimaan vieraita kieliä.* [*Learning to Learn Foreign Languages.*] Helsinki: FinnLectura.

Kalaja, P., Dufva, H. and Nordman, L. (1998) Puhutaan kielillä: Kielet ja kielivalinnat opettajien elämäkerroissa. In M-R. Luukka, S. Salla and H. Dufva (eds) *Puolin ja toisin. Suomalais-virolaista kielentutkimusta.* [*Speaking in Tongues – Languages and Language Choices in Teacher Biographies.*] AFinLA Yearbook 1998 (pp. 131–146). Jyväskylä: AFinLA.

Kramsch, C.J. (ed.) (2002) *Language Acquisition and Language Socialization: Ecological Perspectives.* New York: Continuum.

Lähteenmäki, M. (1998) On meaning and understanding: A dialogical approach. *Dialogism: An International Journal of Bakhtin Studies* 1, 74–91.

Lähteenmäki, M. (2001) *Dialogue, Language and Meaning: Variations on Bakhtinian Themes.* Jyväskylä: University of Jyväskylä.

Lähteenmäki, M. (2003) On the interpretation of Bachtin's linguistic ideas: The problem of the texts from 1950–60s. *Russian Linguistics* 27 (1), 23–39.

Lantolf, J. and Thorne, S. (2006) *Sociocultural Theory and the Genesis of Second Language Development.* Oxford: Oxford University Press.

Latomaa, S. and Nuolijärvi, P. (2005) The language situation in Finland. In R.B. Kaplan and R.B. Baldauf Jr. (eds) *Language Planning and Policy. Europe, Vol. 1. Finland, Hungary and Sweden* (pp. 125–232). Clevedon: Multilingual Matters.

Leppänen, S. and Kalaja, P. (2002) Autobiographies as constructions of EFL learner identities and experiences. In E. Kärkkäinen, J. Haines and T. Lauttamus (eds) *Studia Linguistica et Litteraria Septentrionalia: Studies Presented to Heikki Nyyssönen* (pp. 189–203). Oulu: University of Oulu.

Leppänen, S. and Nikula, T. (2007) Diverse uses of English in Finnish society: Discourse-pragmatic insights into media, educational and business contexts. *Multilingua* 26 (4), 333–380.

Leppänen, S., Nikula, T. and Kääntä, L. (eds) (2008) *Kolmas kotimainen. Lähikuvia englannin käytöstä Suomessa.* [*The Third Domestic. Case Studies of English in Finland.*] Helsinki: SKS.

Linell, P. (2005) *The Written Language Bias in Linguistics: Its Nature, Origins and Transformations.* London: Routledge.

Luukka, M-R. and Pöyhönen, S. (2007) *Kohti tulevaisuuden kielikoulutusta. Kielikoulutuspoliittisen projektin keskeiset suositukset.* [*Towards Future Language Education. The Main Recommendations of the Project on Finnish Language Education Policies.*] Jyväskylä: University of Jyväskylä, Centre for Applied Language Studies.

McRae, K.D. (2007) Toward language equality: Four democracies compared. *International Journal of the Sociology of Language* 187/188, 13–34.

NCCBE (2004) *National Core Curriculum for Basic Education 2004.* Helsinki: Finnish National Board of Education.

Nikula, T. and Pitkänen-Huhta, A. (2008) Using photographs to access stories of learning English. In P. Kalaja, V. Menezes and A.M.F. Barcelos (eds) *Narratives of Learning and Teaching EFL* (pp. 171–185). Basingstoke: Palgrave Macmillan.

OECD (2007) *PISA 2006: Science Competencies for Tomorrow's World* (Vol. 1). Paris. OECD.

Pietikäinen, S. (2008) Researching multilingual visualities: Insights from visual ethnography and discourse analysis. A paper presented at Multilingualism, Discourse and Ethnography, 7–9 April 2008, University of Birmingham, UK.

Pietikäinen, S. and Dufva, H. (2006) Voices in discourses. Dialogism, critical discourse analysis and ethnic identity. *Journal of Sociolinguistics* 10 (2), 205–224.

Roebuck, R. (2000) Subjects speak out: How learners position themselves in a psycholinguistic task. In J. Lantolf (ed.) *Sociocultural Theory and Second Language Learning* (pp. 79–95). Oxford: Oxford University Press.

Salo, O-P. (2006) Opetussuunnitelma muuttuu, muuttuuko oppikirja? Huomioita 7. luokan vieraiden kielten oppikirjojen kielikäsityksistä. [When the curriculum changes, does the study book change as well? Perspectives on the conceptions of language in foreign language study books for grade 7.] In P. Pietilä, P. Lintunen and H-M. Järvinen (eds) *Kielenoppija tänään – Language Learners of Today* (pp. 237–254). AFinLA Yearbook 64. Jyväskylä: AFinLA.

Salo, O-P. (2007) Mistä on uudet OPSit tehty? Eurooppalaisen viitekehyksen kielikäsitys vieraiden kielten uusien opetussuunnitelmien perustana. [What are the new curricula made of? The CEFR's conception of language as the basis for the new foreign language curricula.] In J. Lavonen (ed.) *Tutkimusperustainen opettajankoulutus ja kestävä kehitys. Ainedidaktinen symposiumi Helsingissä 3.2.2006, osa 2* (pp. 578–587). Research Report 286. Helsinki: University of Helsinki, Department of Applied Sciences of Education.

Salo, O-P. (2008) One or many Swedishes? Teacher conceptions of Swedish as a school subject. A paper presented at the conference Mediating Multilingualism: Meanings and Modalities, 3–6 June 2008, University of Jyväskylä, Finland.

Special Eurobarometer 243. Europeans and Their Languages [online]. The European Commission's Education and Culture Directorate-General Unit "Centre for the citizen – Analysis of public opinion". On WWW at http://ec.europa.eu/public_opinion/archives/ebs/ebs_243_sum_en.pdf. Accessed 25.3.08.

Statistics Finland (2008) Education. On WWW at http://www.stat.fi/til/kou_en.html. Accessed 13.6.08.

Taavitsainen, I. and Pahta, P. (2003) English in Finland: Globalisation, language awareness and questions of identity. An essay on the intra- and inter-national use of the language. *English Today* 19 (4), 3–15.

van Lier, L. (1996) *Interaction in the Language Curriculum: Awareness, Autonomy and Authenticity.* New York: Longman.

van Lier, L. (2004) *The Ecology and Semiotics of Language Learning: A Sociocultural Perspective.* Boston, MA: Kluwer Academic.

Voloshinov, V.N. (1973) *Marxism and the Philosophy of Language.* New York: Seminar Press.

Voloshinov, V.N. (1976) *Freudianism. A Marxist Critique.* New York: Academic Press.

Chapter 15

Bringing Home and Community to School: Institutional Constraints and Pedagogic Possibilities

SUZANNE SMYTHE and KELLEEN TOOHEY

> Children like adults, are situated in multiple discourse fields, depending on their personal history, and physical and social location. For the children in my case study, the choice was not simply between "English" or "mother tongue", but they were drawing on the range of registers they had access to across languages, taking up (if only in imaginative play) a variety of positions in a range of different discursive practices. A simple view of children using just two languages, or just two modes of English, spoken and written, is inadequate in this context. The children were operating with many different codes in their spoken language. They were highly sensitive to a range of "voices". What a pity it seems that schools cannot build on this knowledge and competence consciously and explicitly in introducing children to a new range of written registers and genres. (Bourne, 2001: 110)

Introduction

On a Tuesday afternoon in November 2007, thirty children between the ages of seven and twelve gather at the after-school program at the local community center, just four blocks from their elementary school. Some gather around tables in small groups, playing monopoly and checkers, others loudly discuss the meaning of words assigned on a school spelling test. The gymnasium across the hall rings with the sound of basketball. Still other children are working on computers, looking for images of their favorite basketball and soccer heroes. The predominant language is English, although all the children are English language learners (ELLs), and Swahili, French, Farsi, Dali and Persian can be heard as children negotiate and argue over their board games and on the

271

basketball courts. The group leaders sit with smaller groups of children, helping with homework and overseeing arts and crafts projects. Several evenings a week, dinner is served, and afterwards children head home, just as some of their parents arrive home from work and their younger siblings go to bed.

Few children were born in this community; many have recently arrived as refugees and sponsored immigrants, escaping the ongoing conflicts in Sudan, Central Africa and Afghanistan. As they participate in, and create, this multilingual, multiliterate community of learners, so they form new identities as members of both local and global cultural and linguistic networks. What is perhaps most striking to us as ethnographers in their community and school is the contrast between the wide ranging and complex discursive practices evident in their community settings, and the predominantly English-only environment that characterizes their local school. Further, the range of linguistic and cultural knowledge displayed by newcomer children can be obscured in a discursive context in which ELLs, particularly recently arrived sponsored immigrants and refugees, are identified as 'problems' to the school system because they are 'illiterate' (O'Connor, 2008).

Many educators and researchers have called for culturally responsive pedagogy, a pedagogy that integrates children's home literacies and cultures into the school curriculum (de la Piedra, 2006; Lee, 2007; Moll *et al.*, 1992; Moll, 2000; Moje, 2000; Marsh, 2003; Purcell-Gates, 2007; Xu, 2005). Such researchers point out that schooling typically builds upon the skills and activities familiar to and appropriated by majority language and culture middle-class children. Children coming from other back-grounds often do not have the advantage of teachers who are knowl-edgeable of, and able to build upon their out-of-school knowledge and literacy and language practices. Conducting research in two communities where large numbers of ELLs are enrolled in school, we have engaged in various ethnographic activities designed to learn more about the communities' language and literacy uses. As teacher educators working closely with classroom teachers, a central goal in our study was to inform ourselves of the discursive contexts for literacy and language learning in our focal community so that classroom pedagogies could better reflect what children know and value. We hoped that in doing so, we could interrupt the dominance of English-only knowledge and literacy in the classroom, and contribute to the re-valuing of newcomer children's linguistic and cultural resources.

In this chapter, therefore, we discuss approaches that we have used to understand more about the discursive context of one particular school, and illustrate how complex we have found such an undertaking to be. We also describe efforts made by teachers and students to build upon some of the outside-school competencies children bring, and we discuss the mixed results of these undertakings.

We begin this chapter with an overview of the theoretical lenses informing our research, and then provide a detailed account of the methods we used to conduct ethnographic scans of Urban Community and School.[1] The goal of these scans was to learn about the historical and cultural backgrounds of children's schooling experiences, in order to map the out-of-school literacy and learning resources available to children and youth in the community. The third section of the chapter highlights the main findings of this scan. Fourth, we describe one of the school projects that teachers engaged in with students to learn more about children's out-of-school lives. We conclude with some critical reflections on our efforts to link the print and multimodal worlds of ELL children to instructional practices in their school.

Theoretical Framework

We situate ourselves as researchers informed by sociocultural theory as described by Wertsch (1998), Lantolf (2000) and many others. Socio-cultural theorists argue that humans act on the world with socially constructed tools or resources (both physical and symbolic). Such tools include (in the context of Urban School community) multilingual language and literacy practices, books and computers, TV, basketballs, music, song and prayer – a wide variety of multimodal resources that are formed and developed by individuals and the community, and in turn form and develop them, as learners and community members. Learning from a sociocultural perspective is seen as a dialectical and social process in which culturally and historically situated participants engage in culturally valued activities (using cultural tools) and in so doing, change their participation or 'learn'. Observing participants' use of cultural tools or resources in engagements with others, and documenting their changing participation in these practices are, therefore, central activities of sociocultural educational studies. Of great importance as well is learners' access to particular cultural resources, as access in some communities is by no means necessarily equitable. Nor are different cultural resources equally valued in particular settings.

The issue of access to valued cultural resources is an historical, economic and political question. As Holland and Lave (2001: 4) argue, we must pay particular attention to 'historical structures of privilege, rooted in class, race, gender, and other social divisions, as these are brought to the present'. Heller (2008), building on the work of French sociologist Pierre Bourdieu, calls attention to how the resources of particular groups are 'produced, attributed value, and circulated in a regulated way, which allows for competition over access, and typically, unequal distribution' (Heller, 2008: 50). Heller notes the differential value accorded to some tools and practices as compared to others. She notes, for example, that the resources of, in Bourdieu's (1977) terms, 'illegitimate' subjects (e.g. immigrants) are discounted as relevant to participation in the public sphere (e.g. schools). By contrast, the resources of the privileged are accorded elevated status therein.

One of the important projects of much sociocultural educational research is to identify strategies to 're-value' the cultural resources of minoritized or subordinated communities. The field refers to and defines cultural resources in a variety of ways, from the evocative term 'funds of knowledge' (Moll *et al.*, 1992), to 'local literacies' (Barton & Hamilton, 1998), 'cultural and mediational tools' (Hull & Katz, 2006) and 'linguistic resources' (de la Piedra, 2006). For example, Moll *et al.* (1992: 133) developed the concept of 'funds of knowledge' to reference 'historically accumulated and culturally developed bodies of knowledge and skills essential for household or individual functioning and well-being'. This includes knowledge grounded in family members' work inside and outside the home, material and social conditions in which families live, modes of learning and participating in church and community events, health and healing practices, child raising and so on.

This concept assumes that minoritized families have knowledge, skills and practices that are underutilized by schools, and urges researchers and educators to learn more about these foundations for school learning. This perspective on family and community resources has been taken up in a variety of ways. For example, the 'cultural modeling' framework (Lee, 2007; Orellana & Reynolds, 2008) uses ethnographic methods to document the routine language and literacy practices children engage in outside of school, and maps these onto school academic processes. One such practice is 'paraphrasing' (Orellana & Reynolds, 2008), whereby children's bilingualism and their routine practice of translating and transcribing oral and print texts for family members became a resource for teaching academic literacy genres in school. However, descriptions of the 'leveraging' of out-of-school practices into school activities are not common. With respect to the communities in which we work, nothing of this sort is available.

While the funds-of-knowledge concept inspires our inquiry, we are aware of some of its limitations, particularly in the context of diverse multicultural and multilingual community settings. An uncritical 'funds of knowledge' approach risks essentializing communities, obscuring important political, economic, temporal and spatial factors in households' variable access to resources of any sort. Any household of persons who identify with particular ethnic, cultural, linguistic or religious group and/or other affiliations will have their own histories of access to that group's inventory of knowledge, skills and practices. Moreover, as we found in our study, there are also differences within families as to which cultural and linguistic resources and tools are valued. Thus, researchers committed to documenting funds of knowledge in children's lives need to pay attention to the stratifying institutional arrangements of age, work, gender relations and social policies that may shape which cultural resources are valued by and accessible to ELLs and their families, and which are more visible for take up in classroom settings.

In this sense, following Canagarajah (2002: 251), we came to regard children's knowledge and literacy practices not as fixed characteristics, but as 'processes of negotiation of dominant discourses'. Our research methods similarly presented an opportunity to engage in an ongoing inquiry among teachers, children and community educators, about what is and should be valued in classroom settings. However, as we elaborate below, this inquiry and its resulting pedagogic interventions did not result in wholly transformed pedagogic practices, and we increasingly recognize the ways in which institutions like schools are resistant to change. First, however, we describe the methodology we have employed.

Methodology

The project this study reports is part of a larger research agenda of a group we call SILICLE (Sociocultural Investigation of Literacy Instruction for Child Learners of English). SILICLE began in September 2006, and currently involves four university researchers, six teacher-researchers, a videoethnographer, several research assistants, interpreters/translators and two schools. The group meets once fortnightly and has engaged in collaborative planning of classroom activities and collaborative analysis of the enactment of those activities. While we conducted community scans in both the project schools, and have reported on one of the schools in another venue (Smythe & Toohey, 2009), we report here briefly on the scan in the other school and its surrounding community.

As described above, we wanted to document the cultural resources and out-of-school literacies that might inform classroom-based instruction for these refugee and sponsored immigrant newcomers. We began by collecting socioeconomic and demographic data about Urban Community, including census data, municipal reports and school district community profiles. The socioeconomic and demographic information spurred us into more systematic abstract and concrete mapping strategies (Tindle *et al.*, 2005). Abstract mapping refers to data collected about a community from secondary sources. Concrete mapping refers to 'on the street' data collection, through a walking tour of the community, photographs, conversations with people on the street and in local shops, the collection of artifacts such as flyers, newspapers and posters and so on.

In our abstract mapping phase, we familiarized ourselves with the history and politics-economics of immigration in Urban Community. We interviewed community leaders, local service providers, including outreach and immigrant support workers, children and parents. We mapped community assets, such as services, learning centers, community action groups, religious organizations, sports associations and so on. We include some of that information here to show some of what we learned in so doing.

In our concrete mapping phase, Author 1 conducted several walking tours of the community, taking photographs, eating in local restaurants and chatting to residents and shop-owners. Later, Grade 6 and 7 children from three classes in Urban School acted as junior-ethnographers, collecting and sharing information about themselves through photo presentations and collected print artifacts from their homes and daily lives. As we report later in this chapter, children's representations not only informed and deepened teachers' knowledge of children's out-of-school lives, they also provided insights into the cultural tools they use to represent their lives.

Community Scan Findings: An Emerging Portrait of Cultural and Linguistic Resources

Overview of Urban School and Community

Keeping in mind that the concept of 'community' is complex and fluid (Moje, 2000), we adopted a geographical definition of the community as that encompassing the 2–3 km radius surrounding the school, commonly known as the 'school catchment area'. Children living within this school catchment area typically attend Urban School. Notwithstanding the convenience of this definition, the tendrils of this geographic community extend into African, Middle Eastern and South Asian diasporas, the trajectories of refugee and immigrant journeys to Canada, and the educational and social histories the families bring with them.

Significantly, 35% of refugees who settle in the region where we do our research, live in Urban Community, and a large majority of these attend Urban School. The newcomer experience emerges as a significant theme in the scan, drawing our attention to the ways in which global political and economic trends and conflicts shape the everyday pedagogic work in Urban School, as well as the cultural tools, including print literacy, afforded the children in our study.

According to the 2006 Census, 60% of the households in Urban School Community identified as first generation immigrants with 20% having arrived between 2001 and 2005, and 40% reported speaking a language other than English at home. According to the census, Filipino and Chinese represent the largest ethnocultural groups in Urban School Community, although there are significant and growing South Asian, West Asian and African communities. The population as a whole in Urban Community increased by 25% between 2001 and 2005, as compared to the provincial average growth of 6.5%. This is likely a result of widespread condominium development in the community, and the availability of otherwise scarce affordable rental housing (Statistics Canada, 2008). Over the year that we collected data for our scan, significant changes took place as high-rise market condominiums towered over the somewhat dilapidated but affordable low-rise rental flats (and social housing) where many of the children in our study live. See Figure 15.1 for this pattern of 'development'.

This is a highly mobile community, and many households report having moved within the geographical area at least once during the census period. Almost 40% of adults, 15 years and older, report not participating in the workforce, and 40% of adults do not possess any postsecondary certificate, diploma or degree. Community outreach workers note that many new immigrant women experience significant cultural, linguistic and gender barriers to securing paid work outside the home, particularly as they are also responsible for raising and caring for young children. Indeed, Urban Community has larger than average families and larger proportions of children under the age of 10 (13% versus 10.2% in the province) and children and youth between 10 and 19 years of age (14% versus 12% in the province). The majority of residents in paid employment work in sales and service occupations, or in small businesses. The median income in Urban School Community is 20%

Figure 15.1 A community in transition

lower than the provincial average; 30% lower for families with children. Significantly, 41% of people under the age of 18 are considered low income after tax, as compared to the provincial average of 18.5% (Statistics Canada, 2008).

School District officials have asked that the low family incomes and low parent education levels that characterize Urban Community be factored into the provincially sponsored standardized test scores for Grade 4 and 7 children. In 2006/2007, these test scores were on average 20–30% lower than the provincial average. Immigration and settlement groups have called attention to the growing trend of poverty among Canada's newcomer groups, particularly those who arrive in Canada as refugees or sponsored immigrants (who are dependent upon other family members to see to their income and settlement needs when they arrive in Canada) (Creese, 2006).

Indeed, of great concern to the school district are the education histories of these newcomer children. A considerable and growing number of older children (aged 9–14) arrive in Urban School from areas of ongoing civil strife and conflict, and so with little or no experience of formal education. School districts point out that many newcomer children come from homes that do not model family literacy practices of home story-book reading, homework supervision, parental involvement in schools and the English literacy knowledge that are often taken for granted in the North American mainstream (Canadian School Boards Association, 2006). Information about the challenges, deficits and problems associated with children's academic success at Urban School is plentiful and accessible. Less visible and articulated, however, are the cultural and linguistic resources that children bring to learning, and that might be mobilized in classroom settings.

Community literacy and language assets: A sense of place

In this phase of our community scan, we attended to children's participation in social learning outside of school, often afforded in after-school programs, but also at the even more informal basketball and soccer games in the playgrounds adjacent to housing developments. Here we found a tight network of services and supports for children and families in Urban Community, which is characterized by a strong ethos of inter-agency collaboration and a trend toward service integration or a 'hub' model.

As noted above, Urban School is located in a municipality that has retained some affordable rental housing. Although this housing is run-down and substandard by national standards, there is an agreement between immigrant settlement offices and local housing projects to waive the usual requirement for references from previous landlords – a condition that newcomers are normally unable to meet. This agreement also permits 'over housing' – allowing for more than the standard occupancy of two people per bedroom – in order to keep family members together. This practice, in part, accounts for the higher than average housing density statistics cited above. Although often rodent-infested and poorly maintained, we learned in the course of our community scan research that these housing arrangements can offer newcomer families access to common play areas for their children, and opportunities for social networking and on-site education and food programs.[2]

In keeping with many neighborhoods planned in the early 20th century in North America, Urban School Community is designed around a commercial or 'high street', providing walking access to elementary and secondary schools, shops, a medical clinic, a youth drop-in center, community center, Food Banks and churches that offer English as a second language (ESL) classes. Attached to the school is a neighborhood resource center that houses immigrant service groups, a childcare center, a family literacy center and other 'wrap-around' services. In contrast to some suburban communities in the area (Smythe & Toohey, 2009), which are car-dependent and designed around single-dwelling homes, the Urban School community affords older children the opportunity to play, socialize and participate in planned community activities within walking distance of their homes. There is evidence, however, that this mode of urban design is in transition. As shown in Figure 15.1, the conversion of rental and low-density housing to market condominium towers is transforming Urban Community, with implications for housing security and children's access to relatively safe and informal play spaces.

Community outreach workers who have formed close relationships with newcomer families have observed the relative independence and responsibility displayed by older children who are often charged with the care of their younger siblings. These children frequently organize inter-age basketball and soccer games in the courts and fields around their homes and Friday night open-court basketball at the Community Center attracts over 40 children. These informal games seem to provide a context for the development of a children's oral English (especially popular cultural expressions), and illustrate children's identification with popular culture ideals of 'star' basketball players (as mediated on TV), popular music and, what Corsaro (2003) called, 'kid culture' in general.

The circumstances of Urban Community's settlement drive a unique set of social relations among school-based educators, community-based educators and social service agencies in this community. These have resulted in a wide range of out-of-school programs and services in which children in our study participate. These programs are of interest because they seem to afford children with structures of both informal and guided activity that allow them to draw upon and build multilingual and multiliterate practices (Hull & Katz, 2008; Cazden, 2003).

Community workers, including librarians, community recreation leaders, immigrant service workers and school-based settlement workers play important but largely invisible roles as 'literacy brokers' as they help families to negotiate bureaucratic literacies and survive physically and emotionally; they also provide a range of literacy and language apprenticeship activities. We observed these agencies providing: translation of texts; adult ESL classes; opportunities for employment using first languages; homework help; computer classes for children and adults; movie nights and movie making with youth; safe and stimulating places for children to play after school; accompaniment of adults to meetings with government agencies as advocate/assistant; parent discussion and support groups (often specific to ethnocultural groups); early learning programs, including family literacy programs, preschools and childcare, for children aged 0–5; community kitchens and conventional library information converted into codes and symbols for people of all languages and literacy abilities to access.

As the inventory of community literacy and language activities grew, we became aware of the range of cultural tools and resources that were recruited by community educators to draw families into new social networks and learning settings. It became clear that the work of formal schooling could not proceed as it does without this community-based literacy and language work, and the intentional creation of a sense of place and belonging for children in the informal learning spaces that 'wrap-around' the school.

The after-school program at the Community Center, and the Immigrant Youth Group run by immigrant settlement workers, are salient examples. The Community Center offers a range of informal learning opportunities for children, aged 8–14, after school, on weekends and holidays. The program is intentional in its balance between informal learning and opportunities for participation in more structured programs, such as cooking, art and computer classes, in which the children enroll themselves with the aid of a municipal recreation pass. According to the program facilitator,

> The program tries to encourage as much as possible social interaction and play across diverse groups and informally teach the children English in the context of the program. There is no direct instruction, but we support the kids' reading in playing Trivial Pursuit, Monopoly, encouraging them to read game cards, instructions, signs and so on. We also have a "homework time" each afternoon where we encourage peer helping. (Urban Community Center facilitator interview, 7 January 2007)

The facilitator observed that the Community Center does not have as much contact with parents as with children. The children usually come together after school and walk home together in groups in the evening. 'We see all these children, all these communities, coming together and becoming one'. This image resonated with us as we began to appreciate how these children of all ages were creating new 'funds of knowledge' independent of their households or home literacy practices.

We were interested in the activity structures in evidence at the Community Center programs. They incorporated children's interests in basketball and sports in general, music videos, pop 'divas' and 'rappers', while introducing them to new skills and modes of learning. Literacy and language were embedded in authentic contexts and their timing and participation was flexible, building upon the older children's propensity to mentor younger children and work collaboratively.

The Immigrant Youth Groups are similarly structured, but more oriented to building leadership skills. They have recently incorporated the use of still and video cameras to help children document their experiences as new community members and tell the stories of their settlement experiences. Children and youth make movies about the day they arrived in Canada, about their family life in a new country, their parents' struggles to find work. Some children speak about their new identities as Canadians, expressing their love for basketball, soccer, music and their families. These images and videos are shared in community events and represent powerful modes of expression that transcend the constraints of print literacies.

The school district has actively supported these out-of-school programs, recognizing the need for older children in particular, to feel a sense of place and belonging in their communities. What seems more difficult, as others have observed (Hull & Schultz, 2002; Hull & Katz, 2008), is to value these out-of-school programs not just as a social service, but as potential models for literacy and language learning in classroom settings.

Children's linguistic and cultural resources

In formal interviews and informal conversation during classroom observations, the 11- and 12-year-old children in our study described settings outside of school in which they use two or three languages and literacies in the same activities. They reported themselves and others using English, Punjabi and Swahili on the basketball court in after-school community matches. Several are learning Persian or Farsi at the mosque language school, and one has started to learn Trinidadian in a community language school. She does this 'for my uncle, so I can learn his culture'. She attends this school with her cousins and discussed how difficult it was at first to get used to the 'very strict' learning, the many lines she had to write and all the homework: 'Not like this [the public] school!' Two girls reported communicating with families in the Democratic Republic of Congo in Swahili via e-mail using computers at the community center; others use Tagolog and Spanish in church. As recent immigrants, the parents of these children have close social, cultural and linguistic ties to their countries of origin and/or to family members living in the South Asian, African and Middle Eastern Diasporas. However, most are unable to return to their home countries, and recent changes to Canada's immigration laws will make it even harder for family members to join them (Galloway, 2008). While these families occupy multiple linguistic and cultural identities, and are linked to broader transnational communities, they do not maintain these ties as easily as families who have immigrated under fewer political and economic constraints.

In the 1980s, Heath suggested (1983) that involving children as 'junior ethnographers' was an effective way for teachers and researchers to learn more about children's outside-school lives, and we have engaged in several different activities with children in the school to do exactly that. In recognition of children's intense interest in digital texts, and in an effort to build upon the successes of out-of-school programs that incorporate still and video cameras, we collaborated with Grade 6 and 7 teachers to incorporate a range of multimodal projects into their classrooms. These included photo and video representations of children's lives in their community; representations of community literacies, including language 'maps' of their own and families' multilingual communications; podcasts of original stories; and bilingual storybooks of their grandparents' lives as children. Next, we describe the photo project in which Urban School children engaged.

Photo Project

In some ways, of all the projects in which we have engaged, the photo-story project linked most closely to the children's home and family lives. Specifically, the children were given disposable cameras and formed groups of three. They were asked to take photos of their lives, and brainstormed possible topics including brothers and sisters, friends, parents, places they go after school and weekends, such as the community center, school playgrounds, the church, temple or mosque, homework club and so on.

The children were asked to bring back their cameras the following week. The images that came back to school showed friends, families and younger siblings in particular. Teachers and researchers were treated to insights into the importance of space and place in the children's lives: for example, the school playground and the nearby basketball court featured prominently in most of the groups' work. In their groups, the children were asked to select the images they liked the most and to think about how the pictures might be used to create a slide presentation. This gave rise to much discussion and negotiation as three sets of images of families, friends and places were integrated into one presentation.

Children scanned the photos (we did not have digital cameras for them to use) and used computer software to organize, label and present the photos. The result were several series of family, friends and community images set to musical scores of hard rock, rap and hip hop, with labels for most of the slides, and sophisticated transitions. The final three-minute group presentations were shown to families one warm afternoon in June.

While the children all sang along with the music in the background of their presentations, and people laughed at the quirky images of toddlers and birthday parties, a sleeping parent or a group of friends on the swings (with seemingly the most inapt music in the background), for us, the overwhelming impression from these presentations was one of transition, and not the perhaps transition expected from being a newcomer to Canada. The transition these children seemed to be announcing was that they were no longer young children. While in each presentation, pictures of family members were evident and many had photos of children's homes, most of the children's slides were of their friends and the activities in which they engage with friends, in places other than their homes and school. The seemingly gendered selections of music (with boys mostly using rap and hip hop and girls mostly using songs by popular female singers, Beyonce, Natasha Bedingfield and Avril Lavigne), the children's often humorous labeling of their photos (e.g. an overexposed picture was labeled 'Don't let the ghosts scare you'; a photo of a child's house was labeled 'Combat info center'; a photo of a backyard playground was named 'the wrestling ring' (see Figure 15.2) and a photo of the school was entitled 'The Prison') seemed to announce that these children were claiming identities within a multimodal, culturally diverse pop and global culture. This impression of transitional identities was also evident in some of the poses children struck in the photos.

These are children, but they are children who are apprenticing to a larger culture. It is important to note that this impression was underlined by the amalgamation of images, text and music, and the transitions between the images, which we cannot reproduce here. However, Figure 15.3 may give some flavor of how these children represented their current lives.

Discussion

In general, the children's engagement in this project was overwhelming. They learned with enthusiasm new literacy skills of editing, assembling and organizing ideas. They labeled their photos with humor

Figure 15.2 The wrestling ring

Figure 15.3 Friends on the playground

and concern for detail. Their final products were made using a somewhat dated and quite complicated computer program (because their school computers do not have more up-to-date programs), which all the children learned. They were very proud of their products and said in interviews that they had highly enjoyed the project. The children's skillful and strategic integration of image, text and music communicated strongly the potential of these multimodal tools for creating powerful

and generative narratives in classroom settings; perhaps more generative, for pedagogic purposes, than children's usual print-only narratives.

Despite all these positives, we are left with the sense that we stopped
short of exploiting the full range of pedagogic possibilities of this project.
The traditional critical pedagogy question, who/what is missing, has
helped us think about how these projects might have had 'longer legs'
and how teachers might have used them for other classroom work. The
photos might have been used as something like Freire's (1970) codifica-
tions; for example, teachers could have discussed with students the fact
that so few of the photos contained overt heritage cultural references.
While no doubt the children participate in 'heritage' cultural activities,
in the photos taken there was only one picture that referred to
participation in the cultural activities of their homeland: that of a boy
in traditional afghan clothes (embroidered tumbaan [pants] and waskat
[vest]. See Figure 15.4) which he subtitled, "Me in my best clothes".
Whether the children thought such representations were inappropriate to
bring to school, or if they spend little of their time in such activities (one
of the questions the photos raised), is uncertain and could be investigated. Having the children think about this and articulate what it is like
for immigrant and refugee children to bridge a variety of cultural spaces,
may have been very educative.

As we stated in the introduction, an important goal in our research
was to inform us, as teacher educators, researchers and teachers, of the
linguistic and cultural resources available to and used by children
outside of school. In doing so, we hoped to transform classroom
pedagogies to reflect community cultural and linguistic contexts. As
we continue to reflect on why the project seemed to deliver less than its
promise, we have come to see that in designing projects to connect
home/community and school, a number of institutional barriers specific
to school routines and curricular objectives emerge. Even when we
recognize these constraints, they are entrenched and organize learning in
what is possible, or feels possible. For example, the structuring of
learning around timetables and the constant transition from one subject
to the next (we documented an average of eight to 10 transitions per
school day) means that opportunities for critical conversation are few
and far between – as everyone seems perpetually concerned about
what's coming next, be it recess, music, science. The large blocks of time
that were necessary for the children to engage in this project (as with
almost all the multimedia projects SILICLE has engaged in), are rarely
available in schools. The time it required, and, tellingly, the children's
high engagement, made this seem somewhat of a peculiar exercise, not

Figure 15.4 Me in my best clothes

'real school'. Children themselves marked this project as different from their usual school learning, as they formally thanked their teachers in the credit lines of their photo presentations for 'letting us do this fun project'. In spite of teachers' commitment to the project, it was also clear that many schools are not organized to accommodate the production of multimodal texts. For example, this project required significant outside resources to secure access to cameras and to coordinate computer access.

Although Canadian schools are not funded on the basis of the standardized test scores of their students (so that the tests are not as 'high stakes' as they are in other jurisdictions), all the teachers in our project are cognizant of the importance of teaching the provincially prescribed curriculum, and these photo projects did not seem easily translatable into prescribed learning outcomes. Completing these 'un-school-like' projects, showing them to parents and then putting them away to work on 'real' literacy tasks, like answering comprehension questions and writing paragraphs, seemed all too easy and familiar. Our next challenge in SILICLE is to understand more about why such projects, which seem potentially so educative and seem to exploit children's out-of-school knowledge, are so difficult to integrate with school, and to find strategies that will help them become integrated. We see this as a broad policy question, as we consider how school curricular objectives seem so tied to traditional print literacies.

Conclusion

As educational researchers interested in how home and community knowledge can be built upon in schools, as Bourne suggested in the quote at the beginning of this chapter, we have previously argued (Smythe & Toohey, 2009) that schools generally know so little about out-of-school discourse practices that they cannot build upon them. However, as we have come to learn with this project, even when home and community knowledges come to school, it seems apparent that teachers and schools are not quite sure what to do with them. In spite of the best intentions of teachers, efforts to build upon children's cultural and linguistic resources constituted a 'side show' rather than an integrated cohesive pedagogic practice. Returning to the work of Heller (2008) and Bourdieu (1977), the re-valuing of cultural and linguistic resources of minority children requires much more than special projects, or even community scans. From a pedagogic perspective, what seems more promising is a process-oriented view of knowledge, culture and language, enacted in ongoing conversations between teachers and students, rather than timetables that structure disciplinary knowledge. Moreover, as we describe above, community-based learning settings, such as the out-of-school program described at the outset of this chapter, are important, if overlooked sites of multilingual, multimodal learning for newcomer children. Attending to, and valuing the modes and strategies for learning in these informal settings can provide insights into promising classroom-based pedagogies.

The institutional barriers and pedagogic tensions we identify are not insurmountable, and can and do provide the impetus for pedagogic innovation to the potential benefit of all learners. It is clear that newcomer children from places of conflict and instability bring a unique set of learning resources and cultural tools to classrooms. However, these 'challenges' to the usual work of schools, may more fruitfully be regarded as a catalyst for new pedagogies that re-value, in Heller's sense (2008), the cultural and linguistic resources of these multicompetent children.

Notes

1. We refer to the focal school with the pseudonym Urban School and to the community as Urban Community to protect the identity of participants. We also give pseudonyms to parents, teachers and community members for the same reason.
2. It is important to highlight, however, that even this substandard housing is insecure for families vulnerable to poverty. A report on homelessness in the region noted that new immigrant families are most likely to number among the 'hidden homeless', forced to move often to avoid rent increases, and 'couch surf' in the homes of more established relatives (Hiebert *et al.*, 2005).

References

Barton, D. and Hamilton, M. (1998) *Local Literacies: Reading and Writing in One Community*. London: Routledge.

Bourdieu, P. (1977) The economics of linguistic exchanges. *Social Science Information* 16 (6), 645–668.

Bourne, J. (2001) Discourses and identities in a multilingual primary classroom. *Oxford Review of Education* 27 (1), 103–114.

Canadian School Boards Association (May, 2006) Consultation paper on meeting the language learning and settlement needs of immigrant children and youth in Canada's school system. On WWW at http://www.opsba.org/Policy_Program/CSBA_Draft_Consultation_SLL.pdf. Accessed 17.06.08.

Canagarajah, S. (2002) Reconstructing local knowledge. *Journal of Language, Identity and Education* 1 (4), 243–259.

Cazden, C. (2003) *Classroom Discourse*. New York: Blackwell.

Corsaro, W. (2003) *We're Friends, Right? Inside Kids' Culture*. Washington, DC: Joseph Henry Press.

Creese, G. (2006) Negotiating Belonging: Bordered Spaces and Imagined Communities in Vancouver, Canada. Research on Immigration and Integration in the Metropolis Working Paper No. 05–06. Vancouver: RIIM.

de la Piedra, M.T. (2006) Literacies and Quecha oral language: Connecting sociocultural worlds and linguistic resources for biliteracy development. *Journal of Early Childhood Literacy* 6 (3), 383–406.

Freire, P. (1970) *Pedagogy of the Oppressed*. New York: Atheneum.

Galloway, G. (April 28, 2008) New law would put skilled immigrants before families, opposition critics say. *The Globe and Mail*.

Heath, S.B. (1983) *Ways with Words: Language, Life and Work in Communities and Classrooms*. London: Cambridge University Press.

Heller, M. (2008) Bourdieu and "literacy education". In J. Albright and A. Luke (eds) *Pierre Bourdieu and Literacy Education* (pp. 50–67). New York: Routledge.

Hiebert, D., D'Addario, S. and Sherrell, K. (2005) *The Profile of Absolute and Relative Homelessness among Immigrants, Refugees, and Refugee Claimants in the*

GVRD. Vancouver: Multilingual Orientation Service Association for Immigrant Communities. On WWW at http://www.mosaicbc.com/The_Profile_of_ Absolute_and_Relative_Homelessness.pdf.

Holland, D. and Lave, E. (eds) (2001) *Enduring Struggles, Contentious Practice, Intimate Identities*. Santa Fe, CA: School of American Research Press.

Hull, G. and Katz, M.L. (2006) Crafting an agentive self: Case studies in digital storytelling. *Research in the Teaching of English* 41 (1), 43–48.

Hull, G. and Schultz, K. (2002) *School's Out: Bridging Out-of-School Literacies with Classroom Practice*. New York: Teachers College Press.

Lantolf, J. (2000) Introducing sociocultural theory. In J. Lantolf (ed.) *Sociocultural Theory and Second Language Learning* (pp. 8–32). Oxford: Oxford University Press.

Lee, C. (2007) *Culture, Literacy and Learning: Taking Bloom in the Midst of a Whirlwind*. Columbia: Teachers College Press.

Marsh, J. (2003) One-way traffic? Connections between literacy practices at home and in the nursery. *British Educational Research Journal* 29 (3), 369–382.

Moje, E.B. (2000) Circles of kinship, friendship, position, and power: Examining the community in community-based literacy research. *Journal of Literacy Research* 32 (1), 77–112.

Moll, L. (2000) Inspired by Vygotsky: Ethnographic experiments in education. In C.D. Lee and P. Smagorinsky (eds) *Vygotskian Perspectives on Literacy Research* (pp. 256–268). Cambridge: Cambridge University Press.

Moll, L., Amanti, C., Neff, D. and Gonzales, N. (1992) Funds of knowledge for teaching: Toward a qualitative approach to connect homes and classrooms. *Theory into Practice: Qualitative Issues in Educational Research* 3 (2), 132–141.

O'Connor, N. (2008, June 6) Lost in translation. *The Courier* pp. A1–A4.

Orellana, M.F. and Reynolds, J. (2008) Cultural modeling: Leveraging bilingual skills for school paraphrasing tasks. *Reading Research Quarterly* 13 (1), 50–65.

Purcell-Gates, V. (ed.) (2007) *Cultural Practices of Literacy: Complicating the Complex*. Mahwah, NJ: Lawrence Erlbaum.

Smythe, S. and Toohey, K. (2009) Investigating sociohistorical contexts and practices through a community scan: A Canadian Punjabi Sikh example. *Language and Education* 23 (1), 37–57.

Statistics Canada (2008) *Census Tract Profile: Census 06*. Ottawa: Statistics Canada.

Tindle, K., Leconte, P., Buchanan, L. and Taymans, J. (2005) Transition planning: Community mapping as a tool for teachers and students. *Research to Practice Brief* 4 (1), 1–5.

Wertsch, J. (1998) *Mind as Action*. New York: Oxford University Press.

Xu, S.H. (2005) *Trading Cards to Comic Strips: Popular Culture Texts and Literacy Learning in Grades K-8*. Newark, DE: International Reading Association.